From Dictatorship To Democracy

Democracy

Memoirs of a German Expatriate

Hildegard Ziegler Kurz

Blue Water Publishing, Inc.
Tigard, Oregon
1991

Library of Congress Cataloging-in-Publication Data

Kurz, Hildegard Ziegler, 1919– April 3, 2004
    from dictatorship to democracy: memoirs of a German
expatriate / Hildegard Ziegler Kurz.
        p. cm.
        ISBN 0-926524-18-6 : $15.95
        1. Kurz, Hildegard Ziegler, 1919- . 2. Germany--Social
life and customs--20th century. 3. National socialism. 4. Youth--
Germany--Biography. 5. German Americans--Biography. I. Title.

DD256.5.K854 1991
943-086'092--dc20
[B]   91-10321
                                          CIP

ISBN 0-926524-18-6

Library of Congress Catalog Card Number 91-10321
First Edition: 1991

COLOPHON
This book was created using Apple Macintosh® IIci, SE/30 and SE computers,
Quark Xpress® 3.0 software, and an Apple LaserWriter II NTX. The body style is
New Century Schoolbook 10 point on 12-point leading. The cover design was
produced with Adobe PhotoShop and Letraset LetraStudio.

COVER DESIGN: David K. Brunn
David Brunn received his MFA from the University of Oregon in 1986. He began
designing art on the Macintosh when the machine was first released in 1984.
David is currently a consultant to businesses and schools throughout the Pacific
Northwest.

From Dictatorship to Democracy
Memoirs of a German Expatriate

Address all inquiries to Blue Water Publishing, P. O. Box 230893, Tigard,
Oregon, U.S.A. 97224. Printed in the U.S.A.

From Dictatorship To Democracy

Table of Contents

Dedication

This account of my life is dedicated to the memory of my sponsors, Byron and Mildred Gilson, whose generosity, love and guidance enabled me to start a new life in the United States after the painful loss of my German ideals.

Acknowledgments

I wish to dedicate this account of my life to my parents, relatives, husband, in-laws, students, colleagues and friends on both sides of the Atlantic, in particular to those who were responsible for making my life in this country possible and for the success it has been. They all aptly helped me to fulfill my dream.

This book would not have been possible without the professional help of my editor and mentor, Dr. Vincil D. Jacobs, who patiently read my early drafts and provided me with direction, stimulation and encouragement. I also owe my gratitude to Dr. Brian L. Crissey, Chairman of the Computing Science Department at Linfield College, for his kind assistance in the technical preparation and publication of my manuscript. The help of these two colleagues of mine has been of inestimable value.

I also want to thank all my prospective readers for having provided me, in advance, with a forum that allowed me to come to grips with my often disturbing and contradictory thoughts. Your love and support have inspired me and nurtured my writing. Recording my life story was a genuine catharsis, which I sorely needed, and I am deeply grateful.

Preface

When I lived in Germany during the Hitler years and World War II, I was not aware of the fact that, in my own immature and insignificant way, I helped make history. It was not until I came to the United States, first as a student and then as an immigrant, that I realized how important and tragic the years between 1933 and 1945 were, not only for my own country, but also for the rest of the world. Later, when American young people, who were not even born before those years, took a great deal of interest in the historic events preceding their birth, I was glad to share my experiences with them.

When I taught at Linfield College, I was sometimes invited to speak to students of history, especially those who studied history of Germany. After my retirement, my highly regarded colleague and Professor of History, Dr. Vincil Dale Jacobs inspired me to write my experiences in Germany, especially those during the Hitler years and WWII, so that they could be shared with future students. Additional inspiration and encouragement were provided, when I enrolled in a course entitled "How to Write my Life Story," offered by Chemeketa Community College and professionally and insightfully taught by Nyla Booth. Her interest and that of fellow classmates was so genuine and overwhelming that I decided to branch out and add on to my topic by including my childhood years leading up to the rise of Adolf Hitler, and the years from 1945 to the present. I thought that telling my complete life story would be a chance of sharing myself and helping my friends to understand better this strange human being from Germany that I must have seemed at times.

I had a difficult time, especially writing about the Hitler years and World War II, because many of my memories were buried in my subconscious and had to be unearthed. However, the more I pondered, the more I managed to dig up those disturbing experiences that seemed entirely forgotten. I realized that those political events and my youthful and idealistic reactions to them needed to be dealt with, no matter how painful they appeared to be in retrospect. Unfortunately my diaries that I had written between 1933 and 1945 were destroyed in an air raid, so that I was dependent solely on my memory as I was writing about the events during those years.

Apart from personal experiences, I also found it difficult to look at the historic happenings, of which I was a witness, with the objectivity required of a reporter. It was an arduous task to remain objective, when my personal experiences, my subjective reaction to them and strong emotions came in the way. I now realize that I was born at a crucial time in Europe, and that my country has played a significant role in world affairs, although not always in an exemplary way. Even now, 45 years after World War II, today's European history can hardly be understood without adequate knowledge of events that took place decades ago. For that reason, I hope that these memoirs will serve the dual purpose of revealing my personal experiences and also casting some light on historic events surrounding them.

Baby Picture, 6 months old, Nuremberg.

Father in German Army uniform (WWI), 1917.

1

Growing Up After World War I

When I look back on my childhood, it is with mixed feelings. I was an only child, and my parents lavished attention on me while shielding me from much of the pain of growing up in a country that had been psychologically devastated by defeat and morally outraged by the charge that Germany was responsible for causing World War I. As I think about the way in which I was raised, I wonder if my own life reflects in some way the dilemmas of Germany herself as she absorbed the shock of defeat in 1918 and the task of rebuilding thereafter.

I was born in 1919. My parents were Johann Michael and Juliane Ziegler. My father, born October 16, 1888, attended grade school until age fourteen, when he was apprenticed to a printer with the expectation that he would become a printer himself one day. But World War I intervened, and he was drafted into the German army where he served four years. While in military service he was instilled with a deep love of his country and he remained faithful to it in the midst of the very worst adversity. I would have a hard time understanding that later on, but in Weimar Germany patriotism was considered to be an outstanding virtue, and my father always prided himself on being a good German. After the war he was rewarded for his military service with a government job, which was not only more to his liking but also more secure than the printing profession because it offered a higher salary, job tenure and a pension upon retirement.

My mother was a descendant of a Huguenot family which had been forced to flee from France during the religious persecutions of the sixteenth century. She was very proud of her French ancestry. Her native city was Erlangen, which is located about eighteen miles from Nuremberg where I was reared. In her childhood she was able to attend one of the two Huguenot churches in Erlangen. When she married my father, who was Lutheran, and moved to Nuremberg, she embraced the Lutheran faith because there were no Huguenot churches in Nuremberg. I was baptized in a Lutheran church on Christmas Day 1919.

My parents were compatible and they got along well during their 18 years of marriage, so I was spared the trauma that is so often associated with family strife. They were quiet, law-abiding German citizens with a profound sense of moral values anchored in their religious beliefs. Like most Germans during the 'twenties, they took religion seriously and treated their fellow citizens with great gentleness, love and respect. Our household was run frugally, and my parents instilled in me such an appreciation of thrift that even today I cannot easily spend money on nonessential goods without feeling a twinge of conscience.

As I look back over the years, I have come to realize that my mother was the stronger of my parents. She was a strict disciplinarian, who believed in and practiced moderate physical punishment. However, my father always defended me because he could not stand to see me suffer. *"Lass doch das arme Kind allein"* (Please leave the poor child alone), he used to say. I was my father's little princess, and in his estimation I could do no wrong. Oh, how I loved him for that when I was a child! It was not until later, when I was fully grown, that I learned to appreciate my mother's attempts to give my life firm direction and to instill in me the virtue of self-control. To this day I can remember her determined efforts to mold me into a productive and responsible citizen and I think that she did far more to influence the development of my character than my indulgent father did.

The end of World War I and the disastrous Peace Treaty of Versailles brought hard times to Germany and all citizens had to pay a price for our defeat. Like most German city dwellers of the time, we lived in a five-room apartment and never dreamed of owning a home. Our apartment was located on the first floor of a five-story building that was solidly built of stone with cold running water and no central heating. Each room had its own little stove, which in wintertime was stuffed with wood and coal when we used it, but in order to save money, only one room - usually the living room - was heated at a time. Winter nights were extremely cold, and fuel was expensive, so we learned to get by on as little as possible. Every night before we went to bed, we extinguished the fire. The next morning, we would clean the hearth and carry the ashes out to the garbage can. Then we would build a new fire, which we maintained during the day, or as long as someone was at home. A daily chore that befell me was fetching coal from the cellar in big heavy pails. I did fine when we lived on the first floor, but when we moved to a different apartment on the third floor, I had to carry the coal, one pail in each hand, up forty-six steps - I actually counted and can still remember them. On my way upstairs, I had to rest twice on the landings of the staircase to catch my breath.

Every German household consumed enormous amounts of coal. We usually ordered a winter's supply of approximately four hundred pounds in early fall. Burning coal caused soot to accumulate rapidly in the chimney during the winter, so once a month a chimney sweep, employed by the government, would clean out our flue. We always welcomed him as a friend, not only because he cleaned our chimney, but also because we believed his appearance brought good luck. He was a cheerful fellow, who traditionally dressed in a black suit and a top hat. After a short period of work, his hands and face would be as black as his suit, and only a smile and friendly eyes revealed the man behind the coal-dust mask.

Much later, during World War II, when I was living in Vienna, I found out what a hardship it is to be without heat and without the comforts of hearth and home, and I have often wondered how those people who were less fortunate than I managed to cope with the extremities that the war visited upon Europe. I learned to do without the amenities of civilization during the war, and I have learned since to appreciate deeply the luxuries of America, where food, clothing and shelter are available in such abundance.

The lack of central heating was just an inconvenience of my early childhood, along with the lack of central markets and refrigerators. Most households in Germany before World War II had an icebox in the kitchen, which was filled with big blocks of ice delivered by truck every day. They kept the food cool until the ice melted and had to be replaced. Since my parents ran our household on a shoestring, we did not own an icebox. Even this modest appliance was considered an unnecessary luxury, and how I envied my friends who could slip into their flat and grab a piece of ice to cool them off on a hot day! Lacking an icebox, my mother had to go shopping every other day. This was time-consuming because it involved visiting several stores, including the grocery store, the bakery, the dairy, the butcher shop and vegetable stands.

As a small child with all the time at my disposal, I found shopping most exciting and I loved to accompany my mother on her shopping expeditions. On the way we often saw our neighbors, who were also venturing out to do their daily errands. This gave us a chance to gossip, to engage in pleasant conversation and to exchange news of the neighborhood. One nice thing about this was that people really became acquainted. Shopkeepers knew their customers by name and they were experts at anticipating the needs of their regular customers.

My favorite stores were the butcher shop, where the friendly owner always gave me a sample from his vast array of sausages and the grocery store, where every child received a piece of candy with each purchase. The druggist in my neighborhood sold me my first camera, cheap and simple, and sometimes he walked around with me to teach me the rudiments of photography. In general, there prevailed in Nuremberg during the 'twenties a spirit of good will and camaraderie that faded away during the Hitler years and is lacking today. How much of that, I must ask, was a casualty of Nazism and World War II?

In a country where good cooking is prized and the mistress of the house rules supreme in the kitchen, my mother was at a disadvantage. She was a good cook, but because of the conditions under which she toiled, her efforts could hardly have yielded a gourmet dinner. We had only a gas stove with two burners, and our oven in the kitchen could be used only with wood. Furthermore, there was no thermometer on which a cook could rely. The heat generated by wood defied attempts to regulate temperatures, so that baking cakes or roasting meat in the oven was an adventure in itself. Most of my mother's cooking was on the stove-top, because the more difficult dishes could not be left to the vagaries of the oven. When mother made a cake, I took it to the bakery shop nearby and returned to pick up the finished product a few hours later. Bakers would bake cakes for a small fee. My mother never used any recipes and did not even own a cookbook. Her meals were simple and plain, but nutritious. They consisted mostly of vegetables, salads, potatoes, or rice. We lived too far from the coast to be able to enjoy fresh fish or seafood, and meat and desserts were considered special treats to be served only once a week, with dessert on Saturdays and meat on Sundays, and even then only in small quantities.

But we ate well during those years. Breakfast consisted of rolls, butter, jam, coffee or tea. Every morning, long before we awoke, a baker's apprentice delivered rolls to our flat. He put the rolls into a cloth bag that we had attached to the knob of the front door the evening before. At breakfast time the rolls were still warm and they smelled so heavenly that breakfast was worth getting up for. We paid for them once a week, every Saturday at the bakery. It is a commentary on the values of German society that the baker did not keep track of the number of rolls delivered during the week but relied on the honesty of his customers to pay for their goods. I cannot remember ever hearing of a dispute over a bakery bill, even though the system was extremely vulnerable to exploitation.

Lunch was the main meal of the day. School children were dismissed at 1 p.m., before lunch. I usually raced home from school, in order not to miss out on any food. My father, whose office was thirty minutes away, walked home to eat with my mother and me. As a typical child I disliked vegetables, but as a typical mother, mine insisted that I eat my share, which invariably resulted in a spat. How spoiled I was! Eventually I got tired of resisting my mother, and I contrived a way of making vegetables more palatable. I mashed potatoes and mixed them with the vegetables. If I failed to finish the food, which my mother heaped on my plate, I had to eat it for the next meal. The evening meal had greater appeal to me because it consisted of bread, some sausage, cheese, as well as a small salad.

Sunday dinner deserves special mention because it was more elaborate than the rest of the meals and it conformed to the notion that German cuisine is hearty and filling. Because of the absence of a refrigerator, we had to buy food items shortly before preparation. Since stores were closed from 7 p. m. on Saturday until early Monday morning, we planned our shopping hours for late Saturday afternoon. On Sundays we treated ourselves to meat, usually a delicious goulash or Wiener Schnitzel accompanied by a salad, vegetables, a potato dish and gravy.

The meat smelled delicious as my mother prepared it. I was full of anticipation and could hardly wait to sink my teeth into it. Meat was and still is my favorite food, but servings were kept small to make the meat go farther. We savored every morsel, knowing that the next meat dish would not be served until the following Sunday.

Beverages - normally tea or coffee - were served with meals, but the coffee was not made of "mountain-grown" beans but of chicory or malt. It was an awful brew, and up to this day I cannot understand why we drank it. Teas were either chamomile or peppermint and were certainly not very tasty alternatives to the repugnant coffee. Fruit juices could be bought only in health food stores and were beyond our financial reach. Sometimes in the evening my father indulged in a glass of beer for which he sent me to the nearest restaurant. Canned beer was not available, and bottled beer was more expensive than draft beer in open containers. Sending small children to buy beer for their parents was a common custom in Europe. I rather enjoyed buying my father's beer because he always gave me a small tip provided I did not spill a drop of the precious brew on my way home. It strikes me as odd yet today, but I am probably the only German in the world who has never acquired a taste for beer. Strangely enough, neither do I like milk. Even as a baby my parents fed me cocoa because I refused to drink milk. My parents were afraid I would insist on taking my bottle with me upon entering school at the age of six. They tried to wean me from the bottle by covering the pacifier with mustard or some other terrible-tasting substance but it took a long, long time before I let them take my bottle from me — for good!

After having broken my addiction to the baby bottle, my parents sent me to kindergarten. This provided another challenge for them. I did not know what was awaiting me and set out without a great deal of enthusiasm. At the end of the first day, I felt dissatisfied and unhappy by the treatment I had received. I returned home to tell my parents in no uncertain terms that one day of this experience was enough for me. Growing up without siblings and with few friends, I could not easily relate to other children and I did not learn to get along with them. Even in those early years I became a very independent child, certainly in part by choice but in part by circumstance. It was all my parents could do to convince me that kindergarten attendance might prove beneficial to me and provide some badly needed companionship with other children of my age.

I was a lonely child and considered it inconceivable and unfair that my mother grew up with six siblings and my father with three. Why shouldn't I have brothers and sisters? But as I look back at those troubled years in German history, I think that the economic climate of Germany militated against large families. All of my parents' brothers and sisters, with the exception of one, had only one child in their marriage. Economic conditions after World War I made it impossible for people to have large families. They simply could not afford them. How sad!

History books tell us why. Those were hard times, characterized by rampant inflation and a shocking devaluation of the currency in 1923. Years later my father told me that, during the inflationary period, he was able to buy only a loaf of bread or a few postage stamps with a month's salary. One pack of cigarettes sold for up to one billion marks. A week's subscription to a newspaper cost 500 billion marks. Wages were paid on a daily basis, because the money was worthless within a few hours. Germans, who had practiced thrift carefully all of their lives, saw their life savings wiped out in just a few days. It is understandable that under those circumstances families had no choice but to limit their number of children to an absolute minimum, and that many sober and thoughtful Germans would be deeply scarred by their financial misfortunes in the early 'twenties.

Fortunately, all of my nine uncles, aunts and ten cousins lived in the same area in and around Nuremberg, so that we were able to visit back and forth once in a while. In those days, most people continued to live in the same city or village in which they were born. Moving away, even only a short distance from home, was inconceivable. Family reunions American-style which unite all related families, even the most extended ones, were unknown in Germany. Usually just two or three families got together to visit and socialize.

I never knew my grandfathers, because they died before I was born. My maternal grandmother lived in Erlangen, about eighteen miles from Nuremberg. Her name was Margarethe Wrede. I remember regular visits to her along with my parents. The three of us would walk the thirty minutes to the railroad station to take the train to Erlangen. My parents never owned a car in their whole life. German public transportation, mostly streetcars, buses and trains has always been prompt, efficient and inexpensive, and the traveler can journey across the country in one day. Therefore, a car was not the necessity it is in America.

We always walked to the railroad station because we wanted to save the streetcar fare. I vividly remember, when I was three to four years old, my frantic efforts to keep up with my parents' pace as they strode along. Sometimes I would get so tired that I found it difficult to walk. In that case, I would start crying, stomping my feet and refusing to take another step. My father, gentle and sweet as he was, had no choice but to lift me up on his shoulders and carry me. Was I actually a brat? I hope not, but I would hate to have a child do that to me!

I hardly remember my maternal grandmother because I was only seven years old when she died. I have always been under the impression that my family did not feel particularly close to her, and that we visited her only out of a sense of duty or obligation. To this day I cannot understand why we did not enjoy a warmer relationship with her. We had a similar relationship with my paternal grandmother. She lived in Nuremberg, as we did. Her three sons and a daughter occupied different apartments, but never moved away. My father's mother was called Anna Kunigunde Ziegler. She died when I was thirteen years old. My father was her eldest son, but her other two sons eventually became her favorites.

There was little communication between my paternal grandmother and our family. I have only vague memories of her and remember her best when she was about seventy years old. We lived in the same city, but even then we saw each other only twice a year. Transportation may have been a problem. We lived a ninety-minute walk away from *Oma*. Although streetcar fares were inexpensive, visits were made difficult by the fact that neither she nor my family had a telephone. Telephones were considered luxuries, and only rich people and businesses, out of necessity, owned phones.

My father made no special effort to see his mother on a regular basis, such as other German men might. Instead, he made it a point to send me to her apartment with a gift, usually before Christmas. Since she was almost a stranger to me, visiting her was not my favorite thing to do, but as a good little German girl I dutifully followed my father's wishes.

I never questioned the reason why my father did not visit his mother himself. It was not until I grew a little older that his reasons became apparent to me. I remember my grandmother as a heavy-set woman plagued with arthritis, who walked very slowly with the aid of a cane. During the last ten years of her life, she lived in abject poverty on a limited pension, due to the fact that she had sold her apartment house in 1923, just a few weeks before the complete devaluation of the German currency. Almost over night, all bank accounts and investments were wiped out and only people with real estate or other assets, such as businesses, retained their financial stability. Self-respecting citizens considered it a disgrace to go on welfare, so my grandmother chose not to subject herself to it. She barely eked out a living, and gifts to others were a luxury to her, which she could not afford. That explains why I never received a gift or even a birthday card from her. I accepted this as a matter of course without giving it a second thought. Even if my grandmother had had any money to spend on others, I doubt if I would have been a recipient. My father seemed to be *persona non grata* to her and, as his daughter, I was too.

Another factor entered into our relationship with *Oma*. My grandmother did not appear to love her children equally. She played favorites to her two younger sons, because she thought they needed her more than my father did. They were not considered a success by societal standards. In those days, the majority of people lived in poverty. It was up to each individual to raise himself up to a better life without much outside help or encouragement. This is what my father did, but instead of his mother taking pride in his achievements, she gradually withdrew her love and attention from him and took her two younger sons under her wings. My father did not take kindly to being rejected by his own mother.

That situation grew worse, when my father encouraged me to reach for the stars, enter high school at age ten, as was and still is the German custom, and go on to the university. I became the first female university graduate in my extended family. My grandmother did not share my ambition, especially in view of the fact that her other grandchildren did not follow in my footsteps. By going to high school a whole new world opened up to me, and I found myself with many friends and the respect of a society which valued young people with intellectual goals. In my earlier years, I did not miss my grandmother's affection too much. Only later in life, when I came to this country as an immigrant, I observed how beautiful the love between grandparents and their grandchildren can be.

Was I a typical German child? In retrospect, I cannot help but regret my passive attitude and lack of closeness towards my grandmother. I am convinced that, with a different attitude, I could have made a great deal of difference in the lives of my grandmother, my parents and my own. Hindsight always seems better than foresight; but wouldn't it be nice if youth had the maturity and insight of old age, at least to a certain extent?

By writing these few observations about my grandmother I feel that, in spite of our rather cool relationship, I can now express some measure of love and respect to her. Certainly she would never have anticipated being the focus of attention of American readers. This has been my long-overdue and belated tribute to her, and by revealing my feelings I feel somewhat redeemed and relieved.

We enjoyed varying degrees of warmth in relating to other members of the family but somehow we did not act as if we were proud of our ties. I think that, for many of us, feelings of envy and jealousy stood in the way of genuine bonding. My uncles, in particular, seemed to compete for recognition. In a highly structured society, unwritten rules governed relationships. At the top were professionals made up of university graduates, who enjoyed the highest esteem in society. They were followed by a class of less educated persons, mostly in civil service positions for which they received the highly coveted benefits of tenure and a retirement pension. Farther down on the scale ranged tradesmen and owners of small shops, such as butchers, bakers, grocers. Their education usually consisted of eight years of grade school plus three more years of trade school. The very lowest social class consisted of manual workers and laborers, who had attended elementary school only.

These class distinctions were so deeply engrained in German society that the chance of rising to a higher class was rarely available. Even marriages between members of different social classes were frowned on, and any couple who decided to defy tradition encountered the disdain of their neighbors and caused tensions in their families.

This rigid system of class distinctions in Germany contributed especially to strife and envy among families. My father rose in rank when he became a civil servant. His two brothers, on the other hand, remained in the social class of their parents. They became barbers, which ranked below civil service and, as a consequence, they had little in common with my father.

Relations deteriorated when my parents revealed their ambitious plan to provide me with a university education. But I was not alone in my quest for distinction. My father's middle brother had an intellectually gifted son, who also broke the class barrier by pursuing an academic career. He was seven years my senior, studied medicine, and became a well-known orthopedist in Nuremberg, where he now lives in retirement. I admired him greatly for becoming his own person and for transcending the traditional class barriers of German society. My father's youngest brother demonstrated little ambition for himself and less for his only daughter. She worked at menial jobs all her life and married within her social class.

When I was preschool age I had only one close friend. Since most families restricted themselves to only one child, there were relatively few children in the neighborhood. Anneliese became my best friend when I was four years old. She was one year older than I and became a constant source of fascination to me. I stood in awe of her. We did everything together and constantly visited back and forth. She lived only one block from me. Her parents enjoyed a higher financial status than mine, and I spent a lot of time at her parents' apartment. My mother established one firm rule which I found hard to accept and obey. She forbade me to eat with Anneliese's family. Germans considered it an invasion of privacy to stay over for a meal, especially when invited at the last minute.

Quite a change came into my life, when Anneliese entered the first grade. I was devastated because my good friend was no longer available for unlimited hours of playing. My mother taught me how to tell time, so that I could count the hours until Anneliese came home from school. I would wait for her on the street corner every day. From my vantage point, I was able to see as far as two blocks down the street. When I saw Anneliese approach, I would run to her and greet her almost like a long-lost friend. She would then tell me all about her experiences during the school day. I was always suitably impressed and just a little envious of her classmates, who were privileged to enjoy her friendship and attention. I could hardly wait for another year to go by, when I would enjoy walking to school with her every day, even if I could not sit in the same classroom with her.

2

Grade School - Stork - Games

In Germany there were very few women teachers. The reason for this lay in the traditional role for women, in which emphasis was placed on being a loving wife and mother. The mother was in charge of the household and expected to keep the house spotless while cooking three meals a day and greeting her husband with a cheerful smile, when he returned home from work. Then she had to sympathize with her husband's problems and frustrations at work and, later in the evening, supervise the children as they did their homework. No man would be caught dead helping his wife with the household chores or taking care of the children. The male role was always to "bring home the bacon."

Although the pressures on the German housewife could be monumental, no woman would ever think of neglecting her duties, nor would she dream of working outside the home to supplement the family income. My mother used to say that a woman's work is taken for granted and never appreciated. She thought the only way to make the family notice her contribution to the welfare of the household was to ignore her duties. But typically, her commitment to her routine kept her from doing that.

When I first came to the United States, I heard people refer to the three K's of German women. These were *Kinder, Küche, Kirche* (children, kitchen, church). No good German would ever have limited a woman's role to just three areas. There was too much to do otherwise. Even today, I find it interesting that women in German society willingly accepted the role imposed upon them, and it was astonishing that there were no divorces. The marriage vow, *"Bis der Tod uns scheidet"* (Until death do us part) was followed to the letter by all parties concerned.

Personally, I always preferred men as teachers. In my estimation, based on many years of learning, they were generally fairer, did not play favoritism with students, and were less moody than women. Sorry ladies, just my opinion! In my four years of grade school I had only two teachers, each one for two years. I liked them equally well. Their names were Karl Leybold and Wilhelm Hörl. It is a tribute to them that I still remember their names. Those two teachers strictly, but fairly, enforced the rules of the classroom. We enjoyed them because they were not only strict but also gentle and understanding. As young as we were, we always knew where we stood and how we would be treated if we did not follow regulations.

German parents taught their children to follow orders without fail. So when we entered school the same behavior was expected of us, and it proved to be no hardship on the pupils. This does not mean, however, that German children are all angels. Once in a while a child refused to obey the teacher. The ensuing punishment was a *Pfötchen,* a swat on the palm of the hand with a rod. Another less painful but more embarrassing punishment was having to stand in a corner of the classroom for the rest of the period. But generally my classmates and I were anxious to please the teacher as we did our parents, so that episodes of misbehavior were at a minimum.

We attended school Mondays through Saturdays from 8 a.m. to 1 p.m. with two ten-minute breaks, but no lunch period. The school year consisted of 247 school days with two weeks of vacation at Christmas and Easter, another at Whitsuntide (Pentecost), and six weeks of summer vacation, which lasted from mid-July to the beginning of September. Official holidays, which did not fall on a Sunday, were observed by a day off. They included the usual Christian holidays.

We learned so much in school! In the first grade, our curriculum included reading, spelling, arithmetic, nature studies (to make us aware of our immediate environment), penmanship, chorus, physical education, needle work and religion. There was no separation of church and state in Germany, and religion was taught as a compulsory subject every year until graduation from high school. We also received grades in conduct and effort.

Grammar was added to our studies in the second grade, and in third grade composition. Academically gifted students prepared for transfer to high school at the age of ten. Except for physical education and chorus, the curriculum did not include outdoor or extracurricular activities. Consequently, students found it difficult to establish friendships and make contacts with one another. We spent afternoons and evenings working on assignments and reviewing. For that purpose, we needed our books at home, too, so we carried them back and forth every day. In any case, it would not have been possible to leave books in school, because no lockers were available for the convenience of students.

At that time, schools were not equipped with a central heating system. In the wintertime, hours before classes started, custodians kept busy starting fires in the stove of every classroom. During class hours, the custodians walked from room to room to check the temperatures about every hour and, if needed, to shovel more coal into the stoves. Parents, teachers and students accepted such inconveniences without complaint.

A serious blow occurred in my young life, when my father felt he needed to get away from the stress of his job and the family. He decided to spend some time with relatives in the countryside without informing my mother. His strange behavior turned out to be the beginning of a serious nervous breakdown. When he failed to contact us for a whole day, my mother jumped to the conclusion that he might have taken his life, which, fortunately, was not the case. She informed me that, without him, she could not tolerate the thought of going on living. Her plan was to kill me and then herself. She asked me my opinion. I was seven years old at the time and wanted to live, under any circumstances. So I responded to her suggestion by screaming as loudly as I could and refused to comply. Late in the evening, we were notified by our relatives of the whereabouts of my father. A telephone would have been a blessing in such an emergency, but we simply did not have one. My father was referred to a hospital for observation and treatment, and we used to visit him regularly.

I do not know exactly what caused my father's breakdown, but this is how it was explained to me: He worked as a tax collector for the German government. It was his job to go after people who, for various reasons, were not able or refused to pay their taxes. No doubt it was a very stressful job. What bothered him the most was his deep-felt sympathy and compassion for those who lived in abject poverty and could not come up with the funds to pay their taxes. He took their desperate situation personally, and through the years the pressure continued to build up. He was unable to escape from it, because the German civil service system was managed so rigidly that transfers or furloughs were almost impossible to arrange. My father's age (thirty-eight years) and the prospect of working at that same job until retirement became so nightmarish that he could no longer cope with it.

In the late 'twenties, it became fashionable among young German girls to have their hair cut short, but society as a whole was slow to accept this custom. I used to wear my hair in two beautiful long blond braids of which my parents were extremely proud. I looked like a typical German girl! When I asked for their permission to have my hair cut short, my parents adamantly refused. My father was especially disturbed about girls wearing their hair short. While he was still in the hospital, but greatly improved, at least in my estimation, I went to my uncle's barber shop and had my hair cut. Strangely enough, my uncle did not ask if I had my parents' permission. When my mother set eyes on me in my shorn condition, she was shocked, but most of all she was afraid of her husband's reaction to my show of independence. For our next visit to the hospital, she bought me a hat which she pushed way back, in order to conceal as much of the damage as possible. Realizing too late that I had done something to upset my father, I approached him timidly. He stared at me from his hospital easy chair, ordered me to turn around and asked the agonizing question, "What in the world did you do to your hair?" After a hasty explanation, I ran out of the room, as if wanting him to accuse my mother of something that she was not responsible for. Fortunately, he soon recovered from his breakdown in spite of my defiant behavior.

As an only child, one of my most ardent wishes was to have a brother or preferably a sister. In those days, children were kept in the dark about anything that smacked of sex. I was actually told that it was the stork which brought the babies. So I directed my first written notes not to Santa Claus but to the stork to get my wish fulfilled. Almost every night I left notes tucked to an outside window for the stork to see them as he flew by. I pleaded with him to please bring me a sister. When we moved to a more modern apartment in a newly-constructed building, the unbelievable occurred: a baby daughter was born to the family who had moved into our previous apartment. Naturally, I believed that finally the stork had heeded my pleas and brought me a sister. The only problem was that he did not realize that we had moved. One afternoon after school, I went to this particular family and asked for permission to see the infant, whose name was Sieglinde. Much to her mother's surprise and disbelief, I claimed her baby as my sister. Naturally, she refused to hand the little one over to me, although I informed her that everything was above board, because I was the one who had ordered the baby from the stork. My parents teased me about this episode as long as they lived, but whose fault was it for not telling me the facts where babies came from, instead of feeding me the myth about the stork?

After moving into our new apartment, we enjoyed a more pleasant life and a somewhat higher living standard, but we still lived on a shoestring. I owned very few toys. My greatest wish to get a bicycle did not materialize until several years later. Since I was growing rather quickly, my mother bought me very few clothes. In spite of this thrift I always had a Sunday dress and Sunday shoes, which were not to be worn any other day.

Our new apartment had a kitchen balcony where we could sit in the summertime, breathe in fresh air and soak in the sun without leaving the house. It also gave me a chance to grow my favorite flowers in pots, as well as string beans. I had always been a nature worshiper and finally I was able to establish a bond with nature, limited as it may have been. The apartment consisted of five good-sized rooms. One of them, the so-called *Gute Stube*, literally translated the "good room," was set aside for special occasions, such as meals with guests or a special holiday. My mother made it a habit to clean one room every day, whether it needed it or not. She approached these chores with a certain vengeance and always sang while working. I would have liked her singing but, like a robot, she kept repeating the same melodies over and over for hours on end. Her singing may have been an outlet to vent her housewifely frustration or to get some worrisome thoughts off her mind.

In contrast to the daily housecleaning, washing linens and clothes was scheduled infrequently. We did not own a washing machine and instead used a *Waschküche* (wash kitchen). Washing was a tedious and time-consuming process. First the housewives of our apartment building heated plenty of hot water in a huge tub over a wood stove. Then they literally boiled the linens (hence the name "wash kitchen"), rinsed them by hand and hung them up in the courtyard or, during wintertime, carried the heavy linens 82 steps up to the attic. There it was sometimes so bitter cold that the wet linens froze immediately and hung there like huge boards. This old-fashioned way of washing took practically all day. No wonder that every housewife dreaded the energy-sapping procedure and put it off as long as possible.

After years of this drudgery, commercial laundries opened. The closest one to our home was about thirty minutes away, on foot, of course. They did not pick up or deliver, but we had to carry the soiled wash to the laundry in a big clothes basket, leave it there, and the next day pick up the clean wash, still wet, and carry it home. In the wet condition it was very heavy. Upon arrival at home, we had to hang it up to let it dry. It took almost two days to get this chore accomplished, but at least it saved my mother the unpleasant task of washing. An alternative way of easing the burden of washing was to hire a washerwoman, who came to the house to do the wash in our laundry room.

On Sundays, whole families would go for long walks in the forests or in the countryside. Sometimes we treated ourselves to a meal out near a lake or a river. My favorite Sunday outing was to an excellent restaurant that could best be reached, first by streetcar and then by steamboat, on a canal built to connect the Danube and Main rivers.

We lived across the street from a church in which I was baptized on Christmas Day of 1919. The sexton was a neighbor of ours. One of his duties was to ring the church bells on various occasions, such as weddings, funerals and Sunday services. This had to be done by hand, and required three or four additional helpers, depending on the number of bells to be activated. The sexton hired a few young people, a little older and more trustworthy and responsible than I, but I often accompanied them just for the fun of it. There were five bells of various sizes. They could be started by pulling a very thick and heavy rope up and down and up and down many times, depending on the weight of the individual bells. The young bell ringers would let me spin around and around on the rope of the heaviest bell, when it was not needed. There was no danger that it would go off because my weight was not heavy enough. However, as I grew older, my weight increased and, one day, as I was swinging back and forth, all of a sudden, it started to ring, which it was not supposed to do. The other bells were ringing for a funeral. My bell added an overpowering dissonance, which did not harmonize with the other bells. I got a severe scolding and was not allowed to participate in this favorite pastime of mine anymore.

In accordance with our frugal life style, the games I played outdoors did not require expensive equipment. Instead, we engaged in playing hide and seek, cops and robbers, or hopscotch. We also played with glass beads, marbles, or balls. To compete with friends we would run around a block or two and time each other with a stopwatch. Another favorite pastime consisted in attaching a coin purse to a string and lowering it to the pavement from a second-floor window. Usually, persons who walked below saw the coin purse and stopped to pick it up. Before they noticed the trick, we would lift the coin purse to our window by means of the attached string. All this happened when I was about six to ten years old. Then life became serious, because I had to think about mature endeavors, especially preparations for entering high school.

3

Hitler's Rise to Power

I vividly remember January 30, 1933, when Adolf Hitler became the Chancellor of Germany and founded what he called "The Thousand-Year Reich." Thereafter, until the end of World War II, my experiences were inextricably linked with the political events of the time. It is difficult to imagine the pervasive impact politics and government can exercise on a person, unless one has experienced it personally, and it is even more difficult to understand how easily we moved into an unquestioning acceptance of everything that Adolf Hitler demanded of the German people.

I was thirteen years old at the time. Several of our neighbors and my family were huddled together in the apartment of a privileged family who owned a radio. Hitler spoke to the nation from Berlin in such a captivating and charismatic fashion that we were transformed by his words and, after many long years of gloom and doom, felt a sense of optimism about the future. People spontaneously poured into the streets and, with lighted candles in their hands, formed torchlight processions in celebration of the new era in German national life. It was an overpowering experience, and I could hardly wait for the next day to see what kind of reaction my classmates had to the events of that historic evening. As it turned out, most young people were even more impressed than I by Hitler's plans for our nation, and we all looked forward to the future with great enthusiasm.

But the most influential factors that brought Hitler to power was our defeat in World War I and the 1919 Peace Treaty of Versailles which was one of hate and vengeance. Never again was Germany to be given a chance to rise or even fully recover. In the treaty, she suffered severe territorial losses. Her area and population were reduced by 10 percent. Territories lost to France were Alsace-

Lorraine, to Denmark Northern Schleswig, to Poland Posen, West Prussia and the Polish Corridor. East Prussia was shared by Poland and the Soviet Union. In addition, Germany was deprived of all her overseas possessions. Limitations of armaments included reduction of the German army to 100,000 men and prohibition of tanks, submarines and military planes. The initial amount of reparations ranged between ten and 100 billion dollars, which set a historic precedent. A reparations commission eventually set the sum at 33 billion dollars, which generations of Germans would have had to shoulder if Germany had not stopped payments in 1933.

After the war, German feelings of anger and frustration ran especially high because of the loss of so much territory to the enemy. Germans never forgot that their ancestors in the thirteenth century had settled uninhabited and untitled land in the eastern Baltic under the protection of the Order of the Teutonic Knights. Most Germans also conveniently forgot that in the fifteenth century Polish armies had succeeded in conquering those Baltic lands and driving the German authorities out, while allowing only the peasants to stay. Hence, Germans were forced to live under the flag of the hated Poles. Hitler's most attractive goals were to unite all German-speaking people under his leadership and to free the Germans from the "yoke of Versailles."

This had immense appeal to patriotic Germans, who had traditionally felt great emotional and spiritual attachment to their land, and who had suffered through an undeserved military defeat in World War I. The Roman historian Tacitus tells in his book *De Germania* (About Germany) that the ancient Germanic tribes were exceptionally willing to sacrifice blood and life to defend their soil. Hitler told the Germans that they were still a nation of great strength and that they had inherited from their ancestors an indomitable will to survive. In order to preserve and cultivate their strength, there had to be constant inward communion between the individual and the nation. The term *Verwurzlung* (rootedness) was used as a gauge to measure a person's worthiness, and it promoted a sense of German national unity and spiritual superiority, as well as a belief in a special mission, which the Germans were destined to fulfill by spreading German authority all over Europe.

Inspired by these misplaced ideals, many gullible Germans developed an almost pathological belief in the great future of the nation. They were convinced that, under Hitler's leadership, they would finally reach their full potential as a world power, and that

Germany would take her rightful place as the greatest nation in the world.

The collapse of the German economy in 1923 intensified an already serious racial question. Many small businesses went bankrupt and a considerable number were bought up by Jews, who were able to raise the necessary capital from private sources. A very strong and virulent anti-Semitism gripped the minds of otherwise solid and highly moral citizens, and they were willing to overlook the persecutions that began when the Nazis came to power in 1933.

The term "Nazi" needs some explanation in view of the sinister connotation that it has acquired in the United States. It is made up from the first two syllables of "National Socialism" and has retained the German pronunciation, with its spelling with a *z* which is pronounced by Germans as *ts*, rather than like an American *z*. In the United States it is used with reference to everything that pertains to National Socialism, including the Nazi party, party members, newspapers, the Nazi movement, ideology, government, regime, years, etc. But for Germans, the term Nazi was used only in a derogatory sense, and it was inappropriate to employ it otherwise. It would have been inconceivable to refer to a member of the party as a Nazi or to the movement as the Nazi movement. Germans called a party member *ein Parteimitglied* and everyone understood which party the name applied to. This does not mean that the term Nazi was not *au courant* during the Hitler years, merely that it was not tolerated by the people in power and that it had an unsavory connotation. Woe betide anyone - and especially a Jew - who dared to hurl that label at a good party member!

As an impressionable teenager, I took great interest in what the Nazi party had to offer to young people. These included many programs sponsored by the Hitler Youth, a governmental organization that was formed in 1934 to mobilize the support of the youth of Germany for the Nazi party. The activities of the Hitler Youth resembled those of the Boy and Girl Scouts in this country, with the exception that they served the explicit purpose of training and preparing the youngsters for their future role in the nation. But we were less aware of the purpose of the movement than of its potential to rescue us from the dull routine of schoolwork and a staid and unfulfilling family life. Young people readily took part in socially acceptable forms of work and recreation, including parades, marches and raising money for the party on the streets with metal boxes which they stuck in everybody's face. Raising funds for various causes was a constant concern of the Nazis. Besides collecting money on the streets, they also went door to door to raise more "voluntary" *(freiwillig)* money. This kind of fund raising was called "voluntary" because it appeared to be voluntary but actually was not. People were put on the spot to contribute and volunteered, because they did not have the courage to say "no."

Once a month all German families were urged to eat a meatless casserole dish *(Eintopfgericht)* and turn over the money supposedly saved by eating a simple meal to collectors who canvassed all households. The funds raised that way were channeled into an organization called the *Winterhilfswerk* (Winter Aid Effort), which took care of the starving and freezing. Its motto was *"Keiner soll hungern, keiner soll frieren"* (Nobody shall suffer from hunger, nobody shall suffer from the cold). I must say the Nazis were quite compassionate towards the indigent German masses. After all, they called their party "Socialist" and lived up to their commitment.

Young people escaped the confines of their homes and the strictures of parents on weekly hikes or overnight excursions to the countryside, where they spent sleepless nights on straw in the barns of farmers, sang patriotic songs and conceived great plans for the future.

I was not permitted to join the Hitler Youth when it was first organized, although children from the age of ten were eligible to join, and I was already fourteen. My father was adamantly opposed to his little girl gaining too much freedom too soon, attending political meetings in the evenings, and running off on hikes over the weekend. My strongest motive to join came in 1935, when school authorities all over Germany decided that Saturday mornings were to be set aside for youth activities. Members of the Hitler Youth were to be excused from school on Saturday mornings, while nonmembers had to attend school during the usual hours, from 8 a.m. to 1 p.m. Since so many students were excused from school on Saturdays, there was no point in teaching the regularly scheduled courses as before. So those who were left behind read and discussed Hitler's *Mein Kampf* and other books and pamphlets that promoted the Nazi party. These Saturday propaganda sessions had little appeal to squirming, reluctant students, who would have much preferred to be out on adventurous excursions with their lucky friends in the Nazi youth. Thus, when we take into account the many and complex reasons for the success of the Nazi movement, we should not ignore the element of sheer excitement and challenge it offered to bored and tightly constrained German youths.

At the age of fifteen, I told my parents in no uncertain terms that I deserved their full confidence, that I wanted more freedom, and that I especially wanted to join the Hitler Youth. My father's response was sharp and unequivocal *"nein"*, under no circumstances, and of course my mother agreed, negating my strategy of using her to gain what I could not get on my own.

But two years later, in 1935, fate intervened. Our school principal called a special student assembly to announce that he had decided that it was time for our entire student body to join the Hitler Youth. So what was there for a dissenting parent to do but to comply? I was the happiest youngster in the world! Not only had I got my own way for once, I had won a victory over my father, and now I could go running off to join my classmates on their outings! No more attending boring Saturday morning classes, I could join the gang, wear a neat uniform consisting of a navy blue skirt, a white blouse with a black triangular scarf worn around the neck, a brown Suede jacket, a swastika pin, and, last but not least, take part in all those activities away from home. I felt grown up and, charged with energy and a sense of purpose, I prepared to enter a new phase in my life.

In fact, after joining the Hitler Youth, my life did become more interesting and challenging, although not in the way I might have expected. I found myself in an army of like-minded young people, who welcomed me not only because of my willingness to belong and serve, but also, strangely enough, on the basis of my physical appearance. Hitler's physical ideal was the tall, strong, able-bodied, blond, blue-eyed German. I possessed all these attributes and I felt very proud of my German heritage.

We were all expected to attend weekly evening meetings where we sang patriotic songs, studied the Nazi ideology, discussed political events, listened to idealistic lectures and speeches about Germany's future and our role in it, read books and newspaper reports, and enjoyed the camaraderie and fellowship of other young people. On Saturdays, dressed in uniform, we marched through the city streets, singing patriotic marching songs and demonstrating our willingness to serve Germany in whatever capacity we could.

In the early years of the Hitler Youth a strong emphasis was placed on physical fitness. Boys engaged in competitive sports and girls were taught how to march and do gymnastics because strenuous sports were considered to have a negative effect on women's health and prospective childbearing. A high priority was placed on preparing girls for motherhood to the point that couples were granted tax reductions for producing more children. On weekends, we would board a train for a short distance to take us out into the countryside, and then walk and hike for hours on end with sufficient food in our bags, in order to be independent of restaurants. Eating in the embrace of nature was not only cheaper but also more refreshing to the body and soul.

Sometimes we would stay overnight in the barns of farmers or in hay stacks, which, if it sounds wonderfully romantic, was uncomfortable and strenuous. But we comforted ourselves with the knowledge that it strengthened the will and equipped us to endure great hardships, while providing another goal to be accomplished. Weekend rallies were often deliberately scheduled on Sunday mornings in an unadmitted but clear effort to keep young people out of churches.

The creation of the Hitler Youth was a stroke of genius by the Nazi party, and as it spread its tentacles across Germany, its grip on the mind and soul of Germany tightened. As it turned out, our school was only one year ahead of a law, ratified on December 1, 1936, which made membership in the youth movement mandatory for all grade and high school students. No other law was more welcomed by young people. Membership in the movement served strong emotional needs and strengthened a spirit of friendship and community. We took pride in belonging to an organization of enthusiastic young people in a well-ordered society, and it never occurred to us to question the wisdom of our leaders in making the Hitler Youth the center of our teenage world. Hitler's charismatic leadership seemed to provide a special bond among young people, a bond that was even stronger than family ties, against which it had become fashionable to rebel.

My father, a civil servant in the employ of the government, did not see fit to join the Nazi party at the outset in spite of great pressure on the part of his superiors. In order to keep his job, however, he had to prove his Aryan descent several generations back.

It was interesting to see how he resisted the party at first. It was not until some ten years after Hitler's rise to power that my father joined the party. Although not politically active, he was an ardent patriot, who had a great love for his country. During the 'twenties, he witnessed the numerous attempts by the Weimar regime to form a stable government, and like so many Germans, he was deeply discouraged by its failures. The Weimar Republic was Germany's first experiment with a new form of government after the defeat in World War I. It lasted from 1919 to 1933, and its constitution was an attempt to establish a democratic government in

Germany. It was named after the German city of Weimar, which boasted a rich cultural tradition and was regarded as the literary and artistic center of Germany. Although the constitution was similar to the one of the United States and confirmed the basic human rights, it proved unpopular from the start and led to disaster. It failed to make a complete break with the past and provided few fundamental changes. In addition, conditions brought about by four years of war and an ignominious defeat, a harsh peace treaty, unprecedented high inflation, general disorder, economic chaos, steadily rising prices and unemployment caused its demise. After the failures of the Weimar Republic, my father took a wait-and-see attitude when Hitler first came to power and later joined the party when he came to believe that Hitler offered the best solution to Germany's problems. Party membership was considered to be a declaration of patriotism for adult men, and those who failed to join were regarded as outsiders by their peers. Hitler's eventual goal was to counteract the Treaty of Versailles and restore the military power of Germany. This specific goal must have appealed to my father and evoked his patriotic feelings and pride in his country.

It was inconceivable to me that my father, who was such a gentle and loving family man and would not have hurt a fly, could also be the exact opposite, bent on revenge and even war. Only his excessive "love for his country," a false, misguided sentiment of intensely exaggerated patriotism carefully and gradually instilled by the party apparatus within the minds of impressionable and receptive individuals, could be held accountable for his decision.

I was luckier, for I managed to avoid enlisting in the party. This just happened through a streak of good luck. Before I moved to Vienna much later, in 1943, I was urged by the authorities in Nuremberg to be sure and apply for membership upon my arrival. However, my move to Vienna seemed to me a welcome means of escaping party membership. In very uncharacteristic German fashion, I just let things slide and did not report to authorities. At the time, in 1943, the war had already so deteriorated that nobody seemed to care anymore if you were a party member or not. Actually, many people considered it a plus if you did not belong to the party, whereas in the beginning of the Hitler period it was a mark of distinction and a matter of pride to belong. As a member of "only" the Hitler Youth I was treated much more gently after the collapse of the Nazi regime than those who had been in the party. In the process of de-Nazification after the end of the war, I came under the law of "youth amnesty" because of my young age when I joined the youth movement.

The Hitler Youth was divided into several branches, each with its own leadership and organization. Boys between the ages of ten and fourteen were enrolled in the *Jungvolk,* while girls of the same age bracket belonged to the *Jungmädelbund.* Those of the years fifteen to eighteen belonged either to the *Hitlerjugend* (for boys) or *Bund deutscher Mädel* (League of German Girls).

After joining the BDM, I became very interested in politics and its workings without realizing how one-sided my views became. My experience with the world was quite limited and I suffered from an appalling naïveté which I lost only when the war began. Moreover, Nazi Germany was devoid of opportunities for a public sifting of political developments, and freedom of speech and expression were not tolerated. So I more or less slid into the Nazi *Weltanschauung* without noticing how different it was in comparison with other ideologies, or how threatening it was to my own peace of mind. Like so many other Germans, I accepted the restrictions on our freedom at face value and tolerated the strident propaganda of the party without asking questions. The Nazi party glorified everything German and disparaged the achievements of other nations. So we took pleasure in the successes of our country and gave little thought to the outside world.

When I did raise questions about the goals of the Nazi party, they were met with silence or evasions. I realize now that neither parents nor teachers dared to speak out on political issues, for fear of ending up in a concentration camp. Although we have heard little about the voices of dissent in Hitler's Germany, the fact was that Aryan Germans, like Jews, were incarcerated if they opposed the Nazis, and in some cases dissenters disappeared and were never heard of again.

In retrospect, the extent to which Germany came under the control of the Nazi party seems almost unbelievable. The media - radio, newspapers and magazines - were routinely censored. All radio stations carried the same program, called the *Reichsprogramm,* which originated in Berlin, the seat of the government. Switching stations changed nothing, and so we can imagine 70 million people listening to the same radio program, which delivered the same propaganda message in precisely the same way everywhere. Newspapers were severely restricted in their role of dispersing the news and information and they all followed the party line.

So it was that, just as I started reading newspapers in a serious way, my father, in one of his more candid moments, advised me that one cannot believe everything one reads in the papers. Any attempt at discussion in school classrooms were ill-fated because the teachers were afraid of losing their job if they made an imprudent remark or permitted students to criticize the government. Expressions of individual points of view, controversy, or - Heaven forbid - dissent were out of the question.

Some of our daily rituals seem comic and even bizarre today. When we greeted our teachers we would no longer say "good morning" or "good day," but gave instead what was called *der deutsche Gruss* (the German greeting). We would raise our right arm toward the sky in a stiff, awkward salute and say *"Heil Hitler!"* Our teachers responded with varying degrees of enthusiasm - or alarm. Most teachers joined the Nazi Party, called *Nationalsozialistische deutsche Arbeiterpartei,* abbreviated NSDAP, in what must have been an attempt to deflect criticism or even harassment for failing to honor the goals of the state. Some of them wore their party badges proudly. Others, less demonstrative, even dared to omit *"Heil Hitler!"* when they greeted us. Our principal was a party member of long standing, who proudly displayed on his lapel the *goldene Parteiabzeichen* (golden party badge), a round pin made of enamel with the swastika in the center and a wreath of gold around it. Only the first 100,000 party members, called *Alte Kämpfer* (old fighters), were awarded this particular pin and they were held in high esteem by society. Their membership went back to the early days of the party, long before Hitler came to power in 1933.

At that time, I was in my third year in high school (but only 13 years old). The German system had always encompassed several prescribed courses, which all students had to take. However, the Nazis soon changed that. The German language and history were given more emphasis, and physical education was worked in as a regular curricular offering. Classroom instructors were ordered to promote the use of words of Germanic origin instead of synonyms of Latin or Greek etymology. Likewise, the use of German script and print continued to be mandatory. However, when we were taught foreign languages, such as English, French, Latin, or Italian, we had to use the Roman alphabet, which was taught concurrently with the German script.

Since I was a little overweight, I was not very good in physical education, and my teachers were not slow to remind me of my shortcomings. Those children with disabilities were given no sympathy on the playing fields, and those who did well were not rewarded with so much as a word of praise. I was ridiculed by my physical education teachers for my awkwardness and, of course, I learned to hate it. Even to this day I find it difficult to muster any high degree of enthusiasm for sports, even as a spectator.

The godlessness of the Nazi regime in Germany is a matter of historical record. Nevertheless, under Hitler there was no separation of church and state and, ironically, religion was a compulsory subject in each year of high school. The teacher of the first period would have the students recite a prayer in unison before addressing the lesson for the class. We prayed for the *Führer,* whom we considered as having been sent by God, and we prayed to God to guide him and give him strength for his enormous task of leading the nation. I still remember the lines of the prayer, because we had to say it thousands of times throughout high school. It went like this:

Herr, schirme unser deutsches Land
Dem Führer, den Du uns gesandt,
Gib Kraft zu seinem Werke.
Von unserem Volke nimm die Not,
Gib Freiheit uns und täglich Brot
und Einigkeit und Stärke.
Herr, Deine Gnade ist's allein,
Die einem Volke gibt Gedeih'n.
Drum lass uns nicht erlahmen
in Arbeit und in Dankbarkeit
Für unseres Reiches Herrlichkeit,
In Deinem Namen. Amen.

The English translation is as follows:

Lord, protect our German country
Grant strength to the leader you sent us.
Remove the misery from our people,
Give us freedom and our daily bread
And unity and strength.
Lord, it is only by Your grace
That a nation is granted prosperity.
Therefore let us not grow weak
In our work and in gratitude
For the glory of our country,
In Your name. Amen.

As this prayer demonstrates, we were taught to believe that Hitler was sent by God to restore Germany to greatness. The same message was conveyed in sermons and prayers in the churches. Most ministers commended Hitler to God, and invoked His divine guidance for Germany. Hitler himself pleaded to the Almighty to bestow His blessings on the German people.

By all means, play it safe with the Man Above! A prayer from the *Führer* may strike us as paradoxical today, but Hitler had been raised in the Catholic Church and he had been thoroughly grounded in its theology. Christianity by its very message and substance was untenable in the eyes of the Nazis because much of it, especially the Old Testament, deals with the history of the Jews. Moreover, Christian ethics were rejected because they ran counter to the Hitler ideology. The Christian teaching of humility, meekness and universal love, as advocated in the Sermon on the Mount, offered a gentle spiritual counterpoise to the Nazi ideals of strength, aggression and ruthless party politics. In one of his less charitable, if more perceptive moods, Hitler went so far as to maintain that a person could not be both a good German and a Christian, because one excluded the other. But in spite of his disaffection with the churches, he was circumspect in attacking them publicly. Neither did the churches entirely reject the Hitler regime. The relationship between church and the Nazi regime was ambivalent, to say the least, and in some cases they were mutually supportive.

To circumvent the potential embarrassment of honoring the Jews while observing the tenets of the Christian religion, a new branch of Christianity was formed by some imaginative Germans. They called themselves *Deutsche Christen* (German Christians) and completely disregarded the Old Testament, while preaching only those parts of the New Testament that suited their fancy.

The Nazi party probably realized that its political position would have been in jeopardy if they tried to purge Germany of the Christian religion. The majority of Germans were and still are Christians. So we were tacitly allowed to worship God's son and a Jew to boot, in a country whose leaders were vehemently opposed to everything Jewish!

Traditional holidays offered yet another paradoxical element in Hitler's Germany. All Christian holidays, such as Easter, Pentecost and Christmas, were observed and we were free to worship in church and observe the holidays at home as we chose. With the exception of Christmas, most German holidays were celebrated in much the same way as in the United States and elsewhere. The

German Christmas, with its distinctive customs, sheds light on social conditions and life styles, and offers some insights into the German religious psychology.

Generally speaking, Christmas in my youth was celebrated quietly, with less fanfare and less commercialism than in the United States. The Christmas season started officially on First of Advent Sunday, four Sundays before Christmas. I have always been proud of the fact that I was born on a First Advent Sunday, which made the date a special one for me, because store decorations went up that day. Within a few hours, a Christmas atmosphere was created and, as a child, I somehow felt that all this magic was conjured up not only for Christmas but also for me.

The four Advent Sundays were observed in the family circle by the Advent wreath, a forerunner of the Christmas tree. It was made of fir branches, decorated with four red candles and hung from the ceiling by red ribbons or placed in the center of the dinner table. The first candle was lighted on the first Advent Sunday. Two candles burned on the second Advent Sunday, three on the third, and on the fourth Advent all four candles were burning. These candles gave the home a special holiday atmosphere and directed our thoughts towards the Christmas festival. Advent wreaths were also placed in all classrooms of the schools, where they attracted the admiration of all the students. We would also light small candles on our desks and watch carefully to ensure that the braids of the girl sitting in front of us would not catch fire. When we were especially well-behaved the teacher rewarded us by letting us sing a Christmas carol once in a while.

The shopping season in prewar Germany lasted less than four weeks, and even in large cities there were fewer stores than we find today. The selection of merchandise was quite limited, so that Christmas shopping could be accomplished in a matter of hours rather than days. We were restricted in our purchases, not only by the few choices we had to make but also because of financial constraints. Children were kept on an extremely small allowance and were expected to buy gifts from those meager funds. I remember feeling very sheepish when I had to ask my mother for money, so that I could buy her and my father a modest Christmas present. Most parents made it clear to their children that they preferred handmade gifts, in part to keep expenses to a minimum but also as a means of encouraging youngsters to be thrifty and creative. Schools cooperated in that effort - teachers allowed students to work on their Christmas presents while they listened to their teacher's lecture. My choice of gifts never seemed to be the right one, at least as far as my mother was concerned. Deep down, I had the impression that she somehow resented the fact that she had to shell out the money for gifts, which was always a financial sacrifice. I remember that, when I was ten years old, I embroidered her a *Kaffeewärmer*. It never occurred to me that coffee was consumed almost as soon as it was brewed, so that we had no need for a warmer. That present was somewhat less than a hit that Christmas.

The climax of the Christmas season was the *Christkindlesmarkt* (Christmas Fair) on the medieval market place in downtown Nuremberg, where in late summer Hitler's uniformed fans paraded in front of their *Führer* and held their noisy mass meetings. What a change of atmosphere at Christmas time!

The Nuremberg Christmas Fair was the highlight of our Christmas celebration. The city radiated an atmosphere of magic, peace and love. There were innumerable booths with an endless variety of toys, treats for children, Christmas decorations, gifts of all kinds and wonderful things to eat, including sausages on buns, nuts, our favorite candy and exquisite chocolates. The fair usually provided anxious children an excellent opportunity to buy inexpensive Christmas presents. Sometimes, when the weather was bitter cold, and snow piled high on the streets, we thought we were freezing, even though we wore coats, fur caps, wool gloves and high fur-lined boots. When we talked to one another we could see our breath when we exhaled, and we pretended to be smoking.

Cold weather could not deter us from our enjoyment of the Christmas atmosphere, as we milled around in the crowd. At certain hours children's choirs sang Christmas carols, and the *Christkind* (Christ Child), strangely enough in the form of a woman, dressed in white, with wings like an angel and a golden crown on her head, spoke to the masses over the microphone. Not a single child in the city would have missed the excitement of the Christmas Fair.

When we returned home from our shopping expedition, the advent wreath again reminded us of the imminent holiday. Almost every evening my mother was busy baking the traditional Christmas cookies and *Stollen,* a tasty sweet Christmas bread. I helped her clean the pots and bowls by licking the various doughs from the pan. After the goodies were baked they were put into tin cans and cookie jars and then hidden to keep them from disappearing before Christmas. In those days, a cookie was indeed a special and rare treat!

We normally did not exchange greeting cards at Christmas. Instead, we sent New Year's cards to all those whom we loved. This meant that we had a lot of time to enjoy the Christmas season and we took full advantage of it. Our thoughts and innermost feelings focused especially on the three days of Christmas itself: Christmas Eve, Christmas Day and December 26, which was designated a legal holiday. Only two other religious holidays, Easter and Pentecost, were observed for two full days.

On Christmas Eve, the excitement of the holiday was almost unbearable, all the more so because children were kept from taking part in the last-minute preparations. My parents locked themselves in the room, while they put up the Christmas tree. Late in the evening, when the tree was decorated and lighted with real wax candles, a bell was sounded, the door was flung open, and I rushed in to smother my parents with great hugs and kisses. Then mother would solemnly announce that the *Christkind* had brought gifts and left just before I entered the room.

In Southern Germany, children were taught that the presents were delivered to the various homes by the Christ Child, who lived in Heaven except at Christmas time, when she came down to earth to visit the homes of children. In Northern Germany, presents were delivered by the *Weihnachtsmann* (Christmas Man), a figure similar to Santa Claus. I always considered it a remarkable feat that Christ Child and Christmas Man were able to share the chores of bringing gifts to families all over the world in just one magic evening.

My mother always regretted that I was unable to see the Christ Child in person. I was so disappointed! Delivery of gifts was complicated by the fact that German homes were not equipped with fireplaces for the *Christkind* to come through. But in Germany duty always comes before indulgence and enjoyment. In this case, duty consisted of singing in disconcerting disharmony several Christmas carols with my parents. As I stood there singing, my eyes wandered in the direction of the gifts neatly displayed on a table without wrapping. In later years, I played the piano to accompany my parents and I pretended not to be able to play the piano and sing at the same time. Somehow my parents' singing did not sound very cheerful, and I could not warm up to it. Invariably, my mother ended up crying. I was never able to figure out if her tears were caused by joyful emotions or genuine sadness. My impression was that it bothered her that, for financial reasons, she was not able to afford more and better gifts for me.

Eventually I was able to look at my presents - or shall I say present, in the singular? Sometimes I got only one gift, generally a useful one or something that I needed and would have received anyway, Christmas or not. I remember one Christmas I was given a blue woolen slip, which I thought was very unattractive, but no doubt bought on sale at a bargain price. In my child's heart I cried out for something more glamorous. I felt cheated and burst out in tears, only to be reprimanded for being ungrateful. All in all, it was not as bad as it sounds, because I owned a doll kitchen with the cutest little utensils and a toy store that resembled an old-fashioned mom and pop grocery store. Numerous miniature drawers were filled with all kinds of goodies, which I sold in small quantities to friends and relatives, and thus made a little profit.

Because of budget restrictions no Christmas presents were exchanged among friends and relatives other than within the immediate family. Neither did families congregate in large numbers, possibly because few could afford to buy the necessary food. When occasional visitors dropped in, they were treated to a cup of coffee or a glass of wine, and a few cookies or a piece of Christmas *Stollen* filled with plenty of nuts and candied fruit.

Around 9 o'clock on Christmas Eve, I used to leave home to walk to my favorite relatives, Onkel Anton, Tante Anna and Georg, their son, who lived about fifteen minutes away. Christmas trees of German families were traditionally placed inside a window. I enjoyed admiring all the lights in the windows as I walked through the snow. There was hardly anybody else in the streets but it was completely safe, even in this city of 420,000 inhabitants. My uncle was my father's brother and my aunt my mother's sister, which made me love Georg, seven years my senior, like the brother I always wanted and never got. The very presence of this cousin made Christmas Eve much more enjoyable, and I received another gift or two from his parents, who loved me as much as if I had been their own daughter. After an inspiring evening I, all by myself, attended midnight service in a nearby church and then walked home, purged of disappointment and loneliness.

Christmas Day was observed at home to be enjoyed with the family. The candles on the Christmas tree were kept burning all day and had to be replaced frequently. The highlight of the day was a delicious traditional dinner that consisted of roast goose, a salad, red cabbage, a potato dish, and *Stollen* for dessert. All this was followed by a cup of strong, hot coffee. The smell of the goose roasting in the oven made my mouth water for hours. When the food finally appeared on the table we stuffed ourselves to the point of immobility and were grateful for another day, the second Christmas holiday, in which to recover.

Toward the end of the war, meat was extremely scarce, and we were allowed only one pound per month. As was the custom during the war, my aunt went one day to see some relatives of ours in the countryside to help them with the harvest. By then, money had lost much of its value, so instead of paying my aunt for her services, my relatives gave her a live goose, which she took home to Nuremberg and fed to fatten it for the Christmas feast. This particular goose was a very welcome boost to our diet, and we looked forward with great anticipation to eating it. However, my aunt became so attached to the bird that she was unable to kill it, let alone eat any of it. The rest of the family thought it was an especially tasty goose and consumed it with great gusto. I can't help but think of a friend in the small town in Oregon where I live who raised a steer for the table, only to discover the same thing. The steer became so tame that it would approach the kitchen window while she prepared the family meals. She, too, was unable to kill her pet and in a moment of great emotional trauma, she vowed that, the next time she raised a steer, she was going to consign it to the far pasture and call it Hitler!

To all traditional Christian holidays in Germany certain patriotic holidays were added to the calendar. One, January 30, marked the anniversary of Hitler's ascent to power, and the other, April 20, Hitler's birthday. On those days millions of flags were flown across Germany, nobody had to report to work, and all stores, offices, banks and schools were closed. Nazi organizations scheduled noisy demonstrations and thousands of men in uniform marched through the streets and sang patriotic songs to proclaim to the public their utter devotion to the party, its cause and its leader.

I remember April 20, 1936, Hitler's forty-seventh birthday, for a bicycle accident that I suffered on that day. Because of an injury I was taken to the hospital for treatment. In the evening, after I came out of the anesthetic, I insisted on being released from the hospital. On the way home, as I was resting in the ambulance with my mother by my side, I looked out the window and noticed a sea of flags flying from all the windows along the streets. Still a little drowsy from my anesthetic I could not figure out the reason for all these flags greeting me. My mother filled me in by asking, "Don't you remember, today is Hitler's birthday?" I was somehow disappointed because, for a while, still confused, I thought it was the world's way of welcoming me back to life.

4

Nine Years of High School! Ugh!

My high school education spanned the years from 1930 to 1939. "Nine years of high school?" you may ask incredulously. Yes, indeed, not because I was a slow learner, far from it, but because high school attendance in Germany then and now requires nine years. Great expectations were placed on every child, who was intellectually qualified to undergo the rigors of such an education. High school attendance was regarded as an honor and a privilege by society and especially so by parents who, for various reasons, had been unable to go to high school themselves. Secondary schools have always been college-preparatory in Germany. If students were not college-bound because of different career preferences, they did not even choose to go through high school.

This was the case with my parents. They did not consider high school education necessary for their particular purposes but, instead, attended eight years of elementary school. Even now, university graduates constitute only twenty-three percent of German young people.

However, in those eight years of elementary school, my parents received a well-rounded academic education, because no time was allowed for recreation, sports, or other nonacademic activities. My father, very gifted in drawing and painting, entered an apprenticeship as a lithographer and printer upon graduation from grade school at the age of fourteen and he faced three more years of part-time trade school, in order to qualify for a job in that field. My mother was one of seven children, whose parents owned a grocery store. She and her siblings worked in the store, and therefore it was not necessary for them to attend high school, at least in the opinion of their parents.

As I indicated earlier, I was born after World War I, and, for economic reasons and much to my dismay, my parents chose to have only one child. However, there was one advantage to this: they were most ambitious for me and wanted me to receive the best possible education available. As soon as I entered grade school I was groomed to work toward high school and, if at all possible, toward a university education. My grade school teachers, having recognized my intellectual potential, encouraged me in this plan. So I knew from a very early age that I was cut out to become a member of the young intellectual elite. During those four years of elementary school, the highest grades were expected of me, and I was happy to conform because I eagerly looked forward to high school.

Admittance to high school was based on rigid and uncompromising standards, and upon admittance a strong and effective performance in the classroom was necessary for survival. We were expected to have the full support of our parents and grade school teachers; our financial resources had to be sufficient to pay tuition; and we had to demonstrate superior intelligence, enormous ambition, iron discipline and perseverance in our educational endeavors.

At the age of ten, I took the compulsory entrance examination to be admitted to high school. There were three written tests to be passed, in German language, mathematics and, strangely enough, religion. I did well on the examinations, and my parents were extremely proud of me and my achievements in high school. In my first year we were taught English as our first foreign language. I remember walking down the street with my mother and practicing my English on her. She did not know a word of English and looked at me with pride and in disbelief. I was proud also, but for different reasons: speaking English brought me great distinction, I thought, and soon the whole world would be beating a path to my door.

Although that did not happen, I did fall in love with the English language. It became a way for me to see beyond the narrow confines of a highly traditional, conforming way of life to the exciting possibilities of visiting or even living in England or America. Until the war started, I had an English pen pal named Margaret, who lived in Liverpool. She was the same age as I, and for several years we exchanged letters and sent each other small gifts. I still have a handkerchief with an Edelweiss border that she sent me. Writing to Margaret in English was a challenge, and I found that I had to work very hard on grammar and spelling. But the results were worth the effort. I developed an extensive vocabulary while corresponding with Margaret, and I learned to pursue the complexities of English into its deepest, darkest grammatical recesses. That would pay great dividends, when I got to Oregon and needed a job to help pay my way through school. During and after the war I thought often of Margaret, but did not write her, because I was ashamed of what had happened between our two countries. She may have felt the same way. It would have been interesting to meet her or to know what became of her.

All high schools expected a horrendous dropout rate. In 1930, of 220 students in my high school class, only seventeen completed the nine-year grind and graduated in 1939. Academic standards were so demanding that, after each year, students either gave up or were compelled to leave because they did not meet the requirements for moving on to the next class. Students with two fives (equivalent to F's) or one five and two fours (D's) automatically flunked out. These dropouts faced a difficult time, regardless of which of the available options they chose. They could repeat the full year in all subjects, including those they had passed; go back to grade school if they were eleven to fourteen; or leave high school if compulsory school age had been reached and join the job market.

School days were not a happy time for students, because they faced almost insuperable difficulties in passing all of their courses. Learning was not fun; it took place as a form of duty and was carried out with respect and obedience toward both parents and teachers. Students were treated with little respect and were ordered about in a condescending and dictatorial way. After all, young people were considered ignorant or at least lacking in experience and had to prove themselves, in order to be recognized by society. The teacher was always right and the student wrong. Challenging a teacher would have been immensely disrespectful, and so it was never done. We dutifully listened to what the teachers had to say and took everything they said for gospel truth.

Teachers were not available after school hours, and students asked no questions in class, lest we were deemed ignorant and lazy. After all, what were books and libraries for? Only dumb people asked questions! High school counselors did not exist, and career planning lay in the hands of the parents. Students with personal problems were expected either to work out solutions by themselves within their peer group or, preferably, with the help of their parents. That was done with great reluctance. Children who were unable to work out their own problems were considered weaklings.

Some students faced enormous personal problems because of an unstable family life. Since divorce was frowned upon, most families remained outwardly intact, but at what a price! I am convinced that many unhappy couples must have lived lives of quiet desperation and misery just for appearance's sake. In retrospect I find it amazing how much responsibility rested with parents, how many important decisions were made for children by their elders, and what a small role schools and teachers played in the overall development of the children. The only task teachers had to accomplish was to transmit knowledge and promote the intellectual growth of their students. When we attended high school we were no longer as docile as we were as grade school students. Every once in a while, a student or a small group would rebel against a teacher or play a trick on him. But it was always done in a cowardly concealed way, so that culprits could not be easily identified. If the teacher did not have any plausible evidence, he was helpless. Punishment for a proven wrongdoing was either a *"Verweis"*, a written notification of parents, or, in more severe cases, dismissal for the day or suspension with necessary reinstatement.

Given the intensity of the academic environment in the German high schools before the war, small wonder that the practice of cheating on tests was prevalent. I was a diligent and conscientious student and did not have to resort to cheating. Nevertheless, I was an accomplice in so far as I allowed other students to copy from me. My teachers soon caught on to this practice and ordered me from the room, as soon as I had finished my tests. Latin was my favorite subject, and I was very well liked by my teacher. However, he did not like the assistance I gave to some of my friends. During tests he watched me like a hawk, so that it became practically impossible for me to help other students. On one occasion, the girl next to me thought she had found a way to pass a difficult examination. We were to be tested on Julius Caesar's *Bellum Gallicum*, of which there were miniature translations so tiny that they could fit in the palm of the hand, as the student was writing the test. The fingers were held curled over the booklet, so that the teacher could not see it. Unfortunately for the young lady, the teacher had omitted one sentence from the Latin text. Of course, this particular sentence appeared in the German translation from which my friend copied. In her nervousness, she failed to check the Latin text against the

German version. What better proof that she had cheated! It was a very embarrassing situation for the whole class. She ended up with an F on the test, and her parents were notified of her moral lapse.

The high school curriculum was almost entirely prescribed. Everybody sat in the same class with the same students and they had to take the same subjects regardless of special interests they might entertain. The curriculum included nine years of German, mathematics, religion, physical education and art; six years of history, geography, Latin and chorus; four years of French, physics and chemistry; and three years of botany and zoology. Some courses met every day of the week - Mondays through Saturdays - and others four times, three times, twice, or once. School hours lasted from 8 a. m. to 1 p. m. with two ten-minute recesses. Lunch was not provided in school. Daily homework assignments were given in each subject, so that afternoons and most evenings were filled with lessons. The school year consisted of 245 days but, even during vacations, students reviewed earlier lessons or read to increase their general knowledge. Education was considered to be an ongoing process, and lessons were not to be forgotten after tests, because there were comprehensive tests given several times before graduation.

In addition to compulsory subjects, electives could be taken in the afternoon, after the required courses were finished. My electives included violin lessons and Italian, which I continued at the university. This meant a forty-five minute walk back to school after lunch. My parents claimed they could not afford the streetcar fare and buses were not available. I often wondered how much more money they had to spend on my shoes because of so much walking. To my way of thinking my parents were penny-wise and pound-foolish but it may be that they regarded walking as a beneficial activity which builds character. If so, I got a lot of character building from my education.

We were able to choose from three different high schools, depending on our specific interests and future plans, assuming, of course, that our interests and capabilities were already recognizable at the age of ten. The three branches included the *Humanistisches Gymnasium,* which emphasized a classical education requiring a thorough background in Greek and Latin, and involving a study of the linguistic contributions of Greek and Latin to the Indo-European languages and a study of the contributions of the ancient Greeks and Romans to Western civilization. The *Oberrealschule* stressed the sciences and mathematics, with some Latin required along with at least one modern foreign language. The *Realgymnasium* had course requirements in languages, including English, French and Latin, and mathematics, science and the humanities. I attended the *Realgymnasium*.

After nine years, a comprehensive examination, called the *Abitur*, was administered. Students were tested in three foreign languages (English, French and Latin), German, physics, chemistry and mathematics. Each test lasted three hours. The contents of the examinations were kept secret and they might have included materials learned years before. I had the honor of being the valedictorian for my sixteen classmates. We mourned those who, for various reasons, had fallen by the wayside. The *Abitur* carried a great deal of weight, since it entitled the graduate, usually nineteen years of age, to be admitted to any university without further examination.

These were truly no-nonsense schools. The only entertainment we allowed ourselves was the satisfaction we derived from learning. Our social life was severely constrained, except for the opportunity to exchange a few words with our classmates during recess. Extracurricular activities, such as competitive sports, dances and clubs did not exist. We did enjoy our informal associations, and gradually a genuine sense of camaraderie developed among us, largely because we spent so much time together. Most of us spent nine years in the same classroom - teachers rather than students changed rooms - and we got to know each other very well.

Teachers in Germany were awarded great social distinction and treated with high respect by students. We were expected to stand up, when teachers entered the room, even if we despised them, which was the case now and then. University professors were given a traditional greeting by students, which involved young men stomping the floor with their feet, and decorous young ladies knocking on the desk, and when professors left the classroom this rather strange form of applause was repeated. Students even had a traditional way of showing disapproval of their professors' lectures: they shuffled their feet and made a kind of grinding noise on the floor. Those strange patterns of behavior continue in the German lecture halls even today.

5

Georg - My Role Model

Given the absence of meaningful social activities in my high school in Germany, I had to look for a social outlet elsewhere. My cousin Georg was a medical student at the time when I attended high school. He was like a brother to me and treated me with decorum and respect, although I was seven years younger and I must have been rather unsophisticated in his view, especially during my formative years. A highly intelligent young man and endowed with a great measure of common sense, he served as a valuable role model to me for practically all my life, first during his high school years, then as a medical student, a physician in the German army and finally as an orthopedist in private practice in Nuremberg. He had a marvelous way of sharing his experiences with me and made me feel that I amounted to something. Very few people helped me more to develop into a mature, self-confident human being than this man.

For a period of time, Georg and I lived across the street from each other and we visited back and forth often. We spent a lot of time just talking and confiding in each other or playing cards or some other indoor games. Later on, my parents and I moved to a different part of the city, and Georg and I did not get to see each other very much. We made up for it during our summer vacations, which we spent with relatives in the countryside about ten miles from Nuremberg.

The house in which my relatives lived had neither indoor plumbing nor running water. The outhouse provided valuable natural fertilizer for the garden and fields, which made vegetables grow as no other fertilizer did. Water was available in the kitchen, but had to be pumped in from an outdoor fountain, whose main function it was to irrigate the vast area of vegetable and flower beds surrounding the house.

Growing vegetables was the main source of income to my relatives. It was strictly a family enterprise without any hired help. My aunt, uncle and their daughter worked long and arduous hours in the vegetable fields and garden. They welcomed Georg and me every year, because we proved to be hard-working farmhands. The idea of getting paid for our physical labor never entered our mind; we were just happy to be of help and be so much appreciated. During the summer, weather conditions were quite unpredictable, and often considerable changes in temperature occurred within a short period of time, which resulted in frequent electric storms. Very few houses in the countryside were equipped with lightning rods on the roofs, and the danger of fire was ever-present. When thunderstorms hit at night, we prepared ourselves to leave the house in a hurry in case of fire. My aunt took it upon herself to waken her family, Georg and me, and urge us to get up and gather in the living room, no matter how tired and sleepy we were. She then started to pray and read from the Bible to disperse her fear and ours. Years later, during the night air raids, falling bombs reminded me of thunder claps during my vacation time in the country. Although fearful at the time, they were less threatening than the bombs falling out of the sky.

Even though we were tired after spending a few hours awake at night, we enjoyed working hard for the benefit of our relatives the next day. No sleeping in for farmers, even voluntary farmhands. We had great fun working together like one happy family and we especially enjoyed Tuesdays and Saturdays, when we transported the fruits of our labor to the farmers' market in Erlangen. We would harvest the produce the day before and put it in huge baskets to be loaded onto a big horse-drawn wagon.

We had to get up at four o'clock in the morning, in order to arrive at the market for its opening. I was convinced that very few teenagers had to get up that early and sometimes felt a little sorry for myself. However, I would pull myself together and, bleary-eyed, show up at the table for a hearty breakfast consisting of pancakes, ham or bacon, bratwurst, buttered toast, jam and fresh fruits. I took some comfort from the realization that I did not have to get up even earlier to prepare the morning meal. My uncle would quickly devour his breakfast and go out to the barn to harness the horse to the wagon. We would climb on, bundled up in a heavy winter coat and wrap ourselves in wool blankets for protection against the cold early morning temperatures.

We took about an hour and a half to travel to the city. There, we would unload the big heavy baskets full of vegetables onto the rented stall in the market place. The horse had to be taken to a stable nearby, where it stayed until the late afternoon when we prepared to return home.

The produce was displayed in the open air, and we enjoyed little protection from the elements, whether heavy rains or the blazing midday sun. We stood there with umbrellas raised over our heads, waiting for and serving customers. I made it a point to memorize the prices of all produce, which changed from time to time, depending on supply and demand. The customers' purchases had to be weighed on scales that we brought from home. Playing the part of a farm woman was so much fun for this city girl, but I was secretly glad that I did not have to do it all the time!

My uncle seldom stayed around to help with the customers. He usually left my aunt and me to manage the market together, while he took care of business or visited his sister. Only rarely did one of my two cousins accompany us to the market. They had chores to do at home.

The greatest reward for going to market came at noon, when my aunt took me to a good restaurant and treated me to a delicious lunch, which always included a generous piece of *Torte*, a multi-layered rich cake made with butter and eggs and filled with chocolate, fruit and nuts. I also enjoyed our shopping sprees in the various stores. Since the village in which my relatives lived boasted of only one small grocery store, my aunt did her grocery shopping twice a week in the city, and I gladly tagged along.

Later in the afternoon, when most of the baskets were empty and the wallet full, my uncle would come back with horse and wagon. After loading the baskets on the wagon, we proceeded back to the village, ready to resume the daily routine of farming.

The rustic life of a farm family was physically taxing but, in their modest and unpretentious way, my relatives savored every minute of it, deriving an intense feeling of satisfaction from fulfilling a useful purpose in society. How hard they worked! The only piece of machinery they used was a community-owned threshing machine, which they rented after the grain was shocked. These good farm people, with their uncompromising work ethic, have always been a source of inspiration to me, and I look back over those months spent in the countryside of Germany with feelings of warmth and nostalgia.

I remember one day when my mother and I visited those relatives. My aunt greeted us with tears streaming down her cheeks. I was afraid that something dreadful had happened to a member of the family. As it turned out, one of the cows had died just a few hours before our arrival. My aunt's grief knew no bounds. She had been in charge of milking that cow for years and had become very attached to her.

During my summer vacation, I had a chance to provide what I thought was a valuable service to my aunt. The cows, while being milked, warded off with their tails the numerous pesky flies that inhabited the smelly stable. They frequently and unintentionally, I am sure, swatted my aunt across the face as she sat on the milking stool pulling away at the udders. I came to her aid with an ingenious invention. I attached a long piece of rope to the tail of each cow and held it fast during the milking, so that the cows were unable to swat flies, or, for that matter, my aunt. Cruelty to animals? Not really — the ordeal, if indeed it was one, lasted only a very short time, and I am sure the cows did not mind. The milk was poured from the bucket into huge, heavy metal cans, which immediately had to be taken to a central dairy to be transported by truck to nearby cities. My cousin Georg and I used to carry the cans over to the dairy, which was located a fifteen-minute walk away.

Georg and I helped in any way we could to ease the tasks of our hard-working farm relatives, but we also had a lot of fun. While we worked in the fields, Georg taught me all the student songs he knew. German students took pride in building on a century-old tradition of singing and carousing, and to this day university students know numerous student songs by heart and sing them whenever an occasion arises. Although I was not a university student yet, I was anxious to learn those songs, and my cousin taught me well. Every time I managed to memorize a new song, he and I would sing it at the top of our lungs, over and over again, as we worked in the vegetable beds. We enjoyed mixing work and pleasure and when we could find the time Georg would take me deer hunting or on bicycle rides.

An annual event of great importance to the rural inhabitants of Germany was the *Kirchweih*, a festival to celebrate the original consecration date of churches. The event took place in villages all over Germany, and it was matched in importance and intensity only by Christmas. Two days in August, invariably a Sunday and the Monday, were set aside for the festival.

Preparations got under way some weeks before. Women took great pride in sewing new dresses to wear at the festivities. Last year's dress just would not do! My aunt was so loving and generous that every year she designed and made a new dress for me, too. Getting a new dress was such a rare treat for me that I could scarcely contain my eagerness when August approached. I knew that, upon my return to school in the city, my classmates would look at me in my new dress with feelings that ranged all the way from loving and unselfish admiration to overt jealousy.

Another effort of the celebration was devoted to preparation of food, especially sweets, cakes and doughnuts. On the morning of *Kirchweih* Sunday the whole community gathered for solemn church services which gave way to the noise and ruckus of the afternoon and evening. Booths were erected around the church and peddlars offered all kinds of candy, dried fruits, ice cream and soft drinks to eager children. A merry-go-round added to the excitement. Adults congregated in the three restaurants of the village, where dances were held from the afternoon until the early morning hours of the following day. Live orchestras provided the music for old-fashioned dances, including waltzes, polkas, the *Schottisch* and the *Rheinländer*. In later years, the tango and foxtrot also became popular.

As I grew up I developed a passion for dancing and I could hardly wait until I was old enough to try it. But I worried about the dismal prospect of falling all over myself and stomping on my partner's toes. But gallant Georg came to the rescue. He took it upon himself to teach me the various dances and did such a good job that I became quite adept at it, and it became my favorite form of recreation.

My aunt and uncle also liked to dance and they hardly missed a round. Milking cows interfered with my aunt's fun, and she had to tear herself away from the dance floor when the time came. I felt sorry for her, but she took care of that annoying task without complaint. Many couples on the dance floor did not go home for supper, but had their evening meal in one of the restaurants. In true German tradition, at least one pitcher of beer accompanied the meal.

The next day we would sleep late and recuperate. Then the daily chores had to be done, so we could return to the festivities in the evening. Again we danced until the wee hours of the morning, savoring each dance, prizing each precious moment of romance or relaxation, keenly aware that we had to wait a whole year before we were able to indulge in so much fun again.

After I learned how to dance at a *Kirchweih*, I met a fantastic man, about ten years my senior, who was the best dancer in the world. He lived in Tennenlohe near Erlangen, the same village as my relatives. I immediately fell in love with him. We danced together for hours on end but, to my disappointment, he never became romantically inclined towards me. Maybe he singled me out as a dancing partner among other girls because I was from a big city, attended high school, and was probably more sophisticated in my own peculiar way than the country girls who surrounded him in his village. Fred was the first man I fell in love with but to my dismay he did not seem to be ready and willing to date me. Maybe he considered me too young to get more serious. Dating in those days was not as prevalent as it is today and kept to an absolute minimum, at least in public. But I was a scheming girl and wanted to make things happen. Fred was a dentist and commuted by bicycle from his native village to the nearby city of Erlangen, where his practice was located. Even before I knew him, I also often rode my bicycle to Erlangen to go shopping or visit my relatives. So what could have been more natural than taking that bike out more frequently, ride it to the road to Erlangen in the hope of seeing Fred on his way to or from work? Sometimes I rode my bicycle up and down the road at times which I figured would coincide with his, but I never met him that way. It was silly to resort to such a scheme because, even if our two bicycles had met, we could not have done any visiting together, but just ridden side by side. Fred was my first love and it was painful to give him up, without ever having had him as a close friend, let alone as a lover. I was only fifteen years old then, but the pain was deeply felt.

When Georg began his medical studies at the university, his behavior became a little more erratic and much more daring. He had just learned to work on corpses and considered himself a master of the art of dissection. One evening, he brought a skull to my aunt's apartment where he was living, and I was visiting. When I returned from an errand downtown, I found the stairway poorly lit. I cautiously made my way up the stairs when, all of a sudden, I bumped into a macabre skull on one of the stairs. The eye cavities were covered with red plastic and a candle burned inside. Those huge red eyes fixed me with a malevolent leer and I screamed with terror.

Georg promptly came bounding down the stairs to mock me, laughing with glee and unable to hide his malicious pleasure.

On another occasion, he invited me to attend a duel in his fraternity house. Before it was outlawed in the mid-nineteenth century, dueling was a time-honored way for young gentlemen to prove their courage and demonstrate their manhood. A student who had a disagreement or a fight with a rival could challenge him to a duel, which involved fighting with rapiers. In almost all cases this led to bloodshed, which dueling students accepted in hopes of receiving lifelong scars on their faces. To this day, male members of the older generation proudly display their facial scars, which they believe set them apart from "common" people, who did not attend a university. Any attempt to refuse a challenge was considered a sign of cowardice and tantamount to ostracism. To witness a duel was a great privilege and honor, and in my teenage naïveté, I eagerly accepted Georg's invitation.

The duel was secretly held in a dank, poorly-lit, dungeon-like room, and as the antagonists began to fence, I realized I was not as brave as I pretended to be. As the blood began to gush from wounds, I got sick and had to be led from the scene. This incident put an end to my long-standing ambition to follow in my cousin's footsteps and become a physician. I realized then that I would never be able to develop the tolerance towards bloodshed and suffering that a physician must endure. Georg, however, accepted the results of the duel with great aplomb and expressed his satisfaction with its outcome.

One morning, I got up to find my aunt in a very bad mood. When I asked her what was wrong, she simply responded, "You'll see soon enough." Then Georg entered the room, looking embarrassed and distraught. When he started to speak I noticed to my horror that his upper front teeth were missing. He could hardly speak but proceeded to tell me that he had spent most of the night drinking with some fraternity brothers. On his way home, he was in an exuberant mood and decided to jump over a low fence which bordered a park, presumably to keep dogs off lawns and children off flower beds. Georg stumbled on one of the railings, fell on his face and knocked his teeth out. He was a frightful sight.

It would be easy, I think, to attribute these activities to the unrelieved boredom of university life, with its preoccupation with learning and its callous disregard for the recreational needs of youthful, energetic students. At times, I cannot help but think that students resorted to destructive pastimes, such as playing tricks on unsuspecting teenagers, dueling and heavy drinking, because German universities traditionally failed to assume the role of providing suitable leisure activities for the students. But then I note the more than ample opportunities for recreation that American students enjoy and yet they, too, play tricks on the innocent, fight in somewhat less bloody ways and drink too much. Maybe the life of a student demands risky and unconventional behavior.

Wedding picture of cousin Georg and wife Annemarie, a refugee from Soviet-occupied Silesia, 1945.

6

Religion and Ballroom Dancing

As I grew up, my parents consistently had my welfare in mind. The three of us attended a Lutheran church in Nuremberg. Membership as such did not exist in German churches, and we did not have to declare our membership officially. All those who attended regularly and/or were baptized and confirmed in a particular church were automatically considered as "belonging."

When I was old enough to find my own way, my parents encouraged me to go to special services for children, but they did not attend church regularly. It seemed to me that they wanted the influence of religion for me, especially the Christian moral codes, in which they had already been steeped and which they followed - somewhat casually - in their daily lives. At no time, however, did I ever get the impression that they had given up on Christian teachings or the church as such. As a matter of fact, I had always regarded them as good Christians, even though they did not attend church anymore.

I must confess that I tended to follow my parents' casual attitude towards religion even as a child, but German children were expected to follow their parents' guidance in every respect. So I dutifully attended church, although I had doubts as to some teachings of the Christian church. As hard as I tried, I did not feel totally committed to the church, especially in view of the dissension prevalent among various denominations. I have always believed in God as the Supreme Being and all my life I have followed the ten commandments, but have had difficulty believing in the miracles of the Bible and accepting its transcendental tenets, such as the immaculate conception, the resurrection and life after death. All these factors seemed to run counter to my highly-developed reasoning power, which kept me from believing the Bible and its teachings without reservations.

I consider faith a blessing bestowed by God or possibly acquired by one's own efforts during a lifetime. Religion and faith can certainly serve a person well, when it comes to coping with and overcoming the hardships of life, but in my estimation this type of approach is a selfish and cowardly one and I have consistently rejected it for that reason. Whenever I experienced the hard knocks of life, I did my level best to overcome them by my own efforts, as I was taught, rather than choosing what I considered the easy way out, namely to put God in charge and rely on His ultimately solving all problems, both mine and mankind's as a whole.

These observations occurred in my early teens, but I did not think them serious enough to warrant breaking with the traditions of the church, which were also my parents' and as such to be adhered to. Was I a hypocrite or a moral weakling, who did not have the courage to make a decision? Or maybe I did not feel strong enough because I was still so very young, with the hope that things would work out in time.

With these wavering thoughts, I entered one of the highlights of religious upbringing in the Lutheran Church called first communion, or *Konfirmation*. It was customarily observed on Easter Sunday. To be prepared for the event, compulsory religious instruction started the previous September. Classes met once a week for two hours and were conducted by the minister who confirmed the young people the following Easter. I was fourteen years old then. The classes provided an opportunity to become acquainted with the minister and the forty or so like-minded girls who wanted to be inducted into the church. The instruction provided us with an introduction into the Bible and its teachings and prepared us for the oral examination, as a prerequisite for first communion that was held three days before Easter.

Parents took preparations for the event quite seriously. It was the custom for girls to get two new dresses for the occasion; one for the examination and another elegant black velvet dress to be worn at the ceremony on Easter morning. Those dresses must have been quite a financial sacrifice for my parents.

The examination went well for all of us confirmands. It was a matter of honor to do well, even though there were no grades involved. However, I had never heard of anyone who did not pass.

As we walked to church on Easter Sunday for the ceremony, Georg warned me that, in all likelihood, my mother would shed tears during the service. How right he was! I had always thought of confirmation as something positive and had looked forward to it. Certainly in my estimation it should not have evoked tears, and I could not understand my mother's apparent emotional distress - or did she shed tears of joy?

The ceremony was followed by an elaborate festive dinner at home, where we were joined by some close relatives, who had attended the services. They all brought me gifts. I was very fond of my summertime family. From early childhood I had expressed to my parents my desire to own a bicycle. I could not believe my eyes when, on that Easter Sunday, these relatives presented me with a brand-new bicycle. This long-standing wish of mine had unexpectedly been fulfilled! My parents seemed a little less enthusiastic than I, for reasons not understandable to me at the time.

I used the bicycle frequently on weekends to visit the generous donors. Unfortunately, I got involved in two accidents, one of which landed me in the hospital. My bad luck, or lack of skill on wheels, became a great concern for my parents. One day, after my return from school, my beloved bicycle was gone. Stolen? No. My parents had returned it to my relatives without consulting or informing me. It was too dangerous for me. I was crushed, but perhaps I owe my longevity to my parents' firm decision. Fortunately, I have not been involved in any kind of traffic accident ever since, with a bicycle or a car.

One of the greatest ambitions my mother had for me was to learn how to play a musical instrument. A very good friend of mine owned a piano and had taken lessons for quite some time. She lived across the street from us and, during the summer months, when the windows were open, we were able to hear her playing. I was about twelve years old then and dreamed of learning to play the piano, but I never dared hope for my dream to come true.

One summer, on my return home from the country, I heard someone playing familiar melodies on the piano. I could not believe my ears and rushed into the room where the music came from. There sat my father in front of a brand-new piano, playing some tunes, which he had taught himself, in order to surprise me. I admired him for that, because I knew that he had never taken any music lessons in his whole life. That piano was one of the greatest boons of my life. I took four years of lessons and practiced faithfully every day, although the piano stood in a room which, for financial reasons, was not heated during the winter. Nevertheless, I continued practicing in the ice-cold room. To fight the cold, I was dressed in several layers of clothing and a heavy winter coat. The only warm item that I was not able to wear were woolen gloves to warm my freezing and stiff fingers.

With this kind of perseverance, I became quite a good piano player and appeared in several recitals. During the war, music lost some of its appeal because of the seriousness of life and our preoccupation with sheer survival. Today I am lucky enough to play the piano again, and the instrument occupies an important part in my life. Unfortunately, when I came from Germany as an immigrant, I was not able to bring with me my original piano, but my first savings were spent on the purchase of an instrument to replace the one I loved so much.

Taking lessons in ballroom dancing, just like learning to play the piano, was part and parcel of a well-rounded education when I grew up. My parents afforded me both privileges. There were about ten members of each sex in my class taught by a pair of professional dancers once a week in the evening. I was almost seventeen years old then. It was mandatory that the girls were escorted to class by their mother. The escorts stayed for the whole evening, watching with pride and trepidation as their daughters developed from "their little girls" to women, aware of the fact that there were also men in the world besides the female sex. Mothers were seated on a platform overlooking the dance floor. We referred to the place with eagerly watching mothers as the *Drachenburg* (fortress of dragons). A "dragon" refers to a person who is extremely watchful of details, extraordinarily inquisitive and at times even critical, in this case the mothers. When the lesson was over, each mother picked up her daughter to take her home by streetcar. There was no way that a girl could have spent any additional time with her dance partner. Not that we did not think about it! And we did find awkward ways of getting together, as limited as the time may have been. The situation was aggravated by the fact that high schools in Germany were segregated by sex. In my particular case my dance partner and I found it even more difficult to meet after school than others did, because he had to catch a train from Nuremberg back to his home town several miles away. One evening we decided to take the bull by the horn and arrange for a short get-together before my mother came along to claim me. Hans and I agreed to have a brief rendezvous the following morning at my school during my French class. Our classroom faced the street, and Hans told me to be sure to have the window open, because he would whistle for me to come down to meet him in the school yard. I could hardly wait for the next day to roll around in anticipation of our *tête-à-tête*. Instead of listening to the teacher's efforts to teach me some French, I waited for Hans' whistle. German students were not allowed to leave the classroom without permission of the teacher. When I heard the unmistakable whistle, I asked to be allowed to go to the rest room. Permission granted. I ran as fast as I could down the stairs to greet my friend. French was immediately forgotten and instead I enjoyed our rendezvous (French word!) immensely. My French teacher must have had an inkling that there was some hanky-panky going on—maybe I was not a good liar. So he looked out onto the school yard, where Hans and I were happily engaged in conversation. The fun or the happiness, if you prefer to call it that, could not have lasted more than five minutes. I rushed back into the classroom when, to my surprise, the teacher interrupted his lesson, gave me a penetrating look and then grinned with a knowing look on his face. I immediately realized that he had looked through my scheme. This particular teacher had always had a wonderful way of making me blush and now he had a real reason. As so many times before, I blushed again for him and quietly sat down in my seat. Afterwards my classmates were hysterical and in complete disbelief because, over the years, I had acquired the reputation of being a *Musterschülerin* (model student). They complimented me for carrying out such an outrageously courageous deed, and my reputation was never the same. I was rather proud of proving that, after all, I was quite normal.

Both Hans and I finished dancing school together, but never really went on dates as teenagers do nowadays, because of societal constraints. In the spring of 1940, I saw his obituary in the local newspaper. He was killed in France as he served his country in the military. A chapter of potential happiness was sadly closed.

The first devastating personal experience in my young life came with the premature death of my mother in August, 1937, at the age of 46. She died of cancer at our home after three months of excruciating pain. I was only seventeen years old then. In those days, it was the custom on the part of physicians not to tell patients and their family about terminal illness. It was not until my mother's death that my father and I learned of the nature of her disease. The onset of cancer was tantamount to a sentence of death, as no successful methods of treating it had yet been developed. Therefore, cancer patients customarily suffered and died at home rather than in a hospital.

I was emotionally crushed by our loss, and so was my father. I thought the whole world had come to an end and I expected everyone to mourn for my mother as I did. A well-meaning resident of our apartment building took it upon herself to console me, since I did not seem to be able to pull myself together. In an effort to put my grief in the proper perspective, she said to me, "You must learn to come to grips with this tragedy in your life." She then pointed to some apartment buildings in the next block and remarked, "Imagine, the people who live here neither knew your mother nor do they know about her death." Although I considered these words cruel, they were spoken with good intentions and, as it turned out, they actually helped me immensely to adjust to my loss. I learned the valuable lesson that, in the midst of tragedy, life must go on, and we cannot spend our days mourning the losses of yesteryear.

My father and I drew very close in those days of mourning. Neither he nor I could boast of any culinary skills. My mother never taught me how to cook and, whenever I made an attempt to help her, she would run me out of the kitchen, saying, "You'd better do your school work and stay out of the kitchen. You were born for better things." After her death it was up to me or my father to put three meals on the table every day. My mother never used any recipes, nor had she any in her possession. So the first thing my father and I did was to acquire a three-volume cookbook and slowly learn how to cook. My father used to say to me, "You can't even boil an egg!" and he was right.

An irksome German custom required that the family members of the deceased had to wear black clothing from head to toe for one full year. This custom set grieving persons apart from the rest of the population and it certainly marked students in school. To mourn my mother's death, I wore the black dress, which she had thoughtfully bought for me on the occasion of my confirmation. I remember, when I showed up at school after the funeral, all dressed in black, my classmates stared at me and fumbled awkwardly in their efforts to talk to me. What an insensitive custom!

7

Nuremberg—
A Stronghold of Anti-Semitism

Nuremberg, my native city, has played a significant role in German history in the nine centuries since its founding around 1,050 A.D. During the Middle Ages, it enjoyed the distinction of being one of the prosperous trading centers of the Holy Roman Empire and of being called "The Jewel of the German Reich" because of its many historic buildings, among them an imperial castle, several Gothic churches and Renaissance buildings. Many significant contributions to German culture were made by Nuremberg's painters, sculptors, builders and poets. At the time of my birth, Nuremberg boasted of a population of 420,000. Like all cities of medieval origin, it was still surrounded by a high stone wall, which in earlier times had served as fortification against enemy attacks. Before the development of the cannon, the wall was impenetrable and insurmountable and its gates could be closed at night for protection. The people of Nuremberg have traditionally been proud of their medieval city and they maintained its wall until the air raids of World War II destroyed most of the ancient city center.

The city's deep roots in the past became important in the Hitler era with its emphasis on the glory of Germany's early history. Hitler was a great admirer of German history and he was especially fond of Nuremberg because of its medieval ties. We were often told that it was his favorite city, which explains the special role it played during the Hitler years, when it became a stronghold of the Nazi movement. This was due in part to the influence of a Nazi fanatic by the name of Julius Streicher, who became the *Gauleiter* (district leader or area commander) of Franconia. He frequently entertained Hitler in his elegant apartment. We lived about an eight-minute walk from him and, on my daily walk to high school, I passed the building in which he lived. Body guards stood at its entrance around the clock in all kinds of weather.

Streicher was a virulent anti-Semite. He published a weekly tabloid called *Der Stürmer* (The Attacker) which dealt exclusively with Jewish issues and stories and made fun of Jews in unsavory, pornographic comics. Streicher's motto was *"Die Juden sind unser Unglück"* (The Jews are our misfortune) which became a common saying all over Germany. Justice was later served, when Streicher was put on trial and executed in his native city.

It was due to the enormous influence which Streicher exercised on Hitler, that in 1933 Nuremberg was chosen as *Stadt der Reichsparteitage* (City of Party Rallies), which made the city both famous or infamous, depending on one's political views and moral sensibilities. The rallies were held every year in September and lasted about two weeks. During that time, approximately two million party members from all over Germany congregated in Nuremberg.

The annual event required massive preparations. Local families were recruited to house participants, and the idea caught on so well that even non-party members considered it a privilege to offer a room to one or two visitors. Additional thousands found accommodations in schools, which were closed for the duration of the rally. Needless to say, we students looked forward to a two-week extension of our summer vacation.

Even now it is difficult to describe the theatrical effect the various activities had on participants. Some years ago, I saw a film, *Der Triumph des Willens* (Triumph of the Will) produced by Leni Riefenstahl, who was one of Hitler's personal friends and favorites, and I think the film does a brilliant job in capturing the essence of the party rallies. It is pure propaganda, designed to convince the German people of the unity of the Nazi party and of the appeal of the party's goals for Germany. It evokes indelible memories of the pageantry of the party rallies and of the intense excitement generated by the presence of so many national leaders in Nuremberg. I was especially impressed with the awe on the faces of the young people in the film and I am sure that, if I had been filmed with them, my own face would have reflected the same sentiments. The feeling of sheer power, of unstoppable force and irresistible magnetism, was intoxicating and contagious. Each time that Hitler entered the assembly hall, thousands of delirious Germans shouted *"Sieg Heil"* until they were too hoarse to shout anymore. Hitler responded by raising his right arm in a stiff salute, pleased by the adulation of the crowd and in no hurry to begin his speech.

The Riefenstahl film has convinced me of a phenomenon that I recognized intuitively even as a young girl. Hitler was a hypnotic speaker and a charismatic leader without peer, and as the images of thousands of men marching in perfect order flashed across that screen, I could not help but be transported back to the days of my youth and the intoxicating mood of the Nazi party rallies. It is obvious from the film that the German people accepted Hitler and did not question his goals for Germany. A gentler nation seemed to be in the making, and everyone was glad to be a part of it. Good feelings abounded, and we felt and believed that we were now, at long last, at peace with ourselves and confident of the future. Many Germans believe that, if Hitler had not persecuted the Jews, he would be recognized today as one of Germany's very best leaders.

Party rallies were held annually from 1934 to 1939 and then discontinued because of the war. They consisted mostly of daily mass meetings, which were held in giant buildings and arenas located within walking distance of our apartment. As an insatiably curious teenager, I attended many of those meetings and, along with thousands of spellbound spectators, was carried away by the pageantry of Nazi propaganda. We all resorted to every conceivable stratagem to share in the excitement that raged through the city. My teenage friends and I made it a point to count the number of times we managed to see Hitler on his way to the meetings. It was a matter of pride to see him as often as possible. One year, I saw him thirty-nine times within a two-week period. The routes of his motorcade were predictable because, at least one hour before he rode through the streets, the SA (*Sturmabteilung*) cordoned off the streets, and thousands of people would congregate and wait patiently to see the *Führer*.

I joined the crowds with great anticipation. When Hitler finally arrived in his motorcade he would stand in an open and slow-moving car and greet the people with his right arm raised and outstretched and we would shout *"Heil Hitler"* in a frenzy of adulation. Among the participants in the party rallies were even foreign diplomats, who showed up each year in greater numbers. In 1937, forty-nine different nations were represented.

The rallies proved to be an economic boon to the city, and tourists - along with revenues from new construction - became a lucrative source of income. Special buildings and arenas for the exclusive use at party rallies were built, while existing ones were enlarged. One site accommodated 70,000 spectators, and another seated 150,000 persons. The largest facility, the massive German Stadium, provided room for 250,000 people.

In 1935 Nuremberg gave its name to the notorious Nuremberg Laws. One of these anti-Semitic laws deprived the Jews of their citizenship, and another, the Law for the Protection of German Blood and German Honor, forbade marriages between Germans and members of other races, especially Jews, and it proscribed the employment of German servants by Jews.

It did not take long before the city of Nuremberg had to pay dearly for its loyalty to the Nazi party. When the air raids into German territory started, Nuremberg was a favorite target of enemy airplanes. Air raids began sporadically in 1942. They were initially carried out by British planes, whose impact, we discovered, was not half as severe and deadly as those flown by Americans later on. It was painful to see one historic landmark after another destroyed by enemy attacks. Human tragedy became commonplace, as thousands of people perished in the flames or were buried alive under the debris of collapsed buildings. The air raids had a numbing effect on all of us. Making any plans for the future, even for the next day, was useless because there was no assurance that life would continue beyond the next moment. We suffered, but we suffered at a time when human suffering in the death camps reached limits that no one could ever have thought possible.

With the entry of the United States into the war in 1942, air raids became more frequent and more devastating. I remember in great detail an extremely severe U.S. air attack on Nuremberg which took place on January 2, 1945. I had spent Christmas, 1944, with my parents and relatives while on vacation from my job in Vienna, to which I was scheduled to return on January 3 of the new year. For two weeks, the city had enjoyed an eerie calm, and we all felt a growing sense of disaster, as it was apparent that another raid would soon rain destruction upon us again.

I spent the afternoon of January 2 with an old friend, walking in the snow-covered forests just outside the city limits. We enjoyed nature at its best, with clean, pristine air, lovely trees and pure white snow crunching under our feet. I arrived home at 6 p. m. and then, just as we sat down to dinner, the bombs began to fall. In a record time of fifty-three minutes, Nuremberg experienced its worst attack ever.

Unlike earlier attacks, this one was aimed at the city's civilian population rather than at factories and military installations. Wave after wave of bombers flew over the city, dropping explosives and incendiary bombs. Fires broke out everywhere, and buildings crumbled one after another. 2,000 people were killed, 10,000 apartments completely destroyed and about the same number heavily damaged. At least 100,000 persons were left homeless and they took to the streets to wander about in freezing temperatures with no idea as to where to turn. The whole city seemed to be burning. Many buildings inexplicably burst into flames hours after the raid was over, as delayed fuses set them off, just as the damage from earlier bombs was checked. The Nuremberg water supply was nearly destroyed, which made it virtually impossible to fight fires. The eerie glow from the fires in the night sky was visible for miles.

During the last four months of the war, the planes came over nearly every night and many more people lost their lives and homes. Never was I more downhearted and certain that the war was lost for Germany, as it proved to be.

Nuremberg's excessive loyalty to the Nazis resulted in a decision that was ironic, if understandable. It was chosen as the site of the trials of major Nazi war criminals, which took place in 1945 and 1946. For many months, a heavy pall of guilt and grief hung over the city, but finally the verdicts were rendered. A few of those on trial received life sentences and twelve, including some of the men who were closest to Adolf Hitler, were executed. Although I could not quarrel with the justice of the sentences, it was still a wrenching experience to know that these men, who had directed our lives for over a decade, had fallen so low as to be hanged. They were executed so very close to our homes. We could not abstract ourselves from those terrible days, and I remember lying awake with my heart pounding the night the executions took place.

We had not been able to come to grips with the fate that befell so many of the leaders, whom we had respected and honored. For twelve years, we identified with them and their causes, and although we experienced occasional misgivings and sometimes disapproved of official policies, an emotional bonding had occurred between the leaders of the Nazi party and the German people, and we were unprepared to view them as war criminals.

So it was that, aside from the destruction of our city and the suffering of the people, the full impact of the twelve years of Nazi rule had not yet hit us in 1946. The allies tried to counter the

residual strength of pro-Nazi sentiment with statistics on the scope
and magnitude of the holocaust. Along with millions of other
Germans, I found the number of Jewish casualties too high and I
suspected that the figures were exaggerated, in order to impress
upon us our own complicity in the Nazi party programs. I was
heartsick the night that the twelve men were executed and asked
myself over and over "Why?" After all, they had carried out their
orders in obedience to the leaders of the country they loved so much,
so why should they lose their lives for their acts of loyalty and
patriotism?

After the war, Nuremberg had to be rebuilt. Slowly and
steadily, the generous economic aid from the United States made
reconstruction possible. It speaks well for the Nurembergers' sense of
history and tradition that they rebuilt the city according to its
original medieval design, so that today it belies the fact that it had
been reduced to ruins. The population of the city, smaller by 20,000
because of war casualties and evacuations of women and children,
has since increased to 492,000. The city is once again a booming
manufacturing center, specializing in large mechanical and electrical
engineering and in industries producing motor vehicles, bicycles and
world-famous toys. The ancient part of the city is connected with
modern suburbs by means of streetcars, subways and bus service. If I
view the contributions of Nuremberg to the Nazi party with deep
misgivings, nonetheless I do feel a surge of pride at the thought of
the energy and enthusiasm with which the old city was restored.

I feel that I must comment on an inconceivably painful aspect
of life in Nazi Germany, although I do so with the knowledge that
nothing I say can explain or atone for the unconscionable behavior of
Germany's Nazi leaders in their virulent campaign of hatred against
the Jews. My feelings were and are contradictory. I cannot deny that
I enjoyed the camaraderie and sense of purpose that membership in
the Hitler Youth provided, but at the same time I feel a profound
sense of guilt and moral outrage at the way the Jews were treated
during that time. Moreover, like so many Germans then and now, I
feel a residual sense of helplessness when confronted with the awful
realities of the holocaust. No amount of self-abnegation, prayer, or
long, tear-stained conversations with my friends can purge those
feelings or resolve the inner conflicts that I feel when I look back on
those years.

If we approach the issue from the perspective of history, we
learn that anti-Semitism and persecution of Jews did not originate in

Nazi Germany nor were they limited to Germany or the twentieth century. Certainly anti-Jewish sentiments based on religious, social and economic prejudice had existed centuries before the founding of the Nazi party. Ever since the Middle Ages, the Jews had been treated as pariahs in various ways and often denied civil rights. The Catholic and Protestant Churches traditionally took an ambivalent or anti-Jewish position on most issues, because they held the Jews accountable for crucifying Jesus and, moreover, inveighing against the Jews provided a means of rallying Christians to their own religious values.

Modern anti-Semitism dates from the rise of nationalism in the early nineteenth century. Romanticism fostered a deep, if somewhat flawed sense of history in the German people, and it exacerbated the inherent racism of earlier times. The Germans came to believe that they were a primitive, mysterious race which survived by force of will in the fog-shrouded forests of medieval Europe, where violence reigned. Conversely, they viewed the Jews as shallow, arid people, devoid of profundity and lacking in creativity and spirituality. No longer being able to derive strength from their homeland, which they left centuries ago, they were considered uprooted people, doomed to perpetual restlessness and wandering. They were also suspected of conspiracy designed to infiltrate established cultures in Europe to attain power and extend their influence throughout the world.

Toward the end of the 19th century, a biological element was added when the Jews were pronounced a threat to the genetic purity of the so-called "Aryan race," an absurd myth which became a truism for German racists. Nazi party theorists were enamored with the mythology of racism and they conveniently ignored the fact that there is no such thing as a purely Aryan race. They preached that only a racially pure nation can attain greatness. Therefore the state had an interest in keeping the race as pure and healthy as possible. The Nazi obsession with preserving the purity of the Aryan race led to the attempted extermination of several segments of the population, beginning with mentally and physically handicapped and extending to genocide against the Jews, Slavs and Gypsies. At the same time, persons regardless of race and known to be bearers of hereditary diseases, were sterilized by decree of the government.

During the first five years of Hitler's rule, hatred towards the Jews was not too evident. However, I soon developed misgivings about the direction of Germany under its Nazi leaders. More and more of my Jewish classmates dropped out of school under circumstances that were mysterious, to say the least. Teachers did not tell us what happened to these young people, and we were discouraged from inquiring. Later we learned through other sources that these Jewish families had decided to leave Nazi Germany and emigrate to other countries, mostly England and the United States, before they ran the risk of being sent to concentration camps.

I was also very aware of an effort to force Jewish store owners out of business, as "good" Germans were encouraged to boycott Jewish stores. Many large department stores in city centers were owned by Jews. Quite often non-Jewish customers, who wanted to take advantage of lower prices of Jewish high-quality merchandise, were stopped by Nazi guards upon leaving stores with their purchases. The guards, inconspicuously dressed in civilian clothes, photographed customers as they left Jewish stores after their purchases. The next day those pictures appeared in the newspapers, along with the names and addresses of the customers. Soon it was considered a disgrace for "good" Germans to patronize Jewish stores.

Anti-Semitic behavior accelerated over the years and culminated in the outright persecution of the Jews in an effort to force them out of Germany. An excuse for escalating the campaign was found on November 7, 1938, when a young Jew killed a German embassy official in Paris. Nazi leaders demanded brutal reprisals, which manifested themselves in the *Kristallnacht* (Crystal Night) on November 9 and 10, when Hitler's profound hatred of Jews exploded in well-organized violence against them.

The name "Crystal Night" was given to those atrocities by the Nazis to minimize the nature of the criminal activities. It was a euphemism for the broken glass of the thousands of windows that were shattered in the attacks against Jewish homes, stores and synagogues, and it was intended to divert our attention from the appalling lawlessness of the Nazi party on that occasion. The *Kristallnacht* was at once the incipient dawn of the murderous holocaust, which was to last seven years and the beginning of the systematic Nazi campaign to eradicate not only German but also European Jews.

I was a high school student at the time. On the morning after Crystal Night, I walked to school with some friends. Our school was located in downtown Nuremberg, a 45-minute walk from home. On the way we happened to meet a teacher of ours and struck up a conversation, unaware of what had happened until we arrived downtown. We could not believe our eyes. Most Jewish stores had been completely destroyed. The whole downtown area looked like a battlefield. We were terribly depressed by such wanton destruction on the part of the Nazis whom, until then, we considered quite noble and trustworthy. Our disgust was complete when, after a few hours in school, we learned that the night of destruction had been carefully planned and executed and that it was not limited to our town, but affected all major German cities as well as those in Austria and the Sudeten region of Czechoslovakia. We learned of the scope of the devastation only gradually; television coverage did not exist, and radio newscasts were not as frequent or as reliable as they are now.

   After the events of the Crystal Night, more and more open attacks on the Jews ensued. At some later date all Jews were officially forced to wear the "star of David" on their clothing over the place of their heart, to make them readily identifiable and easy to torment or persecute. During the war, persecution of Jews was no longer limited to Germany, but was also carried out in territories which the Nazi armies had occupied. It affected the very heart of Europe, then and for all time, and it remains today the most compelling evidence for man's inhumanity to man.

   Even as a member of the Hitler Youth I found those atrocities shocking and inexcusable. I often asked myself why no voices were raised in protest, but found no answer, and even today I find that many of my contemporaries refuse to think about what happened. The only plausible answer came in the form of another question, "Would you be willing to die in a concentration camp if your death could bring about the release and freedom of the Jews?" The answer was a cowardly "no." Millions of people with a conscience must have felt the same way, but no action was ever taken. Maybe the answer could have been positive, if an individual, courageous enough to intercede in favor of the Jews, had come forward. But none came.

   Like so many Germans, I wondered why the Pope and the Catholic Church did not take a firm stand on the matter. But they remained silent. It is interesting that, as late as 1988, Roman Catholic bishops from East and West Germany and Austria issued a statement that criticized Christian leaders for failing to condemn the atrocities of the Crystal Night and the subsequent program to annihilate the Jews.

   I have also asked myself many times what must be done to make sense out of the German response to Adolf Hitler and the Nazi doctrine. There can be no doubt that the response was passive, but was it passive out of indifference? Or fear? Or traditional respect for authority? Or was there almost universal support for the Führer, such that, whatever he decided was good for Germany, was quickly and uncritically accepted by the German people? I think that all of these explanations have merit and I am unable to say which one offers the best explanation for our behavior under Hitler. For myself, as war clouds gathered across Europe, I experienced an overwhelming sense of helplessness and a nagging fear that events were slipping out of control, and I wondered if Fate in the form of divine retribution was going to reshape our German destiny.

Medieval city wall of Nuremberg, built to protect city from enemy invasion.

8

Compulsory Labor Service And Work Experience

The logical sequence of events after graduation from high school would have been to enroll at a university. The German system of Higher Education makes no provision for colleges, but only for universities and institutes of higher learning, such as trade, music and art academies. In my youth, all high school graduates, who wanted to go on to higher education, were required by law to serve the country for six months in the compulsory labor service and, without pay, six months in a household with many children, whose mother needed additional help. This was intended to respond to Hitler's interest in families which were expected to produce many children to ensure the future of Germany. We accepted without grumbling the fact that we had to interrupt our studies for one year to serve society, which is a measure of how much influence the government exercised in our lives.

I was drafted into the compulsory labor service (Reichsarbeitsdienst = RAD) in April 1939. Between 1933 and 1939, many camps had been built all over Germany to accommodate prospective labor service personnel. There were separate camps for men and women. We had no choice of camps and the government saw to it that we were not stationed too close to our home town, in order to prevent us from visiting at home. Furthermore, an attempt was made to assign high school graduates from all parts of Germany to each camp. This diversity of people made the experience much more worthwhile and interesting, because we could mingle with persons of various backgrounds, geographical locations and German dialects.

The first camp I was assigned to was located in the Bavarian Forest, near the Austrian and Czechoslovakian borders in the Eastern part of Germany. It was about a hundred miles from my home town and difficult to reach by public transportation on which we so heavily depended. Our camp accommodated sixty young women in its dormitories. Only our three leaders enjoyed the privacy of individual rooms. The rest of us slept in bunk beds on straw mattresses. Each morning the straw in the mattress had to be fluffed, because it had lumped up under the weight of the body. The whole setup was extremely primitive. No closets were available, and we practically lived out of our suitcases. This was relatively easy, because we possessed very few personal belongings and did not even bring clothes to camp, because we wore uniforms and work dresses at all times. These were provided by the government. Even on occasional visits away from the camp we were not allowed to wear civilian clothes. We were expected to represent the organization and the Nazi movement by wearing the uniform with pride and dignity.

The "dress-up" uniform consisted of a brown suit, a white blouse with a Swastika pin, hat and brown shoes. This uniform was worn on Sundays and very rare special occasions, such as when we expected a visit of a leader from a different camp. On work days, we wore blue work dresses made of linen, a red bandana and comfortable shoes.

Within a period of nine months, we were assigned to three different camps with a stay of three months each, which meant that we had to move twice. The first camp was so old and dilapidated that it was considered unsafe. We were transferred to the second camp, Murschall near Salzburg, but again we had to move when winter set in, because the camp had no heating system. Late in September we moved to Grafing near Munich. It had been a men's camp but had been vacated when its occupants were transferred to the armed forces at the beginning of the war. All three of these camps were primitive, but we were expected to be tough and, as good citizens, never to complain about hardships.

The three leaders in charge of the camp had received special training by the government, which qualified them to run a camp efficiently. Each one had a different field of expertise, such as home economics, psychology or sports. They were members of the party and had received extensive training in party leadership and governmental matters. The leaders never wore work clothes but only dress uniforms. This meant that they did not participate in physical work to maintain the camp. By virtue of their party membership they were considered to be above manual labor and entitled to special privileges.

A typical day's schedule involved a variety of activities. We were awakened at 5 a.m. every morning and, bleary-eyed, took ten minutes to don sports clothing, much like jogging suits, if not so colorful. Then, regardless of the weather, we had to line up in front of the camp and answer to roll call. We then went out and ran, albeit slowly, for about twenty minutes. In retrospect, I wonder if "jogging" was not invented in Germany during those years. The party strongly advocated physical fitness on the premise that only healthy people could contribute to the future of the nation.

After returning to camp, we were given time to shower and put on clean work clothes. Then we gathered in a circle around the flagpole in front of the main building, sang a patriotic song and hoisted the flag. Breakfast followed immediately. It had been prepared by a crew of six people, who were assigned to kitchen duty for four weeks, after which time they were given a new assignment. Various daily activities around the camp followed breakfast, including discussion groups, newspaper and book reports, songfests with a distinctive patriotic ring, cleaning the camp, washing and ironing work clothes and blouses. Nylon and polyester were unknown in those days. I found ironing especially troublesome. Imagine, ironing sixty dresses and as many blouses all day long, day after day until your four weeks were up and you could be assigned to a different duty.

After we completed our assigned early-morning chores in the camp, we were sent out to various peasant farms to work, which was ostensibly the real mission of the program. Most labor camps were located in poorer areas of Germany, where the greatest need for free help existed. The poorest peasants with the largest families received the most help from the labor service.

Every young woman was assigned to one household, where she worked eight hours a day for four weeks. It was up to the farmers to decide how and where they wanted us to work, which often meant helping the mother with the children, performing household duties, cooking, or working in the fields. It did not take us long to find out that there were desirable and undesirable assignments and significant variables from one family to the next, such as the hospitality of the peasants, the quality of food, the type of work, the sanitary conditions, etc. Our leaders seemed to exercise a certain amount of favoritism when assigning these jobs. The girls they liked best received the easiest assignments and others were sent to households with often almost unbearable conditions, especially from the standpoint of sanitation.

At the end of eight hours of our daily work, we walked back to camp to a regimen of exercise and chores until dinner was served. After the evening meal, we again gathered around the flagpole and ceremoniously took down the flag. Since we had to get up so early, we would go to sleep early, grateful that another day of this rather drab existence had passed.

A German proverb says *"Jeder Arbeiter ist seines Lohnes wert"*(Every worker is worth his wages). This is actually no longer the case. I would prefer the translation "Every worker is worthy of getting paid." We received only a token payment for our labors, and I felt more like a slave than an employee. Every ten days we were paid RM 2.00 (two German marks), which amounted to twenty pfennig per day, equivalent to five cents according to the then existing exchange rate. Imagine, five cents for eight hours of strenuous and demanding work! Although prices in those days were much lower than they are today, we could not buy anything of substance, let alone birthday gifts for relatives and friends. My father sent me postage stamps and stationery, because otherwise he would not have heard from me. It was bad enough to lose a whole year's time by being recruited into the labor service, but as the name implies, we labored and served, and if in the eyes of our leaders no sacrifice was great enough for the country, in our eyes, none was undertaken with less magnanimity.

All was not work, however. On Saturdays and Sundays we hardly worked at all, but we were kept confined to the camp and left to our own devices. Every fourth Saturday afternoon we were allowed to leave the camp, in uniform, of course, for four hours. Attending a church service on Sunday morning was out of the question, because there was no public transportation to and from our camp. The location of the camp way out in the countryside made walking to church an impossibility.

So we spent our Saturdays and Sundays in a variety of ways. There was an opportunity for getting acquainted with other girls, which involved endless conversations extolling the advantages of living a private life at home. We also liked to sing folk and patriotic songs. Or we would write loving and longing letters to our loved ones at home. Sometimes we would sit together in small groups knitting, crocheting, or doing all kinds of needlework, provided we were lucky enough to receive the necessary material from well-meaning friends or relatives because we had no financial resources of any kind.

Visits to the camp were not encouraged, and never in nine months did I see one parent of any of the girls. We were taught self-reliance and independence. Emotional ties between us and those living outside the camp were not encouraged. Sometimes we would go for long walks along the country roads. We would check the license plates of passing cars, trying to determine what the home towns of their occupants were. A car from the home town of one of us would occasionally pass. Then we would cheer as loud as possible and vigorously voice our wishes to go home. Even a stranger's car established a bond between us and home! How impersonal can you get!

Our labor service dragged on for six months, during which time we laboriously counted the days until our freedom but it was not meant to be. On September 1, 1939, Germany declared war on Poland.

The German invasion of Poland prompted the outbreak of World War II. The government acted quickly to decide that members of the labor service were not to be dismissed until three months later, because they were considered a potential work force for the war effort. We listened to the radio announcement of the outbreak of the war huddled together and frightened, not knowing how the war would affect our lives. When Hitler spoke to the nation on the same day, most of us cried because he promised with great fanfare that he would be the first one to lead our soldiers into battle. I have since wondered why we were so emotionally upset. Perhaps, on the one hand, we were so attached to Hitler that we were afraid that he might die and we would lose him, if indeed, he did go into battle. But on the other hand, we were desperately disappointed that we had to serve three more months in the labor service, and that was guaranteed to bring tears to the eyes of the most stalwart!

The relationship between Hitler and the German youth needs some explanation and I fear it can hardly be explained at all. We must bear in mind that the German response to Adolf Hitler was based on emotions which surfaced only from time to time and were not subjected to rational analysis. I have always found it difficult, if not impossible, to express those emotions with words, but I am certain that, until historians manage to identify and analyze the emotional state of the German people during the interwar period, rational explanations of what happened to Germany will be inadequate.

Hitler restored faith and hope in Germans, most of whom admired and adored him, and they responded readily to his charismatic personality. Only those who witnessed Hitler's appeal firsthand can possibly begin to understand the effect of this one man on a nation of 70 million people. Within a very short time after his rise to power, Hitler became the best-loved man in Germany and he seemed to embody all values that most Germans held dear to their hearts. Of those values, love of country was the most intense. Unfortunately for them and the world, it degenerated quickly into unthinking, militant nationalism and resulted in war on an awesome scale. We were drawn to our *Führer* by an unrealistic emotional bond, and we shed tears at the prospect of his going into battle. Our worst fears were not met, however, for he never delivered on his pledge.

We girls had no choice but to settle down and accept the idea that three more months of involuntary labor service lay ahead of us. We comforted ourselves with the idea that, compared with the sacrifices of the troops, our situation was not all that intolerable. *"Einer für alle und alle für einen"* (One for all and all for one) was one of the Nazi slogans we repeated to one another, when our morale began to sag.

During those early months of the war, the enthusiasm of young men for national service knew no bounds. I saw whole trainloads full of draftees on their way to the front. They were jubilant, singing patriotic songs and demonstrating for all to see and hear that they were not afraid to go into battle and even sacrifice their lives for the fatherland. Their motto was the Latin *"Dulce et decorum est pro patria mori"* (It is sweet and honorable to die for one's country).

During Hitler's rule, individuals had learned to consider themselves unimportant, as compared to the fate of their country. A false idealism, which disregarded the welfare of the individual in favor of the interest of the fatherland, and a willingness to lay down one's life for the country resulted.

In the midst of war fever and work-camp banalities, my father announced in one of his letters that he had fallen in love with a wonderful woman, and that they decided to get married in October. He had been a widower for two years and he was lonesome. Quite frankly, I could not quite share his happiness, but despite my misgivings, I planned to travel home for the wedding.

I signed up for a furlough and was granted three days. Before I left camp, I received instructions by our leader to wear my uniform at all times. By wearing the uniform I would display my membership in a very privileged organization and affirm my support for its goals. I was not to wear civilian clothes even for the wedding ceremony in church. Foolishly, I did not dare disregard the leader's instructions, but what a luxury it would have been to don a pretty dress and demonstrate that I was a woman!

Three days of furlough did not allow me much time visiting with friends and relatives, and I was only too aware that my natural mother's sisters, who were not in attendance at the wedding, opposed my father's remarriage. I often thought that, even if he had married an angel straight from heaven, they would still have disapproved of his choice, just because no other woman was worthy of the man who had once been the husband of their sister.

After getting acquainted with my new stepmother I, too, was not particularly pleased, but for other reasons. However, I hid my misgivings and told my father, "I'll be happy as long as you will be," which pleased him immensely. My stepmother did make him blissfully happy, and I soon realized that they were ideally suited for each other. When my father fell in love with my stepmother-to-be he became a new man. No doubt enthralled by her out-going, fun-loving personality, he shook off the recurring depression that followed his nervous breakdown of thirteen years back and he began to enjoy life again. They often went out together, to movies, the theater, folk festivals, family gatherings and they frequently visited her numerous friends.

Indeed, his new wife succeeded in keeping my father happy for the next thirteen years, until his death in 1952. Personally, I found it painful that my father was visibly so much happier than he ever was with my mother. After the end of my three days at home, the thought of returning to the labor camp was appealing to me, because I considered the camp a welcome haven away from the stress of adjusting to entirely new circumstances at home.

But I felt a keen sense of loss. As a child, I was my daddy's favorite and we had become even closer after my mother's death.

Now I had difficulty letting go of him and sharing his delight with his new wife. For her part, no doubt she was jealous of me, but more to the point, her character and personality led her to oppose my idealistic goal of attending the university and preparing for a professional career. She refused to allow my father to contribute anything to my education.

Because she had only an eighth-grade education, our family regarded her as socially inferior. I, as a budding linguist, was shocked by her grammatical errors, especially her use of double negatives in her conversations, and I was embarrassed to introduce her to my educated friends.

What a dramatic contrast to my mother, who never doubted for a moment that a university education was the best possible goal for me and who did everything in her power to make me into an intelligent, self-reliant and self-actuated person, who did not require a man to make decisions. I think, in retrospect, that I must have been a spiritual forerunner of those advocates of women's liberation who came along a quarter-century later.

In those days, unmarried women ran considerable risks, if they chose to leave home and go it alone. My father resented my leaving and thought that my behavior demonstrated ingratitude and selfishness on my part. He blamed himself for having failed me and he would not get over his dismay for a long time to come. With feelings of relief, then, I left for Vienna in 1943, confident that I could manage my life without any further parental guidance. When I finally did move home again three years later, I discovered that my stepmother had thrown away my diaries, given my piano, my mother's beautiful Persian rugs and Rosenthal china to her nephew. Several years later, during a one-year stay at the University of Oregon, I sent lengthy letters home relating in detail the wonderful experiences I was enjoying. My father collected these and saved them for me. When I returned to the United States as an immigrant in 1953, I left that priceless collection of letters at home. You can imagine my dismay, when I learned that my stepmother had discarded it, along with a packet of love letters that my parents exchanged before they were married.

If I had yielded to my stepmother's directive to get married, I would never have discovered America, nor would I ever have discovered myself. She pushed me away, and I was left to spend my holidays with friends and acquaintances rather than with her and my father, and to seek an education as best I could, without their moral and financial support.

After the wedding celebration, I had eight weeks of labor service left. During that time, I tried hard to establish a good relationship with my stepmother. She had never been married before and had no children, which in my humble opinion might have made it difficult to relate to me and my needs. To this day, my relatives in

Germany firmly believe that the only reason why I decided to emigrate to the United States was the fact that I did not like my stepmother. That is far from the truth, but you cannot convince people that they are wrong when their minds are made up. In any case, after being discharged from the labor service I moved back to what was home before, with good intentions of making this new situation work for the good of all three of us. It certainly required quite a few adjustments.

In order to fulfill my obligation of serving the country for a full year, I had to serve three more months under *Projekt Pflichtjahr* (year of duty). The RAD and the *Pflichtjahr* served two different purposes: while the labor service prepared young people to become as physically fit as possible and to serve the needs of peasant families, the objective of the *Pflichtjahr* was intended to instill in young female high school graduates a love for household duties, in order to prepare them for the most important duty of a woman - at least in Hitler's eyes - becoming a competent housewife and a devoted mother.

To fulfill this latter requirement, most young people were assigned to families with several children, but I was sent to an elderly couple with two adult children, who had already left the nest. According to the letter of the law, this particular couple should not have qualified for a free servant. Maybe they pulled some strings, or maybe they were eligible because the lady of the house was deaf. She was able to lip-read beautifully, and did I ever improve my diction when speaking to her. I took care of household chores, shopping and cooking.

The advantage of this assignment was the fact that the couple lived in Nuremberg. Theoretically I could have visited my parents now and then, but I had no time off, even on Sundays. My parents did not have a telephone, so there were actually no contacts with them. But knowing that we lived physically closer again made me feel more comfortable and satisfied with my lot. After three months of playing the role of a servant and learning the skills of a cook, cleaning lady, housekeeper, confidante and companion to an elderly couple, I was ready to embark on life's next surprise. In the meantime, I savored my freedom.

One day in June 1940, I walked downtown Nuremberg with my stepmother when, all of a sudden, the church bells began to chime. We looked at each other, not knowing what prompted this event, especially since bells had been kept silent in deference to the men who had lost their lives in the war. Eventually, news spread that France had surrendered, and the chiming of the bells was symbolic of victory. People on the streets were exuberant and indescribably happy and acted as if the whole war was over for good. They shouted and sang patriotic songs, and strangers hugged and embraced each other in a frenzy of victory.

I realized that now was the suitable time for me to enter a university, but I had no such luck. My stepmother was vehemently opposed to supporting my ambition to go on to an institution of higher learning. Her ideas of the role of a woman in society were hopelessly old-fashioned. They coincided with the Nazi message that the mission of a woman was to get married, be a dutifully submissive wife, bear healthy children to propagate and strengthen the "Aryan race" and be an exemplary mother. In her opinion, this role took precedence over pursuing a career. "You are an attractive girl who will get married. So what do you want an education for? All that money will be spent for nothing," she declared.

Furthermore, my stepmother was not willing to contribute financially towards my support. My father, whose initial hope was for me to become a university student, now changed his mind and agreed with his beloved wife. His decision hurt me deeply, because it ran counter to all the ideals that he and my mother had espoused over all the preceding years. How I wished that my mother were still alive! She would have shared my ambition and encouraged me to reach my goals. I felt completely deserted.

Years later, after I received my Ph.D., my stepmother proudly took me around to all the neighbors and relatives to introduce me as "Frau Doktor Ziegler, my daughter." I was amused but I cooperated good-naturedly. However, I wondered if she may have felt a little sheepish about her earlier insistence that I should get married and give up my academic pursuits.

German universities offered no scholarships to students, and the academic standards were so stringent that part-time work was out of the question. I saw no way out of this emotional dilemma but to give in and look for full-time employment, while living at home under the same roof as my stepmother. Although we were poor, we were considered a middleclass family by society because my father was a civil servant with a safe job with tenure and a retirement pension. My parents believed that a similar job would be just the right thing for me, especially in view of the fact that, because of losses of men in the war, chances for a woman to get married were steadily being reduced. I realized the futility of opposing my parents' wishes, especially since they offered me free room and board, if I consented to do what they wished. So I applied for a government job with the telephone company. I was hired immediately and promptly went into on-the-job training.

In the beginning, this new kind of work was interesting, largely because, as a telephone operator, I was privy to conversations ranging from the passionate confessional of ardent lovers to the cryptic and enigmatic reports of military intelligence personnel. The job also entailed speaking to customers and operators all over Germany. The practice of self-dialing had just been developed, so that I was able to dial any city and telephone number near and far.

For a while it all seemed interesting and fulfilling, but eventually the appeal wore off, and it became boring and lacking in challenge. So I went to my superior and asked for a change of jobs in the technical field. He proved to be sympathetic to my request and offered me a job as a radio engineer.

During the Hitler years, only one radio program was broadcast, called the *Reichsprogramm*, which originated in Berlin and was beamed to all parts of Germany and Austria. My engineering responsibilities included maintaining the technical equipment necessary for a high-quality radio program, supervising the program to ensure that it properly reached all German radio stations, pinpointing technical difficulties, including interruptions and taking care of problems in a minimal amount of time, with the cooperation of booster stations.

The *Reichsprogramm* went off the air at 1 a. m., so that the night hours could be utilized to maintain and repair the technical equipment and the cables. For that purpose I was on duty every fifth night.

Left: Nazi Labor Service members ready to improve their fitness, 1939.
Hildegard in center.
Right: Nazi Labor Service members in work uniforms, 1939.
Hildegard at left.

9

Escalation of World War II

If my narrative of these events seems rather unimaginative, I should point out that, in its early stages, World War II was relatively easy on the population of Germany. Certainly there were food rationings and some other restrictions which, however, were not hard to tolerate. The mood of the country was optimistic, especially in view of the fact that Hitler had promised to have his armed forces back in Germany by Christmas of 1939. As we all know now, it did not work out that way. The news from the fronts was consistently good until, in June of 1941, Hitler broke the Soviet nonaggression pact and invaded the Soviet Union. The news was broadcast as my family joyfully assembled for a family reunion.

When the United States entered the war in 1941, military action escalated. Austrian and German civilians, ever willing to endure innumerable hardships and restrictions, had to get used to a new type of suffering caused by the constant and unpredictable threat of air raids. The mental and emotional burden brought about by the tension of not knowing what the next few hours would bring was almost intolerable. The constant fear of losing one's life or becoming maimed weighed heavily on most people's minds. If some member of our family did not return home shortly after an air raid, our imagination went wild, and we always feared the worst.

In the beginning, air raids originated in Britain and happened only at night, when most people were at home and asleep. To put it mildly, it was an inconvenience or a nuisance to be aroused from your sleep and have to rush to the cellar. Quite often the sirens went off, and we would run to the shelter, but nothing would happen. We sometimes joked by saying that the British pilots could not find

Nuremberg. At other times, there was little damage and very few lives were lost.

However, after the United States entered the war, air raids became increasingly serious and dangerous. We realized more and more that air attacks were another form of warfare inflicted on the German population, in order to break the morale of the civilians, escalate the war and bring it to an end more quickly. To protect the civilian population of Nuremberg, an increasing number of nonworking mothers with small children were evacuated to the countryside. The distribution of food was seriously disrupted, because railroad tracks and highways were bombed, and more and more railroad cars and locomotives destroyed. When food items became scarce, long lines of customers formed in front of the stores. Sometimes it took a few hours, just to secure a loaf of bread, or some item needed for dinner. In some cases certain food items were not available for days, even though customers were in possession of the proper ration coupons that should have assured the availability of the item.

Severe inconveniences occurred in other areas as well. In the face of increased war production, the manufacture of consumer goods had to be curtailed. Shoe and garment stores were stripped of their supplies, and wearing apparel was available only with coupons issued by government offices. Most women's wardrobes were limited to two dresses, one skirt, a blouse, a sweater, a coat and two pairs of shoes. Once I lost a pair of shoes in an air raid. I had only one other pair, and it was weeks before I was able to purchase replacements. Most shoes were made with cork or wooden rather than leather soles.

A rather insignificant example of inconvenience was the fact that grocery stores often ran out of paper bags. In those days, prepackaged food items were not available. Most grocery items such as sugar, flour, rice, pasta, beans, lentils, etc. were weighed by the grocer and then put into individual small paper bags. Without bags a customer could not take those items home. In order to avoid this nuisance, people saved their paper bags from previous purchases and took them to the grocery store at the next visit. The bags were used again and again until they wore out. Once in a while when you were lucky you could add an occasional new one to your supply to replace the ones that had become unusable with time.

These everyday inconveniences caused by the war paled in comparison with psychological stress. All of us have stress in our lives, often caused by relationships with people whom we love or who are otherwise close to us. However, this particular stress I am going to write about had nothing to do with disappointments, such as broken friendships or worries about family members, but it was inflicted by people I did not even know. They carried on this war on nerves for about four years of my young life.

The war on nerves was an undeclared war within a declared war. For us, it started literally "out of a clear blue sky," when enemy airplanes began to drop their destructive and deadly freight on innocent women and children, while young husbands and fathers fought the declared war, which only the Nazis wanted, on the fronts. Based on my personal experience, I came to the conclusion that no government should be allowed to start a war without consent of the people. This would take care of the scourge of wars that have caused the loss of hundreds of millions of lives throughout history, not to mention ruining economies and leading to senseless destruction all over the globe.

Imagine you are sitting with your family at the dinner table. Mother is serving the tempting food she has prepared with love all afternoon. Judging by the aroma that emanates from the serving dishes, it promises to be an especially delicious meal. The children are home from school and daddy from the office. The whole family is ready to relax and enjoy the harmony of close family relationships. Or you have just managed to fall asleep at 1 o'clock in the morning and you have to get up at 6:30 a.m. to go back to work. Both of these scenarios are rudely and cruelly interrupted by an air raid siren, which goes off with an ear-splitting noise, as if it were located right outside your home. All this and many more similar nerve-racking episodes happened all the time. The air raid siren was a messenger of doom and an instrument of destruction that spared no one. You, your cherished family, neighbors, relatives, colleagues, classmates and friends were all at risk all the time.

Every citizen had a small suitcase full of paraphernalia necessary for daily living, such as clothing, shoes, a coat, underwear, soap, toothbrush, etc. It also contained valuable jewelry, often of sentimental value, and important documents which would have been difficult to replace. Every time there was an air raid we each grabbed our suitcase to take it to the air raid shelter. In most cases this was the cellar with heavy stone walls, which provided fairly good protection from bombs. In the cellar we waited for agonizing hours till the all-clear was sounded.

Before we hurried to the cellar, we hugged and kissed each other, as if this were our last chance to express our love. The thought of being killed or losing loved ones was always with us. We would rush to the cellar, our hearts pounding with terror. Sometimes the bombs would fall, and we would hear the explosions around us before we reached the shelter. Upon arrival we were packed like sardines and had to endure an almost unbearable feeling of claustrophobia. In the wintertime, we suffered in the cold damp cellar, and the cold made us shiver and our teeth chatter.

Under this sort of strain it was difficult to be friendly or civil to people around us. Nobody smiled, and with stony faces we would say unimportant things, such as, "Here we are again" or, "What will happen today?" or, "Do you suppose our turn will come today?" While waiting for relief from the stress, the minutes or even seconds just seemed to creep by, and an hour felt like eternity. The air alerts took anywhere from half an hour up to four hours at the most. Sometimes a single stray plane would keep millions of people waiting under duress.

No two people reacted the same way in the face of danger. Observing other people's strange and unusual behavior became a source of additional stress. One woman always prayed without interruption in a high-pitched, nerve-jangling voice. In retrospect, I imagine that my own behavior must have been annoying to others, too. I always sat there with my gas mask over my head. It was large enough to cover my ears tightly and saved me from hearing the whistling of falling bombs, the terrible explosions and the nerve-shattering panic afterward. Some people cursed after each explosion, and children, who could not get their way and whose needs could not be met, were whining and screaming. Sometimes the shelter was so excruciatingly silent that one could have heard a pin drop. I do not know which was easier to tolerate, the silence or all the hideous noises around us.

When the air raids occurred at night, I often would assume a fatalistic attitude and refuse to get up and go to the shelter, although I realized that it was one of the safest places to be. My absence caused my father great grief. He was an air raid warden, whose responsibility it was to see to it that all residents of our five-story apartment house, about 100 people, were accounted for. Naturally, he worried about my safety up on the third floor, but he was also annoyed when people asked him about my whereabouts. As the daughter of this dedicated air raid warden, I was supposed to set an example for responsible behavior! It often occurred that a nearby city or even Munich, as far away as 130 miles, was bombed. I am reluctant to admit that, in this case, our anxiety was greatly lessened, and we heaved a sigh of relief, when it turned out that Nuremberg was not targeted. Nevertheless, we had to stay in the cellar, because sometimes our turn did come after another city had been bombed.

After we were finally allowed to go back to our apartments, we checked for possible damage. Once, the two stories above our apartment caught fire after being struck by an incendiary bomb, but fortunately we were never completely bombed out, as millions of other Germans were. Our windows were often broken because of the air pressure of falling bombs. In the beginning we had the window panes replaced, but when the air raids increased in number, we just boarded them up until the end of the war. Among other hardships, we experienced broken water pipes, no electricity for days, no heat, no public transportation, no phone service.

My main worry after survival was the well-being of my favorite aunt, who lived a twenty-minute walk from us. After my mother's death of cancer before World War II, my aunt had taken me under her wings. We had a beautiful and loving relationship, which was enriched and strengthened by the fact that she was not only my mother's sister, but she was married to my father's brother. In those days we did not have a telephone. Therefore the only way to contact people was by seeing them in person.

After every air raid, I set out to look for my aunt and uncle, which was a dangerous and foolish thing to do. My father's and stepmother's protests and attempts to keep me at home were of no avail. Often I went on my dangerous walk even in the middle of the night, disregarding the explosions of time bombs and having to force my way over debris and rubble piled up from collapsed buildings. The only lights that guided me were burning buildings and the moon and stars on clear nights, which provided an eerie contrast to all the destruction surrounding me. I found it to be a consolation to be able to look up at the peace and calm that emanated from the skies. The moon looked down at us earthlings, as if to say, "What fools you are! Why in the world are you fighting those senseless wars?"

On the way to my aunt, I had a chance to look over the damage on buildings that were so familiar to me. Some had completely collapsed and buried apartment dwellers beneath them;

some were still burning and smoking; some were left with the façade, and holes instead of window spaces. It was a dreadful sight. The agony of the war on nerves was mitigated only slightly, when I found my aunt and uncle well and unhurt. After the summer of 1942, a feeling of disillusionment and defeatism swept the nation. A large segment of the population feared that the war was already lost, although very few openly admitted their fear. A strong loyalty towards Hitler persisted, and a lack of confidence in him and his policies would have been regarded as treason by his fanatic supporters. However, there was no denying the fact that living conditions had become increasingly difficult and discouraging. We were keenly aware that Germany could not fight a two-front war indefinitely and, as time wore on, the realization that the nation was weakening began to take hold. The increasing frequency of air raids, ensuing destruction and death served notice that the government was not able to protect its citizens from the enemy.

Left: Cousin Hans Wrede, 1940, missing in action in the Battle of Stalingrad, 1943.
Right: Boyfriend Alfons Biehmer, killed in action in France, 1940.

10

Viennese Interlude

In early 1943, I decided to leave Nuremberg and move to Vienna. My decision to leave my native city was motivated in part by personal circumstances and in part by an intense desire to improve my language skills, which I hoped would provide me with an opportunity to escape the confines of hearth and home in Nuremberg. I hated the nerve-racking air raids that rained down death and destruction on our city and I did not want to die a young martyr to the ambitions of Germany's leaders. But I also wanted to attend evening classes at a prestigious school for interpreters in Vienna, while working during the day. Theoretically, it should have been easy to transfer from one town to another, because all communication media, including radio, telephone and telegram services, were centralized and run by the German government. But my superiors in Nuremberg refused to release me from my job, because trained female workers were scarce and, if I left, they would have had to train someone else to take my place. Therefore, in defiance of my employment contract, I walked out, went home, packed my suitcase and took the next train to Vienna. As I prepared for my departure, my stepmother displayed no emotion whatsoever. If she had any feelings at all, they probably were of relief that I was finally leaving the nest. My father, however, was devastated. He took my decision personally, and thought he must have let me down, but he did not chide me or blame me for his personal suffering.

It was no easy task to get to the railroad station. Streetcars no longer ran because of damaged tracks, taxi service was difficult and unreliable, but I wanted to be sure to get to the station in time to catch the train to Vienna. Walking was out of the question, as I was taking three heavy suitcases with me. In spite of his heavy heart, my father came to my assistance. He borrowed a handcart from a neighbor, loaded my suitcases on it and escorted me to the station. We hugged and kissed and bade each other a tearful farewell. My departure was a heart-rending experience for both of us. Would we ever see each other again?

When I reported to the authorities in Vienna, I was greeted with open arms and put to work in the same type of job that I had held in Nuremberg, namely, as a radio engineer, but this time working in the office, which was in charge of supervising the radio broadcasts.

Vienna had not been a target of Allied bombers before 1943. American bombers normally attacked German cities from bases in England and, because of the great distance involved, they were unable to reach Vienna without refueling. The situation changed, however, when Italy surrendered to the Allies in 1944 and U.S. air bases were established in Italy, which shares its northern border with Austria. Air raids on Vienna were now possible and they were carried out in increasing numbers. I felt as if I had jumped from the frying pan into the fire. Moreover, my dream of attending the Viennese school for interpreters never materialized, because the intensity of the air raids forced people to stay home during evening hours, and the school was closed.

In fact, night life in this formerly joyous city of two million inhabitants came to a standstill. A strictly enforced blackout left the streets of the city dark and foreboding. Buses did not run, and streetcars had to proceed very slowly and cautiously to avoid smashing into various obstacles or derailing on damaged tracks.

As the raids continued, damage to historical and cultural landmarks made emotions run high in the hearts of the Viennese, people who by tradition were dedicated to cultural pursuits. The famous Opera House burning for hours and smoldering for days, brought tears to my eyes, and I will never forget the pitiful sight of St. Stephen's Cathedral after it was hit by a powerful bomb. Its beautiful mosaic roof collapsed, and parts of the venerable old Gothic structure were reduced to rubble.

As soon as the air raid warning sounded, we had to retreat to the nearest shelter or cellar for safety. When an air raid occurred during my working hours, I often defied the rules and left the building to run to my apartment, which was located only two and a half blocks away. I simply could not face the thought of spending long hours with 1,800 co-workers in a very limited area, or being buried alive or dead with them. My apartment building was more comfortable, for only twelve people normally sought shelter there. Sometimes bombs would fall so quickly that residents could not reach the relative safety of shelters and cellars, and the thought crossed my mind more than once that I might be hit by a bomb, as I rushed homeward. While we waited for the end of the air raids, the sound of falling time bombs and explosions so unnerved us that we had to force ourselves to leave the shelters and assess the damage caused by the attack.

Across the street from our office building, a huge building that had been struck by a bomb collapsed, and an unknown number of people were trapped and feared dead. We tried to be optimistic about the prospects for survival of its inhabitants and we knew that in some cases people buried under debris had miraculously survived for days. However, those people across the street from us were not so lucky. One hundred and eleven of them were brought to the surface and they were all dead. Death sometimes came by other means; every once in a while, a building would remain standing, apparently undamaged after an attack, but the people inside killed by the enormous air pressure caused by exploding bombs.

The war in Vienna had its lighter side, too. We normally ate lunch in the cafeteria of the building in which I worked, where we were able to buy inexpensive meal tickets and enjoy generous and reasonably good meals. However, every Monday we were served horse meat, which I simply could not endure. My boss, in an effort to avail himself of my meal ticket and eat double rations, used to say jokingly while referring to the horses, "Well, such is life; yesterday the horse was still in the races and today we eat its meat." This went on a year or so, during which time I went without lunch every Monday. But as food supplies dwindled, so did my determination not to eat horse meat. One Monday I caved in and decided to eat in the cafeteria. My boss was there, his appetite honed to consume not only his portion but mine as well. My very presence made him realize that I had finally decided to try the horse meat. His reaction was one of disappointment. It is amazing how a very undesirable type of food can assume such significance in the face of hunger. I did not find the taste of horse meat too repulsive, but after the war ended I chose not to eat it again.

Daily reports from the fronts were followed carefully, and the situation deteriorated noticeably. Consequently, most of us quietly waited out the war, hoping that it would end sooner rather than later. It is amazing that Germans put up with those kinds of conditions for almost three years, and I find it hard to believe that we did not demand that our government withdraw from the war. Unfortunately, too many Germans still trusted Hitler and strongly identified with his goals and ideals. The propaganda machine worked overtime to bolster the morale of the people and to discourage pacificism. Josef Goebbels, the clever and demonic propaganda minister of the Third Reich, delivered a famous speech in the Berlin Sportpalast on February 18, 1943. The building had been filled with carefully selected party members, who were coached to greet Goebbels' speech with a tremendous ovation. The speech was a masterpiece of propaganda and skillfully addressed itself not only to those present, but to everyone listening on the radio all over Germany. Goebbels led up to the climax of the speech by asking the audience, *"Wollt ihr den totalen Krieg"*? (Do you want total war?) and the crowd enthusiastically shouted *"Ja!"* This sent the message to the whole nation that Berlin stood firmly behind Hitler and his design to continue the war to its military end. Berlin, the capital, was offered as a model of exemplary dedication to the party. "Total war," of course, meant stepping up the war efforts and making greater sacrifices. Hitler still exercised an inexplicable hypnotic effect on the public, a phenomenon that defied any logical explanation, but fostered an uncanny degree of loyalty and subservience toward the *Führer.*

Goebbels seized another means of encouraging the Germans to believe that the war could still be won. This involved the promise that "secret weapons" or "wonder weapons" were being developed in Northern Germany which, when employed, would assure Germany of the final victory. Everybody knew the names of those weapons of the future (V 1, the flying bomb; and V 2, the flying rocket), but nobody could predict how soon they would be available to the German war effort.

Finally, it was the fear of the unknown which kept Germans from giving up on the war. This fear had become an almost engrained characteristic over the years. It was partly based on what was considered the cruel and inhuman treatment that Germans had suffered through the Peace Treaty of Versailles at the end of the First World War and it was strengthened by the Nazis' message that the Allies were monsters and criminals devoid of any human qualities. More irresponsible Nazi propaganda! We were convinced that we would all be sold into slavery to foreign countries if Germany lost the war.

If, on the surface, Hitler was still universally accepted, it would be naïve to think that he had no adversaries. One particular group, which came closest to admitting that they were dissenters, was the officer corps of the armed forces. Hitler had never been on good terms with them, because he did not trust them or their expertise. He always found it very difficult to submit to any individual, let alone a whole group. The resistance to Hitler within the army was quite well-known to the average German. Hitler had become so intransigent towards the officer corps that, in spite of a deep and almost unthinking loyalty to their civilian government, they made plans to remove him.

A small group of officers, under the leadership of Graf Claus von Stauffenberg, carried out an attempt on Hitler's life on July 20, 1944, by placing a bomb in the conference room where Hitler consulted with some officers. Miraculously, the attempt failed and he escaped, badly shaken, allegedly with only minor injuries. We were never told the extent of his injuries, but the rumor circulated that he was never the same afterwards. To everybody's surprise, he addressed the nation after midnight from East Prussia and assured us that everything was all right and that the perpetrators would be severely punished. Many Germans interpreted the fact that he had survived the assassination attempt as proof that God was with him and wanted victory for Germany.

In view of various setbacks, we Germans hoped against hope that Hitler, in the interest of the people and to save further lives, would surrender sooner or later. But he was determined to fight to the bitter end. He claimed to have survived seven attacks on his life and he thereby strengthened his claim that he was sent by Providence to lead the nation into the future.

The German people deserved better. Until the very end, Hitler called for sacrifices beyond belief, while refusing to admit defeat. Millions of German lives were wasted, and the country was left in ruins. How could he have inflicted such a tragedy on a nation which he allegedly loved so much? The German people should never have allowed him to go to such extremes. But how do you oppose a dictator who unites complete and absolute power in his own person as Hitler did?

It may be appropriate to conclude this sad chapter with a quote given to me by a friend. The source is unknown. "When the

Germans are in a mess, it's always the fault of their emotional life, not their minds. When they think, they can't be beaten. When they indulge their feelings, any idiot can lead them around by the nose." It is sad but true that the German people acted very emotionally in their acceptance of Hitler's leadership without thinking of the consequences.

Toward the end of March, 1945, the Russians rapidly approached Austria from the East, just as the U.S. army advanced on the Western part of Germany. Surprisingly, life in my Vienna office went on more or less as usual. Within a matter of a few days, the Russians came so close to Vienna that we could hear their artillery, as they forced the German army to retreat. During the late evenings and on into the night, the sight of fires on the horizon reminded us of the imminent siege of the Russians.

We now suffered air raids inflicted by both Americans and Russians, but came to fear the American raids and to dismiss the Russian attacks. The Russians were so inefficient in hitting their targets, and their bombs were often so weak that we could casually continue with our duties without fear of harm. No such carelessness attended the American raids. When we heard the familiar sound of American bombers, we headed for the shelter as fast as we could move our feet.

The gravity of the situation became more evident when, one morning in early April, 1945, the government announced that the work force of Vienna was to be released from their jobs to enable them to seek refuge in the countryside, if at all possible, with friends or relatives. A mass exodus from the city followed within a very short time. My boss, very concerned about my safety and well-being as a German citizen, suggested that I try to return to Germany. He had learned from a good friend, who was a high-ranking officer in the German army and stationed near Vienna, that the last German army truck was to leave the city within hours. The truck driver had agreed to take me along on his retreat westwards. Frightened and heartbroken, I had to make an almost instantaneous decision. Everybody in the office deemed it sensible for me to take advantage of the offer. So I raced home, packed a suitcase in a hurry and said good-bye to an Austrian friend, with whom I had shared the apartment. We both burst into tears, realizing that we might never see each other again. She indicated that she could not possibly let me go out alone to meet the truck, so she decided to accompany me. We realized that the army truck would not be able to get very far with the U.S. troops pressing into the western part of Austria. Ideally, but unrealistically, I had hoped that I would be able to reach Germany on the truck. However, I had to admit this was simply not possible. Without having reached a decision as to what steps to take, we walked to the prearranged location to meet the truck. With great hesitation we got on. The driver was not there yet, so we still had a few minutes of deliberation. Then it started to rain, as if God wanted to send us a message or at least help us make up our minds. We had not brought an umbrella, so we got wet as we were sitting in the back of the truck.

Even such a small hardship as rain felt quite uncomfortable, so how could we possibly face further and more severe hardships ahead of us, without food, surrounded by strangers and military enemies, in the midst of grave dangers? Our mood turned to despair and my friend asked me, "Do you really want to leave?" I answered in the negative. When the driver arrived we told him of my decision. We grabbed my suitcases, got off the truck and, relieved but frightened of what the near future might hold, walked home to our apartment to make preparations for the imminent Russian takeover and siege. With enemy troops entering the gates of Vienna, what could be done to ensure survival? Since the city was to be attacked as well as defended for quite some time, our main concern was to set up a shelter in the cellar of the apartment building, take canned food and other provisions there, as well as mattresses, blankets and warm clothing. About fourteen other apartment dwellers joined us in our efforts to prepare for the Russians, and we no longer felt so alone. As a matter of fact, we were almost certain that, with courage and determination, we would not only live through the crisis, but also come out stronger for the experience. We spent two weeks in those surroundings, cut off from the rest of the world almost entirely, not even able to communicate with neighbors, and lacking electricity, heat, radio and newspapers. It was not even safe to go upstairs and look around to see what was happening in the streets. What an existential experience!

The worst was yet to come. Life in the cellar became uncomfortable, primitive, frightening and boring. Most of the apartment dwellers, especially families with children, had left the city. The only young people among us were two teenage boys, one fourteen and one sixteen years of age, whose fathers were away serving in the German army. Their mothers were with us as well. The two boys found life in the cellar uninteresting, to say the least.

The war that was being fought in our streets proved to be more exciting and interesting to those young people. They could not contain their curiosity, so one morning, much against our warnings, they decided to leave the cellar to go upstairs and see how the war was progressing. We could hear artillery and explosions all around us. The boys did not return for hours, and we all feared the worst. Unfortunately, our fears came true. As we found out after many anxious hours, they had been killed by gunfire and were found lying in front of our building. Nobody can imagine the grief of the mothers and its effect on all of us. The worst thing was that, since casualties were running so high, funeral parlors, if indeed they had not shut down entirely, could not handle the burial of so many street victims. So we people in the cellar had no choice but to take it upon ourselves and bury the boys. I cannot remember which brave souls among us carried out this mournful duty, but I was not one of them. There was a small strip of grass across from our building. There our two volunteers dug shallow makeshift graves and buried the two boys. It was not until months later that the city fathers undertook the excavation of bodies killed in the last days of the war to give them a proper burial in cemeteries.

Left: Opera House in Vienna, Austria, bombed during U.S. air raid, 1945.
Right: An idealistic member of the Hitler Youth in uniform.

11

Brush with the Russian Bear

We realized that the Russians were very close, but we did not have any personal contacts with them until mid-April when, one morning, we heard them shouting upstairs. Soon they came to the cellar, and we got our first glimpse of Russian soldiers. It was a most frightening experience, because we realized that they were enemies and we could not anticipate how they were going to treat us. Instinct told us to try to cooperate with them and do whatever they ordered us to do. But how, if you could not communicate? Suddenly, I had an idea. Why not try English on them? I was the only person among the group of Austrians who spoke some English. With the approval of the others, I asked a Russian officer what they expected of us. He responded that they wanted to search our apartments for weapons and German soldiers, who might have defected and be hiding in our civilian dwellings. I told my group of the Russian plans. We were afraid that the soldiers, in an effort to gain entrance into our apartments, might break doors and windows. In order to prevent this from happening, we decided to hand over our keys to them. Much to our amazement, the soldiers refused to accept the keys. Why? we asked ourselves, but no one knew the answer until later. The Russians told us to stay in the cellar, while they searched our apartments. It was still a mystery to us how they were going to manage to get in. Several hours later, still waiting in the cellar, we concluded that they had finished their search and left the building, because we could not hear them anymore. We decided to go upstairs and see what damage they had done. We soon found out how they had entered the apartments: they had sawed a large hole in the front doors and crawled through the opening. Unwilling to follow their example, I opened the door to my apartment with my key. I could not believe my eyes! The apartment looked as if it had been hit by a tornado. Some of the furniture was overturned, the contents of all the drawers in the kitchen, living room and bedroom had been emptied onto the floors, so that I could hardly walk through the mess. It took me a couple of days to put things in order again. In the process, I found out that certain items had been taken, such as my complete set of sterling silverware, my genuine gold and silver jewelry, my alarm clock, an elegant tailor-made suit and - - - my bathing suit!

Since there was no one available to board up our doors, they stayed open for weeks. That was exactly what the Russians wanted. They wanted the apartments to be accessible to them in order to re-enter at their discretion, day or night. In order to be relatively safe at night, I moved a piece of heavy furniture against the entrance door every night, hoping to be somehow protected against any intrusion. Frightened as I was, sleep did not come easily. The Russian soldiers did not go to sleep early, because they had too much fun moving about in the streets and frightening us with their shooting throughout the early hours of the mornings.

All of us apartment dwellers kept in close touch, in order to exchange our experiences with the Russians and to provide mutual moral support. Among those people there was a lovely middle-aged Jewish lady whom I came to regard as a close friend. She was concerned of what might happen to us younger women, because word had spread that the Russian soldiers were out to satisfy their sexual desires by raping women. Because of her concern for us we called her *Mutti*, which in German is an endearing word for "mother."

The second wave of Russian soldiers, who entered our building, came with the express purpose to find German citizens, and that included me! They did not appear to blame Austrians for the war but they certainly had it in for the Germans, including civilians. As a Jewish lady, *Mutti* must have been outraged at the Germans for what they had done to her race all over Europe. But she protected me by repeatedly saying to the Russians that there were no Germans among us.

I will never forget her loving kindness towards me. As for the Russians, she regarded them as liberators from the Germans, but she soon realized that she was mistaken. She was certainly not treated better than anyone else. As a matter of fact, she even suffered more indignities than the rest of us. She had beautiful oil paintings, some of them quite precious, hanging on the walls. One day, when the Russians again entered her apartment, they kept saying to her "*du bourgeois*", which meant "you are a bourgeois," a term of contempt. They severely damaged her beautifully framed pictures by repeatedly shooting at them with their rifles. To add insult to injury, they relieved themselves on her Persian rugs.

Once the Russians had swept into Vienna, it did not take long before the city surrendered, but things did not go back to normal for a long time. The war was still going on, as the Russians marched farther towards the Western part of Austria. In our own selfish way, we were just grateful that military actions, including those scary air raids, were finally over for us. This did not mean, however, that our lot was a happy one. There was complete chaos and lawlessness in the city. It would have been futile on the part of the police to try and enforce any degree of order, so they did not even try. Many Austrian civilians took advantage of the situation and, along with the Russians, looted the stores, which were kept closed to the public.

There was a store in our building, whose Nazi owners fled before the Russians conquered the city. Prior to their departure, they loaded all non-perishable food items onto a van and encouraged us to help ourselves, when we were in great need of food. The van just stood in front of our building, but we did not dare take the food out for fear of the Russians. One day, the van had disappeared, stolen either by Russian soldiers or some courageous but dishonest Austrians. In order to acquire food for their families, some people resorted to stealing, because groceries were not otherwise available for quite some time. Factories were closed and farmers were afraid to bring vegetables and fruits to the city because of unsafe conditions on the roads. When men ventured out on the streets, they were in danger of being arrested, and women ran the risk of being abducted and raped.

The first food item that became available after a few weeks was bread, if you were lucky. Soon after the Russian occupation, some bakeries began to bake bread again on a limited basis. We usually heard about it by word of mouth. The bakeries opened at 9 a.m., but in order to secure a loaf of bread, hundreds of us lined up as early as 5 a. m. and waited patiently for four hours till opening time. Even this was a risky business. All too often Russian soldiers would inspect the lines and pick out attractive young girls to take them away. I soon found out how to escape this danger. Whenever I lined up for bread, I would dress literally in rags and, Heaven forbid, no make-up, to make myself utterly unattractive. Another way of avoiding the Russian advances was not to look at them. They used to beckon girls because of the language barrier and force them to come along. So I stared at the ground and never looked at them whenever they approached.

Bread and potatoes were our mainstay. To this day, Germans use a lot of potatoes in a variety of dishes. It used to be the custom to buy a large supply, about 150 pounds per person, in the fall. This quantity lasted till the end of the following spring and was stored in the cellars. It was fortunate that my landlord in Vienna, before fleeing to the countryside, had offered me the remaining quantity of potatoes in his cellar. Never had potatoes tasted so good to me and never will they again.

Apart from the problem of acquiring food, there were certain conditions, which made life miserable. We had no electricity for months and therefore did without warm water or heat. For the whole winter of 1945 to 1946, the luxury of taking a hot shower or washing one's hair in warm water was unavailable. Natural gas for cooking purposes was supplied only during certain hours of the day.

As a German citizen, my life was made even more difficult. My bank account was frozen, so that I could not withdraw any money. In addition, I was jobless, because German citizens were no longer employed in Austria. I was considered an undesirable alien. In the absence of newspapers, orders given by the Russians were posted at strategic locations. One day, news was spread that all German citizens had to report to the Russian authorities. Since I was raised to be a law-abiding citizen, I was going to comply, no matter what the consequences. My Austrian friends, bless their hearts, advised me against it. This good advice may have decided my fate in a favorable direction. A few of my German friends, who reported to the Russians, disappeared without a trace, never to be heard from again.

For someone who had been raised in a protective environment, I found the behavior of the Russians absolutely bizarre. One day, I walked into the bathroom of my apartment and saw a Russian soldier washing his hair in the toilet bowl. On another occasion, after some stores had re-opened, I took my watch to a repair shop. The repair man seemed to be in an exceptionally good mood. When asked what made him so happy in those days of hardships, danger and suffering, he told me that, just a few minutes before I entered the store, a Russian soldier brought him one of those big old-fashioned alarm clocks and ordered him to make five wrist watches from it. Some other time, I was at a beauty parlor to have my hair styled. Suddenly, a Russian soldier entered and gestured to the beauty operator to indicate that he wanted a permanent. The trouble was that he had a crew cut, and his hair was not nearly long enough to put up in curlers. The beauty operator was frantic because he became increasingly irritated. No matter how hard she tried, she could not get through to him. He misinterpreted her gestures and jumped to the conclusion that she was simply unwilling to comply. He showed his disapproval by shooting into the air. Then he left, much to our relief.

The Russians employed women in uniform to direct the traffic of their military vehicles. When the weather was quite hot, those women wore sleeveless blouses. You could see their arms covered with watches from their wrist to their upper arm. No doubt, those watches, considered status symbols by the Russians, had been stolen from the Austrians. Some of those traffic policewomen were dressed in dirndls, which are dresses consisting of a colorful full skirt gathered to a tight bodice and worn with a half-apron, first by girls in the Alpine regions. Now the dirndl is the national costume of Germany, worn by women young and old in all parts of Germany and Austria. Russian women in that type of costumes looked quite out-of-place, especially when they wore them with silver or gold-colored high heels, as they directed the city traffic.

Many Russians did not seem to be familiar with conveniences that we had taken for granted for decades, such as indoor plumbing, hot and cold running water, etc. The Austrians predicted that, once those soldiers returned to the Soviet Union, they would certainly start a revolution and demand all the good things that we people in Western Europe had appreciated for decades but which were still unknown in the Soviet Union. Of course, no such thing happened, because the Soviet system was so repressive.

After the surrender of Vienna, we considered the war over, although the fighting continued in other parts of Austria. The government, which had been run by Nazis since 1938, ceased to exist practically overnight. Until a new government, especially a new form of government, could be established much time went by. The only evidence of someone functioning "up there" was in the form of ration cards providing for 800 calories per day, which was a starvation diet, if you actually lived on it. The majority of people, however, had some contacts with friends or relatives in the countryside, who were able to supply them with some additional food. Those who tried to live on 800 calories soon lost their physical strength and some of them actually died of hunger edema or malnutrition, among them an elderly gentleman in our apartment house. Another way of getting some extra food was barter. This practice led to an exchange of goods on the black market, which meant that food could no longer be purchased for money. For example, if you needed a dozen eggs, a pound of meat, flour, sugar, a new pair of shoes or any type of clothing, you needed to come up with some merchandise that you were willing to trade. One of the hottest items on the black market were cigarettes, which were practically the main currency.

In order to acquire some food, people would part with the most unbelievable belongings, such as porcelain, silverware, genuine jewelry, Persian rugs, pieces of furniture, framed pictures, toys. The list could go on and on, but it is obvious that, in the face of starvation, even the most treasured possessions lose their meaning and much of their value.

One day, a group of Austrian men, in their early twenties, came into the courtyard of our apartment building. They were pulling carts loaded with kitchen articles, such as pots and pans, pails, dishes and all kinds of utensils. To our astonishment, they admitted that they had looted a store and were now trading their loot for food. Since we were not bombed out, we had no need of those items. We were curious about the activities of those young men and engaged them in a friendly conversation. They confided that they had worked as members of the Austrian underground movement against the Nazis. *Mutti*, being Jewish, immediately sympathized with them. On the other hand, I, being a German, was leery of those men, who, in my opinion, had somehow sabotaged the German cause. Consequently, I decided not to participate in the conversation, at least initially, in order not to show my annoyance. However, much to my amazement, *Mutti* introduced me as "a very nice German lady," who needed protection from the Russians.

The young people promised to help me by providing a safe place to live, if I was willing to leave my apartment. It turned out that they were looking for a housekeeper, whose responsibilities were to cook three meals a day and keep their apartment clean. In return, they offered room and board, but no pay. They insisted on an immediate answer, but I was reluctant to accept their offer, especially since there was no way of telling what I might be getting into. Was I ever scared!

My fellow apartment dwellers, who had gathered around the very unusual group of men, to find out what was going on, encouraged me by saying, "It's better to be raped by an Austrian than by a Russian." This was an example of the grim humor we engaged in during those depressing days! To me it was hardly a consolation. When the four men promised to treat me like a queen, I finally accepted their offer. They wanted me to come along with them right away, so I did not have much time to put a few items of clothing in a suitcase. Then they took me to their apartment. I was assigned my own room, which made me feel better immediately. The young men laid down the rules of the house: they would acquire sufficient food on the black market, and I was to cook the meals. To my dismay, some Russian soldiers were camping downstairs in the courtyard. I was warned not to be seen at the window and not to turn the lights on in the evenings until my protectors returned home and, above all, not to leave the apartment. My presence in the house was to be kept a complete secret.

I had no idea what kind of work these young Austrians pursued and I was still uncertain whether I had made the right decision. One day went by pretty much like the other. My routine was boring and I felt like a prisoner, without any freedom. The only comforting thoughts were that, for once, I had enough to eat and I was safe from the Russians. The Austrian men did keep their promise and acted as perfect gentlemen.

I endured this comfortable, if unrewarding, situation for six weeks, but then I decided that, in the long run, freedom was worth more than food and safety. One day, I informed the men that I would prefer to live at home again, which, under the circumstances, they were able to understand. In order not to fall into the hands of the Russians, while leaving the building, I waited for an opportune moment to sneak out. I raced through the deserted streets of Vienna and back to my apartment, a run of about fifteen minutes. Free at last, but no longer safe! Which was more important? I had made my choice and did not regret it.

The political and economic conditions in Vienna stabilized very slowly. The Russians had complete control of the city from mid-April through mid-August of 1945, four long months! When I needed to leave the house for some reason or just to go for a walk, I would take at least one escort along. Quite often we would walk in groups of four or five. One beautiful sunny Sunday in August, we were out enjoying the lovely Vienna summer. It was so good to be alive! Suddenly, we heard the rattling of tanks and we looked at one another in astonishment, not able to believe our eyes and ears. There were actual tanks moving through the streets, and this after the war was already over for three months! And, lo and behold, the soldiers wore different uniforms from the ones we were used to. They were neither Germans nor Russians, but Americans!

We were euphoric, because we realized that their arrival portended the re-establishment of law and order, as well as more satisfactory living conditions. Even though Americans were enemy forces to us, just like the Russians, we cheered and greeted them as our liberators from the Russian yoke. There was some uncertainty among the Viennese as to how to react to this new "invasion," but generally people established an immediate kinship with the American forces.

With the arrival of the U.S troops, life in Vienna improved in every respect. Like Germany, Austria was divided into four occupation zones but, unlike Berlin, Vienna was not made into a divided city. Instead, it was administered alternately by Russians, Americans, British and French. The city government changed hands every four weeks, depending on which occupation force was in command. We liked the U.S. administration best, because from them we received the best food. The quantity remained limited, but the quality changed according to the occupation force which was in charge of the city. Adequate food supplies continued to be a major problem for the Viennese.

The possession of ration cards did not guarantee the availability of the food, because stores were not fully stocked yet. One type of food I remember best was the dry yellow peas we received from the Russians. The peas were so hard that they had to be cooked about three hours and, in the process, tiny worms came floating to the surface. We jokingly referred to them as our extra allowance of Russian protein.

Austria was now completely separated from Germany after a happy union from 1938 to 1945. For seven years Austrians had been German citizens, until their Austrian citizenship was restored at the end of the war. Diplomatic, political and economic relations between the two countries were forbidden by the Allies, and for me, as a German citizen, this was especially difficult. I was no longer able to exchange letters with my parents, relatives and friends in Germany. For months, I did not even know if they had survived the war. Naturally, my parents were equally worried about me. Some hardy souls, however, occasionally crossed the borders between the two countries illegally. Eventually, some six months after the end of the war, a letter from my father reached me in Vienna. It had been smuggled across the border and mailed in Austria. I was able to send a reply back to my parents in Nuremberg the same way. This was probably the most precious present we received at Christmas, 1945. It took a long time before the postal service between the two countries was re-established.

In the latter part of the summer of 1945, I came down with a case of hepatitis. I went to a physician, who confirmed my self-diagnosis, shrugged his shoulders and informed me that I would not be able to buy the needed medicine, because Austria had been dependent on Germany for its pharmaceutical supplies. With borders closed, no business could be transacted anymore. I went home in complete misery and took to my bed for a few weeks until nature's healing set in, and my symptoms disappeared.

12

Academic Studies and Manual Labor

 Years earlier, when I was ten years old and brought home my first A in English, my parents promised me to let me study languages at the university after graduation from high school. In my nine years of high school, I earned nothing but A's in English, French and Latin. My parents' promise provided me with the greatest motivation. However, after I finished high school in 1939, my academic studies had to be postponed for six and a half long years due to the war effort, which made it necessary for every qualified young woman to fill a man's job. But now, after all this waiting, my dream finally seemed to come true. It was the summer of 1945, and I was free to apply for admission to the University of Vienna as a foreign student. I was informed that German students, who applied for admission, had to work twenty-five days, four hours a day, in the streets of Vienna, much as if we had to earn our entrance into the university by performing humiliating manual labor. It has befuddled me again and again how individuals can be held responsible for the actions of their government. To this day, I find it extremely hard to understand collective guilt.

 However, I was so anxious to be admitted to the university that I would have consented to any hardship. A hundred hours of strenuous menial work without pay was awaiting me. The city had been so badly destroyed that narrow-gauge tracks had to be laid across town, so that lorries could run like little locomotives through the streets. The German students' job consisted of shoveling the rubble of collapsed buildings onto the lorries and cleaning up the streets. We were also instructed to save all the bricks and remove any cement from them with a little hammer, so that they could be used again for rebuilding purposes.

After finishing my hundred hours of work on the streets, I was able to enroll at the University of Vienna. I majored in French and English with a minor in philosophy, the latter being required of all prospective high school teachers, regardless of major. I was on cloud nine! Since my bank account was still frozen, I was not able to come up with payments for tuition and the purchase of books, let alone living expenses. Fortunately, I had several wonderful Austrian friends who had helped me out in many a precarious situation before. Once again, they came around and offered to loan me the needed money to attend the university. I hasten to add that most universities in Austria and Germany were and still are state-supported, so that studying at an institute of higher learning has been rather affordable, quite in contrast to the relatively exorbitant fees of comparable U.S. institutions. There were no dormitories at Austrian or German universities, and students lived either at home or in rented rooms with a nice landlady to watch over them. I was still hanging on to my apartment which I had occupied during the war years. It was located only half an hour's walk from the university, which helped me to save on transportation fees.

I pursued my studies with a great deal of ambition and a full measure of gratitude for the chance that I had finally been given to build my career. The first semester went very well. We were already into the second semester, when university officials announced out of a clear blue sky that the university had to close down because of a lack of fuel. The classrooms could no longer be heated. Immediately, the professors handed out extensive course outlines and reading assignments. We were admonished to keep up with our studies, even though classes would no longer be in session for the rest of the winter semester. Since it was not the custom at German and Austrian universities to give regular tests, closing the school for a short period of time was not as much of a problem as it would be if the same had to happen at an American university. Personally, I considered losing out on lectures given by illustrious professors another serious disappointment of my life. Fortunately, credit was given for the full semester, provided we handed in a number of research papers to the professors. We felt honor bound to do the assigned reading at home. My home was an ice-cold apartment. Consequently, I spent most of the time in bed, fully clothed, including coat, gloves and woolen cap on my head to protect myself against the cold, while feverishly engaging in my assigned work.

I had planned to stay in Vienna indefinitely and hoped that, eventually, relations between Austrians and Germans would improve to the point that Germans would be granted equal rights along with other aliens. However, at the end of the second semester, I was dealt another blow. One day, I received a summons for a hearing from Austrian authorities. Naturally, I was quite apprehensive, but had no choice but to appear. I was asked my reason for being in Vienna and was told that I could just as easily pursue my study of languages at a German university. Of course, I could not refute that argument. My love of Austria and her people could not convince the officials to let me stay there. I was given ten days to leave Vienna.

The process was called "repatriation." I was to appear at the *Westbahnhof*, the railroad station from which trains to the Western part of Europe departed. To my surprise, I was in the company of about 250 other Germans, who were also repatriated to West Germany. We were allowed to carry only two suitcases, so that I had to leave most of my belongings in Vienna, never to get them back.

The train which we boarded was not a regular passenger train, but a freight train without benches. We sat on our suitcases all the time. Normally, the trip from Vienna to Nuremberg lasted about six hours. This time it took us three days and two nights. Since I did not expect such a long journey, I had not brought much food along. The reason for the delay was that, every once in a while, the Russians stopped our train whenever the locomotive was needed for another train. There was a shortage of trains and locomotives, because so many had been destroyed by bombs. There we stood for several hours without a locomotive, before our trip could be continued. Later, during our stops in the U.S.-occupied zone in the Western part of Austria and Southeastern part of Germany, some well-meaning American soldiers tossed us packages of cookies onto the train to supplement our otherwise meager or nonexistent food supply. What a godsend those cookies were!

Although order was largely restored in Germany, it was still impossible to communicate either by letter, phone, or telegram. Thus, my parents were not informed that I would be coming home after three years of absence. On my arrival in Nuremberg, I did not have any German money to take the streetcar or a taxi to my parents' apartment, which was a 45-minute walk from the station. I had to walk all that distance with two heavy suitcases, and this after two nights with hardly any sleep. No words can describe the surprise of my parents when, ghostlike, I stood in front of their door. They were aware of the fact that German citizens in Austria were being repatriated, but they had no idea when I might show up. The repatriation process was very slow, largely because well-trained, trustworthy bureaucrats, who had not been tainted by membership in the Nazi party, were hard to find, and also because damage to transportation facilities was so extensive that train service was sporadic and unpredictable.

My father took me in his arms and welcomed his prodigal

daughter. My stepmother was uncharacteristically gracious and kind. We had all survived the war. How lucky we were! Everything else, even the memory of our earlier strained relations, mattered little, at least for the moment.

Burgtheater, Vienna, Austria.

Street scene in Vienna, Austria, with swastika flags, 1939.

13

The Sting of Guilt and Postwar Problems

Defeat is a most painful experience. In my case, it not only brought an end to our hopes for victory, for prosperity and stability, for values to build on in the future, it also left me in a psychological no man's land, where the traditional values no longer fit and no new system was attractive enough to gain my respect. But it did not end there: I could not deny the legacy of twelve years of my life, especially when they had such a tremendous impact on me. Suddenly, everything I had believed in was wrong, and it was criminal to identify with a government which I thought had functioned in the best interests of the future of our nation. I felt a terrible void and found nothing to replace my untenable values. Neither did I know where to turn for comfort, nor how to find new ideals on which to build a new life.

In my efforts to come to grips with my situation, I asked myself where the Germans had gone wrong. The "new" journalism, with its greater openness in reporting than we had ever experienced under Hitler, helped somewhat to set the record straight. It was an eye-opening experience. In the process I asked myself, "What and how much did I actually know?" It soon became apparent to me that a great deal of information had deliberately been withheld from us by our government. For example, I did know that concentration camps existed, but I was not aware that people were actually killed there. I thought that those camps were similar to detention camps or prisons, at worst, to keep certain elements of the population away from the rest of the people for more or less justifiable reasons. It was not until the end of the war that the real truth emerged. Having been deceived once before, the question came up, "How much of the information is indeed based on facts, or are we being brainwashed again?"

As new truths entered my mind, another question, this time hypothetical, arose. "If what is presented to us at this time as the truth, why didn't I or anyone else do something to keep the Nazis from committing those atrocities?" And another, "Did we actually want the war and why did we go along with Hitler as long as we did?" One question led to another without pointing the way to plausible answers, which led to more questions and more frustration. Then I tried rationalizations: "Even if I had known all the facts and tried to oppose the Nazi misdeeds, I would have been imprisoned or possibly executed. The Nazis had a tight rein even on the average citizens."

The realization that I had failed to act in a moment of grave crisis produced an agonizing feeling of personal guilt and irresponsibility. But it also inspired more rationalizations. Obviously, the Jews were not the only ones who suffered and lost their lives. Millions of Germans, both soldiers and civilians, had been killed in the war. I used to refer to this phenomenon as "the Aryan holocaust." And what about those millions of brave Americans, Frenchmen, Englishmen, and Russians, as well as members of other nationalities who had to sacrifice their lives? And what about the total destruction of our cities and our country? We admitted that we Germans had inflicted untold suffering on much of the world, but something within me said, "Look at us, we suffered, too. And how!"

All these rationalizations could not remove the sting of guilt which, multiplied by seventy million Germans who felt the same way I did, added up to a mountain of collective guilt. But the recognition that others also had to shoulder the guilt did nothing to alleviate my own distress. The damage had been done and could not be reversed. The futility of these reflections troubled me even more, when the events of the Hitler era and World War II began to flood the media. Eventually, we began to experience media overkill, as old wounds were opened again and not allowed to heal. Young Germans especially, who were not even alive when Hitler was in power, resent the fact that they are held accountable for the deeds of their fathers.

I still find the continuing fascination of the media with events of the Nazi years almost unbearable after more than four decades. Although I have been a proud American citizen for thirty-two years, an unsettling feeling overcomes me when asked by strangers what country I am from. I have developed the ridiculous habit of responding by "guess." Quite often I am mistaken for a member of a different nationality, probably based on my physical appearance. People will take me for Swedish, Norwegian, or Dutch. I bask in the warmth of wishful thinking for just a moment and even allow myself to feel flattered. Then I come down to earth again and identify myself as the German that I was and will always be, regardless of citizenship. I cannot escape my past, nor can I change it. Like so many of my fellow Germans, I carry an almost insuperable burden of guilt for our collective sins of the past.

All that notwithstanding, I wish to stress the fact that Germans experienced the most humane and, may I say, unexpectedly generous treatment from the U.S. occupation forces. Those Germans who were able to look ahead several years even foresaw the possibility of being protected by Americans against the Soviet threat in the Cold War and possibly long-range protection for decades to come.

On the other side of the ledger, many disconcerting events followed in the wake of the occupation. The following is a list of negatives brought about by the American occupation as seen through the eyes of a German observer. I regret that the list is so long.

In the beginning, the U.S. forces were regarded as enemies and as such were resented. Their privileged life style was constantly on display. They drove huge, fancy cars, dressed well and had plenty to eat, whereas thousands of Germans faced starvation and routinely raided garbage cans outside U.S. military installations in search of discarded food. The presence of military personnel was deeply felt, especially in view of the fact that Germans had been demilitarized and ammunition factories were closed. Murder, prostitution, rape, use of narcotics, vulgarity and rowdyism shook the normally law-abiding German citizens. Thousands of German homes were confiscated to accommodate the influx of U.S. soldiers and their families, while young German women, untrained for other jobs, willingly served American families as domestic help and, thus, were no longer available to German households. Americans could afford to pay higher wages, and the dollar enjoyed a higher purchasing power than the German mark. Relationships between U.S. forces and German civilians were complicated by the language barrier, and U.S. denazification efforts were especially stringent when compared to those of the other allies and were considered ineffective and even senseless by many Germans. We received food stamps only after being able to prove that we had watched a film on concentration camps.

Although fraternization between U.S. soldiers and German citizens was not allowed, many German girls teamed up with American GIs for various reasons, mostly to obtain food for themselves and their families. This restriction was later removed. German girls found it easy to get acquainted with American soldiers. An amorous American male made advances to attractive females by addressing them as "sweetheart," "darling," *Liebling* or *Fräulein*. When the girl indicated that she was interested, a friendship easily developed. The frequent use of the word *Fräulein* in this context gave it a pejorative connotation from which it has never escaped. Therefore, it was dropped from official usage. According to a new law, all women are to be addressed and referred to by *Frau* (Mrs.) even though they are not married.

Liaisons between U.S. soldiers and German girls occurred frequently, but they were not endorsed by good upright German citizens. Thousands of children were born out of wedlock to U.S. fathers and German mothers. Germans frowned upon this, but for the most part they accepted the consequences, as long as both parents were white. On the other hand, Germans, having been made aware of race distinctions by Hitler, considered it appalling, when girls threw themselves into the arms of black soldiers and gave birth to babies of mixed races. About 10,000 German illegitimate children were fathered by black U.S. soldiers.

This proved to be an especially difficult problem to deal with, because it was unprecedented and unthinkable under Hitler. At first, children of mixed races were segregated, and it was even planned, but not carried out, to send them to live in some black country. Many years passed before the German public learned to look at those children with a somewhat open mind.

Another problem surfaced among Germans employed by U.S. military forces. The Germans often felt as if they were treated as second-class citizens because they were paid less than those people who worked in identical jobs for German employers. At the same time, German business interests resented the influx of American businesses into Germany, because wartime setbacks left them unable to compete.

Even the life style of the Americans came under close scrutiny. One case in point was the use of make-up. One day, a rich uncle of mine, who drove a beautiful, expensive Mercedes, invited me for a Sunday drive. In those days, very few Germans owned a car, so going for a ride was a special treat for me. I dressed up in my Sunday best and, to top it all off, I put make-up on my face and thought I looked quite nice. However, wearing make-up was not fully accepted by Germans. When I eagerly joined my uncle for the ride, he looked at me with disgust and said, "Come here to me." At first I did not understand the meaning of his strange behavior, but I soon found out when, with his hand, he smeared my lipstick all over my face. I felt deeply humiliated! Then he gave me a lecture on how German girls were supposed to be proud of their natural look without the help of make-up. Needless to say, my Sunday was ruined. This incident was characteristic of the way many Germans reacted to American idiosyncrasies and customs that they themselves did not practice. Upon my return from Vienna, my parents filled me in on a few more happenings in connection with the arrival of U.S. occupation troops.

Nazi party members were afraid of the kind of treatment they might expect from American troops. Therefore, former Nazis tried to remove anything in their household that revealed sympathy with or even support of the Nazi cause. For example, in practically every German household the customary framed Hitler portrait disappeared from the wall. This happened in my parents' home also. Furthermore, my father destroyed all photos taken at party rallies, as well as our swastika flag and the family genealogy, which he had to submit to Nazi authorities, when it came to prove his Aryan descent, in order to be able to retain his job with the government. I regret having lost the information on our ancestry, especially in view of the fact that nowadays genealogy and search for family roots are quite popular. In the absence of detailed information on my ancestors, I now jokingly refer to myself as a "pure German," a "distinction" which relatively few Americans can claim.

Two items we lost because they were stolen by U.S. soldiers, were a copy of Hitler's *Mein Kampf* and my father's bicycle, which was badly needed to get to and from work.

During my three years in Vienna, I had developed a great affection for Austria and her fun-loving, culturally aware people. Indeed, it was a traumatic experience to leave. If I had not been expelled, I might still be there because I was happy despite the hardships I had gone through. However, Germany was my native land and in a way I was glad to be home.

The full impact of the loss of the war did not hit me until I returned. I find it almost impossible to describe the depth of my emotions, because my country had lost the war. The optimism of the prewar era was almost completely destroyed and massive war casualties offered a grim commentary on the ideals of the Nazi party. A completely new beginning had to be made somehow. I remember my father saying that Germany would be annihilated. "Believe me, there is no future for Germany," he would say over and over again. He came to that conclusion in part because he believed that Germany would be severely penalized for her frequent involvement in wars and her atrocities committed against Jews all over Europe. But he also based his predictions on Germany's treatment after World War I.

We all realized that World War I was a mere warmup for the slaughter of World War II. Like naughty children, we thought we had a lesson coming and we knew what we deserved. There was a terrible feeling of guilt among most Germans. We found it almost impossible to believe that we had followed the wrong leader and a false ideology. So we struggled hard to build a new and different life for ourselves, not quite knowing how to go about it.

Amidst all this despair, some positive feelings still prevailed. We were happy to have survived the war and grateful for the small courtesies and generous aid that the Americans provided. I came to believe that you can be a survivor, no matter what the odds are against you, and that this conviction can be a source of strength in any difficult situation in life. It has repeatedly proved to be a great consolation to me.

And, like so many Germans, I had to find a way to be tolerant of others, regardless of nationality, race, creed, or political convictions. Our associations with foreigners and former enemies took us beyond the stereotypes of the Nazi ideology, and we discovered that they were human beings with hopes and aspirations that were much like our own. Despite the defeat of my country, I came to feel a kinship with other peoples and I formed an intense desire to become a citizen of the world.

Ironically, the German authorities in Nuremberg raised the first obstacle to my dreams. Nuremberg suffered an extreme shortage of housing after the war, due to the damage caused by Allied bombing, and because approximately 13 million refugees from the Eastern part of Germany and the rest of Europe had sought refuge in West Germany. I had assumed that I would move in with my parents on my return from Vienna. What could have been more natural than that? As it turned out, a refugee from East Germany had been assigned to my former room in my parents' apartment. The German housing authorities - my own people! - refused to let me move in with my parents. The person in charge said to me sarcastically, "It's your

own fault that you are in this quandary. You should not have moved
to Vienna in the first place."

Then I faced the problem of obtaining ration cards without
which I could not survive. Municipal authorities told me that, in
order to get a residency permit and ration cards, I had to have a job.
Since I was a student between two semesters and on vacation, I was
classified as unemployed and as such not eligible for ration cards,
and I could not be granted permission to live in Nuremberg with my
parents. What a blow!

Georg, by then an influential physician in the city, pulled
some strings and, fortunately, he was able to strip away these
bureaucratic restrictions. However, I had to sign a statement
agreeing to sleep on the sofa in the living room rather than claiming
a room of my own. How happy I was to receive ration cards, which
enabled me to eat without feeling guilty for taking food away from
my parents! Another hurdle had been overcome, but certainly not the
last one.

Before leaving Vienna, I had finished my first two semesters
of study, so it seemed only logical to continue studying at a German
university. My choice fell on the University of Erlangen. It was the
native city of my mother and I had spent many happy days there.
Furthermore, it was located only about eighteen miles from
Nuremberg. I could have commuted by train, but I preferred to stay
with an aunt who lived in Erlangen. She welcomed me, not only
because she was fond of me, but also because she was physically
handicapped, and I could be of great help to her. I did her shopping
and kept her apartment clean in exchange for meals and overnight
accommodation. Since her bedroom was occupied by a female refugee
from Silesia, we both slept on sofas in her living room. We enjoyed
little privacy, because this lady's bedroom had no separate entrance,
which made it necessary for her to walk through our living room. It
was an awkward situation on both sides, complicated by the fact that
she had to get up much earlier than we did. She always woke us up
at a very early hour, no matter how quietly she tiptoed through our
bedroom.

When I applied for admission to the University of Erlangen,
my application was turned down, much to my dismay. I was already
twenty-six years old, anxious to finish my studies and get on with my
career as a high school teacher. My application was rejected, because
refugees from the East had flooded West Germany and its
universities, and they were given preference over native West

Germans. Again, I was devastated! Once more, a door had been closed, but as fate would have it, another one opened. The very same day that I was rejected by the university, I returned to Nuremberg by bus. There, to my surprise, I happened to meet a former high school classmate, whom I had not seen for seven years. She was a medical student at the University of Erlangen. I poured my heart out to her. She comforted me by telling me that she would be able to intervene on my behalf, because she knew a professor in the Division of Liberal Arts who served on the Admissions Committee. Knowing me from high school, she was able to give me a very good recommendation. I was extremely happy, when I was informed that my application had been reconsidered, and I was admitted to the university after all. I started at Erlangen in the winter semester of 1946.

"Divided into three parts? Never!"
A road sign protesting the postwar division of Germany.

14

Arriving Where I Always Wanted to Be

University life after the war did not conform to our contemporary notions of what student life should be. It was quite bleak and not conducive to much fun and excitement. Millions of young men had lost their lives during the war, and the majority of students were women. Most of them were my age and, like me, they had not been able to continue their studies right after high school. Gradually, more men, who had been detained in prisoner-of-war camps and eventually released, joined the ranks of the students. There were no student activities to participate in. We got to know each other only by brief conversations during breaks between classes. Those of us who commuted by bus or train had a further opportunity to get better acquainted on the way to and from the university, but otherwise there was no social life of any consequence.

No unit tests, midterms, or finals were given. Naturally, under those circumstances, some students faced a great temptation to let things slide and to lead a happy-go-lucky life. However, most of us were extremely well-motivated and we used our time to study as much as possible. The main activity of our undergraduate studies was to gather as much material in our field as possible, both by taking copious notes during lectures and wading through assigned readings. There were only two occasions when tests were administered. The first came after four semesters, when students had to prove that they were sufficiently prepared to do advanced academic work and to write term papers. This was an oral exam given by the professor to whose seminar the student wanted to be admitted. Then, after eight semesters, the state examination was administered. It consisted of six comprehensive written tests, each four hours in length, given over a period of six days. Tests consisted of essay questions only. True-false and multiple choice tests were unknown.

All prospective language teachers were tested on English literature, an English-German translation, a German-English translation, Old English, History of the English Language and History of England. French was my second major, which required being tested in the same categories pertaining to French. This amounted to forty-eight hours of testing over a period of two weeks. If we passed with an A or a B average, we were exempt from oral exams. Students who had a C average or lower on their written tests were able to repeat them after one year. This included the whole sequence of tests, even the ones passed the year before.

This university system had one great advantage. Students did not have to spend a lot of time reviewing and preparing for tests during the semester. Consequently, they could take a heavier course load than is customary in the United States. The average load at Erlangen was twenty-five to thirty credit hours per semester. When I graduated after four years, I had accumulated 220 semester hours of academic credit, which is nearly one hundred hours more than is now required for a bachelor of arts degree in an American university.

Unlike today, schools kept educational expenses to an absolute minimum. Tuition was relatively low, so that most students could afford it. Expenses for room and board practically did not exist for the majority of students, because most of them lived in the area, commuted by train or bus and lived at home with parents or relatives. Therefore no dormitories were needed. All German universities were run by the state, which ensured the same academic standards throughout the country. This made it unnecessary for any student to single out a specific university for an academic specialty or the expertise of a particular professor.

Living close to home may not have been as much fun as living independently, but it certainly kept expenses down. The number of students who needed housing was very low. Some rented rooms from private families and, in some cases, received their meals there, too. The university ran some sort of student cafeteria, called the *Mensa*, but it served only one meal a day, at noon. The noon meal was the main meal all over Germany. During the rest of the day, the facility was closed.

For many years after the war, an acute shortage of any kind of paper proved to be a handicap to our studies. At times, we were not able to buy notebooks, typing paper, or even required textbooks.

Publishers had to keep the printing of books to a minimum. Students proved quite resourceful in their efforts to overcome the problem. Whenever one of us was lucky enough to get hold of a much needed textbook, he or she would share it with fellow students, sometimes at a small charge, but always according to a schedule carefully worked out and strictly adhered to. Another way to circumvent the shortage of books was to buy them from students who had taken the courses before us. When we no longer needed the books, we passed them on to younger students. The shortage of books, notebooks and writing paper also helped to keep expenses low.

Professors were keenly aware of the situation and kept students' needs in mind. Most classes were lecture-type courses and provided us with a maximum amount of valuable information. In an emergency, they could even serve as substitutes for textbooks. Each and every word the professor uttered was important and faithfully recorded by the students in shorthand, then neatly transcribed and typed at home. Thus, lectures were easy to study and review when necessary.

Our professors were also very helpful providing us with long reading lists of books pertaining to our field and available in the library. Ordering books was quite inconvenient. The library was kept open only a few hours of the day and never in the evenings. Students had no access to the stacks. There were no browsing rooms or study areas. The only function of the library was to issue books. To order a book, a student had to fill out an order form, turn it in and come back the next day to pick up the book, provided it was not checked out by someone else. In order to ensure a particular book recommended by a professor, we would sometimes race to the library after the lecture and order the book that was needed by so many. Sometimes we had to wait for a book for weeks and months and quite often we did not have a chance to read it until vacation time.

In spite of the relatively low costs of education, financing my studies proved to be quite a problem. I had lost two years of savings in Austria but, fortunately, had accumulated savings in a German bank between 1940 and 1943. However, this fund dwindled more quickly than I had anticipated. My aunt in Erlangen helped support me from her meager earnings by knitting sweaters and socks for neighbors, friends and acquaintances. Because of her physical handicap, she was unable to make a normal living for herself. She was too proud to apply for welfare payments to which she would certainly have been entitled. One of her brothers, who was a farmer nearby, regularly brought us fresh vegetables and fruits, when in season, and three hundred pounds of potatoes in the fall that lasted us through the winter and into early spring.

We actually lived on a shoestring. My aunt and another brother of hers lived in the same house. He owned a prosperous business and died as a millionaire. It would have been easy for him to support his invalid sister but, due to a family feud dating back to the death of their mother in 1926, he refused to communicate with any of his siblings. I was not inclined to carry on the family feud. Therefore, I paid him and his wife occasional courtesy visits, which he did not seem to appreciate much. He always looked down on my family, because my father did not make a fraction of the money he did. His only son was an underachiever in school and not qualified to study at the university, to his father's great disappointment. This unfortunate cousin of mine lost his life in the Battle of Stalingrad in 1943, we assume. Actually, he was reported as MIA, "missing in action."

Until 1948, I managed to support myself, if somewhat precariously. That year the currency reform occurred. On June 29, the *Reichsmark* was declared invalid and taken out of circulation, in order to restore the German economy. Under Hitler, the currency had lost much of its value because of the exorbitant costs of the military and the war. Consumer goods were extremely scarce, and store owners hesitated and even refused to sell goods for worthless money. Now, new money, the *Deutschmark* (D-Mark), was printed and issued, which proved to be a stable currency, but at what a price!

Under this new currency system, every person started out with an initial allotment of DM 40, which was equivalent to $10.00. All prior savings lost their value, which meant that all Germans, with the exception of those who owned real estate or businesses, started out equally poor. I had two more semesters left at the university and no funds. Scholarships were not available, even for the best students. Neither were there such things as student loans, or part-time or summer jobs. The academic demands were so high that all free time, including vacations, had to be spent studying, reading the assignments and pursuing research in our field. Fortunately for my education, when my mother died in 1937, I inherited a building site near Erlangen. With the postwar expansion of the city, which miraculously had not suffered any air raids during the war, it was easy to foresee that my property would considerably increase in value, when it was ready for development. Unfortunately,

I could not wait for this to happen, because I needed the money immediately, to finance my last year at the university and the following year of student teaching. I sold the lot at a great loss, which I did not realize until later, when it more than tripled in value.

My senior year brought increased academic demands and preparations for the state examination, which was compulsory and led to the equivalent of a Bachelor's degree in the United States. There was no speculating as to the contents of this particular examination. Traditionally, it included subject matter learned years before, so we constantly reviewed all the material taught and studied over a period of four years. Certainly, we were all familiar with favorite topics and special research of our professors, but these comprehensive exams, consisting of essay topics only, were not prepared by the professors but, as the name indicates, by the State Department of Higher Education. Under those circumstances, coaching and last-minute cramming were of no avail.

The atmosphere leading up to the state examination was feverish, to say the least. We were fully aware of the fact that our future career and a specified desired job depended on the grade we would receive in this one particular exam. On the day of the first exam, we were assembled in a huge room, seated far apart from each other to prevent any cheating, prepared for the ordeal. In order to encourage each other and provide a certain atmosphere of camaraderie, beer and wine were passed around, and we seemed to feel less nervous right away. When the professor entered the room, he held up a large envelope for everyone to see that it was still sealed and that he did not know the topics of the exams. Then, very ceremoniously, he opened the envelope and distributed the exam topics.

Old English was my forte and I sailed through that exam in three hours. When I handed in my paper, the professor was surprised and urged me to go over it again, with the possibility of making some improvements. His frown indicated to me that he surmised that I was not in full command of the subject matter and I had given up. Firmly, but politely, I assured him that there was no need to add on another hour.

After a few days, I received a congratulatory note from him. He requested a meeting with me in his office at a designated time. It turned out that he wanted to get acquainted with me because of my "superior achievement" on the test. That was the first time that a professor took notice and showed a special interest in me. German professors traditionally do not make an effort to get acquainted with their students. Naturally, I was quite thrilled. German parents and professors were of the opinion that, the less attention students get, the more of an effort they will make to achieve and prove themselves. Students normally did not get any recognition until they had become successful on their own, with little or no encouragement on the part of their elders.

How thrilled I was! I had the distinct impression that I had arrived and was overjoyed. At the end of our conversation, the professor urged me to write him a letter once in a while to tell him what and how I was doing out in the world. What an honor! He was a distinguished scholar in his field, well-known and highly respected in academic circles all over Germany. His request led to a rewarding correspondence, which later spanned the Atlantic until his death a few years later.

Indeed, I had arrived where I always wanted to be. Those long and seemingly never-ending years of struggle and ambition had finally paid off. I graduated from the University of Erlangen in 1949 with *magna cum laude*. English and French were my majors and my minors were in Italian and philosophy. My father was ecstatic, and my beloved mother would have been extremely proud of me, had she lived to see the day.

After my graduation from the University of Erlangen, I decided to go on to graduate work. Master's degrees were unknown at that time in Germany, so the next higher degree to aim for was a Ph.D. I intended to teach foreign languages in high school and high school teachers with a Ph.D. were not unusual. As a matter of fact, about 60 percent of German high school teachers hold a doctorate. Having been trained to reach for the stars in all my intellectual pursuits from early childhood, regardless of obstacles, it again came natural to move toward this crowning achievement of my education. I was convinced that nothing else would do.

In my sophomore year, I had attended a lecture in French medieval literature, which dealt, among other topics, with the status of women in French society of the Middle Ages. The professor pointed out that, in literature, the role of women was portrayed in a different light from the one played in the real world. Medieval authors seemed to delight in drawing a negative picture of the women of their time. Women were regarded with contempt, and unrealistic accusations were levied against them. A literary concept, called misogyny in the vocabulary of the scholar today, describes a situation in which all women, starting with Eve in the Bible, were held responsible for any misfortune which ever befell men, or even mankind.

Misogyny ran through French medieval literature for approximately two centuries. According to my professor, no systematic treatment of it had ever been undertaken. He added that he would be pleased if a student of his would write a doctoral thesis on the topic, as it was one of his favorite literary interests. The nature of the subject matter had an immediate appeal to me and, although I was only a sophomore at the time and almost three years from the decision of choosing a topic for a dissertation, I made a mental note of the opportunity.

After concluding my undergraduate studies, I went back to the professor to ask for his permission to pursue the topic he had thrown out so casually two and a half years earlier. He was delighted with my interest in the subject matter. Students who worked toward a Ph.D. were required to seek out an original theme which no other student in Germany (and in France, if the thesis dealt with French Literature) had treated before. For this reason, I was glad to have found such a topic, pleased when the professor gave me the go-ahead, and overwhelmed by this new challenge that faced me over the next four years.

It was not the custom for postgraduate students to take additional courses or do any work on the graduate level to prepare for research on their dissertation. As a matter of fact, graduate courses as we know them in the United States, did not exist. Neither did doctoral advisors, so for four years I worked completely on my own and did the necessary research by reading primary and secondary sources. The title of my thesis, written in German, was *"Antifeminismus in der Französischen Literatur des Spätmittelalters"* (Antifeminism in French Literature of the Late Middle Ages). The greatest difficulty that I faced was that I had to read the medieval literature in the original Old French language because translations did not exist. Modern French is a Romance language based on Latin. Old French, very unlike modern French, is almost like another foreign language. It occupies a linguistic position somewhere between classical Latin and modern French. If I had not been able to fall back on my Latin studies of ten years, it would have been impossible for me to read my Old French sources. Three cheers to my competent and angelic teachers and professors of Latin! They never tired of teaching us a language now regarded by the majority as "dead," a point of view that I certainly do not entertain.

Top: Hildegard Ziegler (maiden name) ID card, University of Erlangen.
Bottom: Favorite student hangout, University of Erlangen, 1947.

15

Go West, Young Lady!

The next step in my career was a one-year assignment as a student teacher in a boys high school in Erlangen. A whole year of student teaching seemed fair enough, because German institutions of higher learning do not offer courses in education. Instead, they are taught by outstanding high school teachers, who have had many years of practical experience in the field, rather than by theoreticians. The courses taught are comparable to those in this country, ranging all the way from Adolescent Psychology to Methods of Teaching. The education courses were presented concurrently with practical introduction to and experience in teaching. Since I had majored in two languages, I was assigned to two supervising teachers, one in English and one in French. I encountered some difficulty in the person of my supervisor in English, who happened to be a young lady like me, in love with the same gentleman, a fellow student of mine, who was also under her supervision. Pius and I were very much in love with each other and he dated me exclusively, which did not endear me in the eyes of our jealous supervisor.

Thirty-two student teachers were assigned to our school. They represented a broad spectrum of academic subjects, not just languages. In Germany, a much higher number of language teachers is needed because high schools require two to three foreign languages over a period of four to nine years. In the type of high school I chose I was required to take nine years of English, six years of Latin and four years of French.

During student teaching, we attended each other's classes, took notes and later offered constructive criticism, a practice which I found extremely helpful and valuable. Student teaching proved a most satisfying and rewarding experience to me. There is nothing like hands-on experience when it comes to teaching.

The German high school system divides teachers into seven ranks. They are *Studienreferendar, Studienassessor, Studienrat,*

Oberstudienrat, Studienprofessor, Studiendirektor and *Oberstudiendirektor.* English equivalents do not exist. Advancement in rank constitutes a promotion and a raise in salary. In a society, which placed great emphasis on class distinctions, it was important to rise in the ranks on the basis of merit. During my year of student teaching, I took great pride in my first rank, which carried the impressive label, *Studienreferendarin* (the ending *-in* is indicative of the female form of *Studienreferendar*).

After one year of student teaching, the rank of *Studienassessor* was automatically bestowed. Ranks three to seven could be reached on the basis of teaching success, dedication to teaching and students, and service to the school. I went as far as the rank of *Studienassessorin*, but did not stay long enough in the German system to be eligible for further promotion.

I enjoyed student teaching tremendously, but I will never forget the day that proved to be the highlight of my assignment. On that day, the principal of the school entered the room in which all thirty-two student teachers were assembled for an education class. He announced that the Institute of International Education in New York City had made scholarships available to German teachers, and we were free to apply. Some of us were already married and anxious to enter the teaching field as soon as possible for financial reasons. Others, like me, had lost several years of their desired career or preparation for it and preferred not to apply for that reason. It seemed like a real sacrifice to postpone gainful employment for another year but, on the other hand, the United States was beckoning! Indeed, I was interested! Besides the challenge and the opportunity to broaden my horizon significantly, I welcomed the chance to put my knowledge of English to practical use and to acquire more fluency.

On my way home that day, I daydreamed of traveling to the United States as if I had already been granted the scholarship. When I arrived at home, I enthusiastically told my father about my dream. He looked at me in disbelief and said, "You are putting me on. Today is *Faschingsdienstag."* Shrove Tuesday is the culmination of the period known as *Fasching* or *Karneval* (English Carnival or Mardi gras), a period set aside for merrymaking, all kinds of foolish pursuits and numerous masquerading balls. On *Faschingsdienstag,* people seize the last opportunity to carouse before the beginning of Lent. They dress in crazy costumes so outlandish that nobody is able to recognize the other person. Men liked to dress in women's clothes, women as men. It often happened in the ballroom that husbands did not recognize their own wives in costume and vice versa. It was a day of complete craziness, and nobody took the other person seriously. My father was convinced that, because of my reveling in the spirit of

Mardi gras, I had lost my marbles. It took a long time before I was able to convince him that I was sincere in my desire to go to America. From the standpoint of a German ex-soldier, he still considered Americans dangerous enemies. "Do you realize," he would say, rather unconvincingly as it turned out, "that you will be going into enemy country?" A couple of Americans we happened to know, jokingly added to his qualms by telling him that the Western part of the United States (which I favored) was still occupied by cowboys and Indians.

I decided to discuss the pros and cons of studying in the United States with a good friend of mine, who had just returned from a year at the University of Arizona under the auspices of the same program. She was absolutely enthralled by her experience. Naturally, she could not make up my mind for me. At the end of our conversation, she flippantly remarked, "Why don't you apply? Chances are you won't get it anyway." That did it for me! I applied for the scholarship the following day. There was fierce competition from applicants all over Germany. I had no idea how many applicants there were and how many scholarships were available, but I happily threw my hat into the ring.

After undergoing some screening, I was to appear before U.S. civilian and military committees. It was an interesting experience because of the nature of questions I had to answer. They were mostly of a political nature, for example my ideas on the position of postwar Germany and her role in the future, my attitude toward the U.S. occupation forces, my ideology, philosophy of life and many others. I must have made a good impression and answered the questions in an acceptable way, because I stayed in the running for several weeks. Eventually the list of applicants was down to two in my high school, myself included. The final decision was made on the basis of the fact that I had passed the state examination with an A in English. I was ecstatic!

One of the questions of the application form was, "Where in the United States would you like to study?" which I answered by, "As far West as possible." I soon found out if my wish would come true when I was sent to the office of a high-ranking military officer in Nuremberg. On his huge desk an equally large map of the United States was spread out. He congratulated me on receiving the scholarship and then informed me that I was chosen to study at the University of Oregon in Eugene, Oregon. I must have drawn a complete blank, because he smilingly asked me if I knew where Oregon was located. I was embarrassed to own up to my ignorance of American geography. The officer added to my suspense by asking me the location of California which, fortunately, I was able to point out on the map. Then he informed me that Oregon was bordered by

California in the south and by Washington State to the north. With true American graciousness, my ardent wish to study in the West had been fulfilled!

I was to leave Germany early in September, some four months away. The wait taught me a good lesson in the relativity of time: too much time for anticipation and yet so little time to make proper preparations for the adventure. I had to make so many decisions, to answer so many questions, to gather so much information! I needed so many material goods that today we take for granted, especially a nice wardrobe, travel utensils, suitcases, a camera, films, to name just a few.

My existing wardrobe was pitiful, made tolerable only by the fact that most Germans were in the same situation. For almost ten years, I had not been able to buy anything new. During the war, the main thrust of the German industry was on manufacturing weaponry and the war effort in general. Consumer goods were not a priority. Whatever was produced was assigned to refugees or people who had lost all their belongings in air raids. The rest of us simply had to make do with what we had. After the war, millions of refugees from the Eastern part of Europe had to be clothed, and I did not qualify for an allotment of new clothes.

I do remember two specific items of my wardrobe because of a rather unusual way of acquiring them. One was a dress handed down to me by a lady who was engaged to be married to an American GI. She let me have this "Made in the U.S.A." dress, which was no longer fashionable. The quality was still good and I was proud to wear my first American dress. The second piece of clothing obtained by me in an unorthodox fashion was a coat made of the uniform which my cousin Georg had worn during the war. He was a lieutenant and as such the fabric of his uniform was of superior quality, as compared to the uniforms of common soldiers. When Georg came home from the front at the end of the war he wore this particular uniform, including a coat, for the last time. All German soldiers, who were lucky enough to have survived the war, returned to the country in uniform, because civilian clothes were not available to them. Georg was gracious enough to let me have the coat of his uniform. First I had it dry-cleaned, then I took it apart by ripping open the seams and had a tailor make a very handsome coat for me. It did not bother me that the color was reminiscent of German uniforms. Many other Germans were in the same boat and wore similar outfits. However, I realized that I could not possibly look presentable in the United States wearing a hand-me-down dress that might have been in fashion some six to eight years before, and a coat made from a German uniform.

In the meantime, the German fashion industry had recovered sufficiently to fill the needs of all German people, and new clothing was no longer rationed. Eventually, everything became available, provided one could afford to buy new clothing. Unfortunately, my financial problems, which had accompanied me during my years of study, still haunted me. After all, I had not held a job from 1945 to 1950. During this time, every penny I had saved went toward tuition, books and living expenses. Somehow, I managed, though. My father and stepmother, who had held a tight financial rein on me during my years at the university, became more generous and were willing to shell out some money to buy me respectable clothes, because they finally felt proud of my academic accomplishments and they shared in the honor I gained in winning a scholarship to study in the United States. After all, this did not happen to just anybody.

My anticipation of studying in the United States was marred by having to tear myself away from Pius and leave him behind after one year of dating. We took comfort in the thought of seeing each other again after a year. Little did we realize that it would take two years rather than one, because Pius received a scholarship to study at the University of Nebraska, one year after my return to Germany. On the occasion of our eventual reunion, we became painfully aware of the fact that we had drifted apart. Two years of overwhelming experiences in the United States, including our dating American students, had changed our love for each other. Maybe it all turned out for the best, since Pius' mother preferred a Catholic mate for him.

My initial sadness over our separation became mitigated by the enormous excitement of things to come. The first step toward the great adventure was a three-day orientation period in Frankfurt, West Germany, which provided much valuable information about the trip, the United States and a chance of getting acquainted with numerous other young German teachers lucky enough to have been chosen as participants in possibly the greatest adventure of their lives.

After the end of the orientation period, we boarded a train to Cannes, a French harbor on the Mediterranean coast, whence we were to embark on the voyage. The novelty of the experience was overwhelming: crossing the German border for the first time in my life, admiring the French countryside, having a chance to speak French, eating meals in a French railroad dining car, getting to know more and more fellow travelers. My whole outlook on life and the world seemed to change within just a few days.

Upon arrival in Cannes, we had time to admire the luxury of the resort. The heat of this Southern part of France was almost intolerable, but I wanted to see as much as possible of the scenery, so I forced myself to remain outdoors most of the time, exposed to the burning sun for hours on end. In the process, I acquired a painful sunburn which later resulted in a fever. What an unpleasant way to start my great adventure!

As much as I was impressed by the beauty of Cannes, I welcomed boarding our ship, the *Argentina*. We travelled through the Mediterranean to Barcelona, Spain. Unfortunately, my health problem had become worse aboard the ship, so that I was not able to enjoy the city of Barcelona along with my fellow travelers, who disembarked for three hours. I felt quite sorry for myself. The next highlight was passing through the Straits of Gibraltar where I said "hello" to the continent of Africa of which only the coastline was visible. The change of color from the blue of the Mediterranean to a muddy gray indicated that we had arrived in the Atlantic. It was exciting to me because I had never been on an ocean before.

The painfully slow voyage from France to New York took twelve days. However, it did not go according to schedule, because we got caught in a frightening storm, which made most of us seasick. I remember going to the dining room clinging to a railing and tables to steady myself. The ship rolled so badly that it was difficult to walk straight. Eventually, I became so sick that I lost my appetite completely, and there was no use to go to the dining room for meals. I stayed in bed most of the time. Sympathetic stewards would look after me in my cabin and throw an occasional orange on my bed. Fruit was the only food that I could tolerate and felt like eating. Toward the end of the voyage, the storm had grown so severe that the captain declared it unsafe to approach New York as planned by schedule. Instead, he steered the vessel northward and we docked in Halifax, Canada. At last, I was in America, if somewhat farther north than I had planned.

The slowest voyage across the Atlantic aboard the "Argentina" with 300 German students, 1950.

16

A Stranger in a Strange Land

Eventually, the storm subsided, and we sailed into the New York City harbor. I was thrilled by the sight of the Statue of Liberty. It was a deeply moving experience for me. After all, I was about to enter the country in which liberty is one of the loftiest ideals. The fact that the statue was made in France, another "enemy country" to me, made it an even more impressive experience. Not only was I able to identify with the former enemies of Germany, but also with their ideals.

On disembarking, I was astonished to find that customs officials greeted us with a friendly, "How do you like America?" and, "Welcome." A far cry from my father's notions of America, the "enemy country." What a kind and gracious people! There were no signs of prejudice toward their former enemies who, under Adolf Hitler, had inflicted so much misery on other people. For the first time in my life I felt like a worthy human being, finally harboring feelings of dignity and self-respect on account of my mere existence.

After passing through customs, we were taken to hotels. The luxury of our accommodations was overwhelming. I had a television set, a rarity in 1950, right in my hotel room. Should I watch TV or go sightseeing in New York City? The latter, I decided. On the way out, I saw a cleaning lady in the hallway and I impulsively spoke to her in English. Such bold behavior would have been swiftly censured in Germany.

The cleaning lady was very gracious and eager to talk. After a few casual remarks, she asked me, "Madam, are you from England?" I was flabbergasted and made no attempt to conceal my delight. In Germany, we had been taught British English, but I had no idea that I could be mistaken for an English lady. This humble cleaning lady gave me all the confidence I needed to dive in and speak English with great aplomb. As a matter of fact, I felt so confident that I ventured out on foot to do some sightseeing and to practice my English. It did not take long before I got lost in the vastness of the city. I asked a gentleman for directions, again in English, of course. He smiled immediately, recognizing my German accent.

He said, "*Sie können ruhig Deutsch mit mir sprechen*" (You can speak German with me). What a blow! My newly acquired confidence in my language ability suffered a severe setback. On the other hand, I had many rather satisfying experiences in New York City. As I walked around in the streets, I did not feel in the least intimidated by the skyscrapers, the hustle and bustle and the noise of the city. Even the language barrier did not disturb me anymore. I walked proudly, my head up high, feeling good about all these new experiences. New York City was human too, in spite of its foreignness. I almost had a feeling of *déjà vu*. Was it possible that I had lived in this city in a previous life? The very thought of having been a U.S. citizen in a former existence excited me no end.

After three glorious days of sightseeing and watching TV, we went on to Chicago by train. But my shyness returned and I was afraid to speak to strangers. My German background haunted me: unless you are perfect in any endeavor, I told myself, don't embark on it at all.

Seats on the train were reserved, but I decided to sit in the rear to avoid speaking to people. I was frightened! Upon arrival in Chicago, I went sightseeing. Some fellow traveler had recommended to me "Marshall Fields" as a must. I had no idea what Marshall Fields was. Least of all, I expected it to be a huge department store. How could "Fields" be a department store? I took "Fields" literally rather than as a family name.

On I went to the Wild West. When the train made an unscheduled stop, the passengers were informed that there would be some delay, and we could leave the train. I was hungry and took the opportunity to go to some establishment that in my German eyes looked like a restaurant. Mustering all my courage, I walked inside to order a sandwich. There was only a bartender. To my surprise, I had entered a bar and again made a fool of myself. Another setback!

The midwestern landscape turned quite monotonous, and I was finally able to go to sleep sitting up in my coach seat. When I awoke, I could hardly believe my eyes. The most beautiful scenery greeted me. I do not recall whether we were in Montana, Idaho, or Oregon, but I was impressed!

I had been on the train for three days and two nights, when we arrived in Eugene, Oregon. A representative from the University of Oregon was supposed to meet me, but not a soul was in sight. I had no idea as to how to get to the university and I was afraid to ask. So I started out to walk carrying my two suitcases. Asking for a bus schedule and inquiring about fares was too much of a language challenge for me. I decided to walk like a good German, facing all hardships with equanimity. Little did I realize that it would take me about forty-five minutes to get to the University of Oregon campus. There is no better (or worse) thing than German will power!

I finally arrived at the university and reported to the office of the Foreign Student Advisor, where I received the key to my room. Some helpful soul took me to my dormitory by car. On the door to my room, a sign had been posted with my roommate's name and mine. Unfortunately, she never showed up. After all the experiences of traveling alone in a foreign country and not knowing a single person, I felt desperately lonesome. I threw myself on my bed and cried pitifully, like a little girl. An evening meal served downstairs had no appeal to me.

Suddenly there was a knock on the door. Four foreign students stood there, wondering if they could be of some assistance to me. They took me under their wings and I enjoyed my very first meal in an American dormitory. Right away, I felt much better. After about fifteen minutes, I found out that one of those four students was a German! What a comfort! She hailed from Berlin, and we became fast friends. Now she is married to an American university professor in Bowling Green, Ohio, and we are still in touch with each other after forty years.

As I indicated in an earlier chapter, neither I nor any of my friends ever received a scholarship from a German school. When I became the proud recipient of an AMERICAN scholarship, my astonishment and gratitude knew no bounds. It was not until I arrived at the University of Oregon that I learned how generous my scholarship was: the whole year in the United States would not cost me one dollar! I received round trip transportation, full tuition, room and board, textbooks, plus $20.00 incidental money per month. I am quick to admit that $20.00 does not buy much nowadays, but in 1950 it went a long way. I was able to buy one piece of clothing every month, as well as those items needed for everyday use. In addition, I could afford to send a food package home once in a while. The most coveted item in Germany was coffee, which sold for exorbitant prices there. I bought it at 39 cents per pound in Eugene and sent it home at low postage fees. The same was true of cigarettes, which I sent to my delighted father on a regular basis.

Soon after my arrival on campus, I was informed of the purpose of my studies. The program was called "Reorientation Program for German and Japanese Teachers." The title was obvious and spoke for itself. The U.S. government disapproved of the political orientation which young Germans and Japanese had received in their countries under the nondemocratic leadership of Hitler and Emperor Hirohito, respectively. It was time that young people in both countries were re-educated by more enlightened teachers and taught the democratic values of this country, so that they might oppose autocratic governments in the future. The program was administered in a tactful way, but I could not help but think that it was a form of brainwashing, although I generally approved of the teachings of a democratic society.

For the first time in my life, I had an academic advisor, named Elaine, who guided me in my decisions and had to approve my choice of courses. I soon found out that I was expected not to take any courses in my majors, which were English and French. I regretted this because I was anxious to increase my knowledge of conversational English and I hoped to take a course in French medieval literature to give me new insights into my research on my dissertation. Instead, my advisor steered me to such varied fare as education, political science, philosophy, psychology, religion and mass media. Those courses greatly expanded my general knowledge, and I was grateful for the new perspectives I gained in spite of my initial disappointment.

Perhaps more than anything else, I enjoyed the interaction between professor and student and the many discussion sessions at the university. German universities, even after Hitler's rule, did not engage in the verbal give-and-take that is so much a part of the academic world in the United States. Possibly that was a holdover from the Hitler years, when no differences of ideas and opinions were tolerated. Now I was not only permitted, but encouraged to express my opinions, even if they ran counter to those of other students or even of the professor.

I really blossomed under the American system. For a change, I gained some respect from others and, in the process, my self-respect increased as well. No longer was I afraid of expressing my ideas and defending my viewpoints. American students proved to be very interested in and tolerant of my opinions. I also learned a valuable lesson in how to balance various points of view, including my own, and to think more objectively. How my eyes were opened! For the first time in my life, I conceded that Hitler and his faithful followers were wrong in so many fundamental ways. I must say that I soon felt comfortable with my new way of thinking and I eagerly looked forward to imparting my newly acquired outlook to my future German students. The reorientation program already started to work!

As far as my grades were concerned, I received mostly A's and B's in my classes, not too bad for a foreign student, who was still struggling to improve her English skills. I could follow lectures and discussions without difficulty, but my oral skills were clumsy and I had difficulty with American slang. Likewise, my English reading skills were not up to par, which meant that I had to spend inordinately more time studying for tests than my American counterparts. Once I walked out of an IQ test, much to the astonishment of the professor, because I was not familiar with some of the vocabulary. I was frustrated throughout most of the test, and the word "pageant" provided the proverbial straw that broke the camel's back. My self-esteem hit an all-time low!

I had never lived in a dormitory before and had to get used to all kinds of regulations and strange behavior. In Germany I was able to stay out all night if I chose to do so. One evening, very soon after my arrival, members of a Lutheran church invited me for a discussion. I cannot recall the topic but we had a good time and did not adjourn till about 12:30 a.m. I walked back to the campus and, to my dismay, found the dormitory locked.

How could they do that to me? Maybe they did not even miss me, because I had not signed out. Naughty! Fortunately, a friend in the dorm, who was ambitious and liked to study at night, heard my call through an open window and ran downstairs to open the door for me. I was not familiar with the practice of signing out, signing in and closing hours and I felt incensed about this curtailment of my personal freedom in the land of liberty. Something was wrong here, at least in my estimation. When I discussed the matter with the Foreign Student Advisor, he fully understood my point of view, realized that I was about thirteen years older than the average American university freshman and offered to make an exception in the future and to allow me to stay out beyond closing hours, if I wished. However, I did not expect special treatment, but wanted to conform, which came easy after growing up under Hitler.

Life in the dorm was generally quite enjoyable, with some very few exceptions. One of them was the customary "rowdy night"

every Friday evening, when students partied until 1 a.m. to get the
frustration of the week out of their system. Having studied under
extremely quiet conditions in Germany, I was quite sensitive to and
intolerant of noise. Besides, I could not understand the need for
acting like frustrated little children. After the first experience of this
kind, I planned my Friday evenings carefully and very seldom stayed
in the dormitory, but I watched the time, in order to comply with
strange American rules and sign in before the dormitory was locked.
It felt so good to be inside on time!

Learning to get along with groups and roommates on a social
basis was quite a new experience to me. During the academic year of
1950 to 1951, I had four roommates, counting the first no-show of
whose existence I knew only by the name plate on the door of my
room. The second one was more interested in her fiancé than in her
studies. She stayed out for days and nights at a time, and I never
knew when I would have the pleasure of her company. She
eventually gave up returning at all. Our housemother informed me
that she had dropped out and got married.

My third roommate was a lovely girl from the Philippines,
who was very intelligent and ambitious. But she planned to stay at
the university for only two terms, so I knew ahead of time that I
would lose her, too. It was a pity because we got along beautifully.
When the first snow fell, she responded like a little child because she
had never seen snow before. Her enthusiasm was contagious, and I
set out to teach her how to build a snowman. She was so much fun
that I hated to see her leave in the spring.

By then, I was a little apprehensive as to what kind of
roommate I would have after her departure. In order to be on the safe
side and prevent any disappointment, I asked the Foreign Student
Advisor for his permission to let me move in with my German friend,
who also happened to be without a roommate at the time. I was told
that it was against the rules for two foreign students of the same
nationality to room together. My German stubbornness prevailed
eventually, and, to my delight, that kind man caved in. For the rest
of the year, Gisela from Berlin, roommate number four, kept me
company. We had no problems whatsoever and were most
compatible.

Because of the differences between German and American
students, I must have made a fool of myself more than once. When
some students invited me to attend my first football game, I dressed
up for the occasion, high heels and all, as if I were going to a dance.
My American friends tactfully advised me that heels might not be

appropriate to wear to sporting events. I had never before changed clothes in such a hurry!

Meals were served in the dormitory, which was a great convenience and a timesaver. Although the war had already been over for five years, when I left Germany, the food supply there was still limited at times. I was amazed to see the quantity and vast variety of food in the dormitory. For once, I was able to eat as much as I wished and to choose whatever I liked. In Germany we never got enough eggs, so this was my opportunity to make up for it. Some mornings I would eat as many as three eggs for breakfast. I now wonder how high my blood cholesterol was at the time. Ignorance is bliss!

On Sundays, an early sit-down, dress-up dinner was served. The meals were always tasty and of good quality. My favorite beverage was coffee, of which I never got enough in Germany because it was so expensive. After finishing my two cups, the student waitress came around and asked me if I wished another cup. I really thought two cups should be enough and simply answered by saying "thank you" which in German is equivalent to "no, thank you," but apparently in this country was interpreted as meaning "yes, please," because she poured me a third and later a fourth cup of coffee. The same thing happened the following Sunday, until I mustered enough courage to ask a friend what I was doing wrong. She told me to try "no, thank you" and, like magic, it worked! The coffee spell was broken.

The Christmas season was an especially uplifting time. I remember a beautiful Christmas party for international students where representatives from numerous lands spoke about the various Christmas customs of their respective countries. The climax for me came when, all of us in unison, sang "Silent Night" not in English, but in thirty-two different languages from all over the world. It was a deeply moving experience for me because I was proud of my German heritage, and this most popular of all Christmas carols was originally written in German. After all, I decided, my native country did have something positive to offer to the world other than guilt and anxiety because of what happened during the Hitler years. It was a real catharsis to me!

Another moving experience of a different nature happened when an elderly lady, a complete stranger to me, looked me up in the dormitory and presented me with a pair of slippers as a Christmas gift. Again it proved to me the wonderful American spirit of hospitality, kindness, generosity and tolerance. Little things meant a lot!

About a week before Christmas, the Foreign Student Advisor informed us foreign students that several Oregon businesses had approached him and requested applications from foreign students, who could work as salespersons during the Christmas rush. I immediately volunteered and was assigned to Miller's Department Store in Roseburg, Oregon. I stayed with a very lovely family who also shared their meals with me. Again American generosity prevailed. Never in my whole life had I been treated more gently and lovingly than in this country of "enemies!" I wished my father could have had similar experiences.

The media had done a good PR job in announcing my presence to the people of Roseburg. German immigrants, their children and grandchildren came in droves to speak to me and try out their German. In between socializing, I actually managed to make some sales for the store. A radio station invited me to speak about German Christmas customs and to play German Christmas carols on the piano. The most exciting event of my stay in Roseburg was a flight in the mayor's private plane. Flying today is no big deal for most people, but in 1950 it was a rare happening, at least to me. It was an elating experience to be able to admire the beautiful scenery of Oregon from above. When my assignment in Roseburg was over, I was lucky enough to travel by car to San Francisco with an American fellow student, who provided transportation and superb sightseeing. We spent all our Christmas vacation in the Bay Area and in Yosemite Park.

Besides learning all about campus and student life, I was expected to branch out and participate in off-campus activities. Quite often, high school teachers invited me to speak to their classes, mostly about my experiences in Hitler Germany and during World War II. Students always seemed to enjoy it, when I showed up dressed in my native costume. Once in a while, I was asked to address school assemblies in Eugene, which scared me to death. I had never spoken over a microphone before, which in Germany was reserved for real celebrities. My audiences invariably met me with a great deal of respect but, in all honesty, I was never sure if they understood a single word of my speech.

On two occasions, a Eugene radio station invited me to play the piano over the radio. I was quite good at playing but never in my whole life would I have performed on the German radio. I almost felt like a celebrity, which certainly had a beneficial effect on my self-esteem. It was beautiful to realize that, in these United States, individuals had more of a chance to be recognized and allowed to stand out than in Germany, even when they had not reached the point of perfection yet and maybe never will.

The hospitality of Americans continued to be evident on other occasions also. A professor of political science and his family regularly invited groups of foreign students to their home for parties throughout the year. Every once in a while, fellow students invited me to spend a weekend with them at their parents' home. The Interstate 5 freeway had not been built yet and a trip to Portland from Eugene took more than four hours on the back roads. I especially enjoyed the chance of meeting parents of students, because I was already scheming to come back to the United States to live after my year at the university was over. It was important for me to make contacts with people other than students in my search for a potential sponsor!

As I became better acquainted with students, professors, high school teachers, business men and townspeople, the demands on my time became greater and greater. More and more people wanted me to share my European experiences with them and they included me in their social activities. In addition, my part-time work at the University of Oregon library took quite a few hours every week. I also took the opportunity to do some research on my doctoral thesis by checking out certain library books, which I surmised were not easily available in Europe, and I ordered some books through Interlibrary Loan, mostly from the Library of Congress. Last, but not least, I kept up my self-imposed academic standards in my classes: I was satisfied with A's and B's, but a C was unacceptable. Sometimes I wished that the day would have forty-eight hours to get everything done. Toward the middle of the third term, I had worked myself into a frazzle, which resulted in health problems, and I had to spend several days in the infirmary. When the nurse measured my temperature she reported it to be 102 degrees. Of course, I realized that it was measured in Fahrenheit. But when I notified my father of my illness, I purposely did not refer to it as Fahrenheit. He was shocked and wrote back asking me if I was serious about my extremely high temperature as he conceived it. He emphasized that in Germany people died, when the fever reached 45 degrees, Celsius, of course.

Similarly, when I first wrote home about the Oregon summer weather, I reported temperatures up to 90 degrees. As before, I did not specify Fahrenheit or Celsius, so my father was confused again, realizing that, measured in centigrade, water boils at 100 degrees and an air temperature of 90 degrees (Celsius) was unheard of in Europe. Once again, I had my fun reacting to my father's confusion, but he did get used to "those crazy Americans" measuring temperature in Fahrenheit, especially after I pointed out the differences between Fahrenheit and Celsius in a follow-up letter.

I recovered quickly but, on the advice of the physician, I had to curtail my outside activities. The academic year all too soon drew to a close. Since I had been classified as a "special student," my studies were not expected to lead to an academic degree.

After the end of the academic year, my scholarship expired, but my passport was valid till September 15, 1951. The thought of severing the ties with my newly adopted country and its wonderful people weighed heavily on me. I had fallen hopelessly in love with everything American, the people, their good deeds and exemplary treatment towards me, the democratic system with its freedoms, the higher standard of living, the Oregon scenery, the vastness of the country.

Wanting to stay in Oregon as long as possible and savoring every minute of it, I had to make some difficult decisions. First of all, I was no longer able to live on campus, which meant that I had to rent a room in town. Secondly, there were no more payments coming from the Institute of International Education, and I had to find a means of supporting myself.

Finding a suitable but inexpensive room proved to be easy. A friend of mine with whom I shared the same first name (Hildegard - very rare in this country) recommended renting a room in a boarding house near the campus where she lived. I followed her advice and had no regrets. The owners of the house were most hospitable, and the renters surrounded me with love and concern. I still had no job, however. One day, I decided I might as well be bold and apply for a job with the Eugene *Register Guard,* a daily newspaper, which had run a few articles and pictures of foreign students. Finding my picture in an American newspaper flattered my ego, and I have harbored positive feelings toward reporters ever since. I knew a couple of them, although not very well.

It had always amazed me that the Germans could come up with a proverb to fit practically every life situation. The one applicable to the situation I found myself in said *"Frisch gewagt ist halb gewonnen"* (Nothing ventured, nothing gained). Relying on my newly acquired self-image I made an appointment with the personnel office, introduced myself and explained the purpose of my visit. It was an ambitious undertaking because, except for an interest in journalism, I had no practical experience whatsoever. The personnel officer's initial response was negative. Naturally, what could I expect under the circumstances? However, in talking to me he seemed to develop an interest in my background. Realizing that I could be available for only less than three months, he could not possibly have me trained for a job. He told me that the only job opening was one as a proofreader, but he had doubts about my qualifications for that type of job, because English was not my native language.

The job as a proofreader sounded intriguing, and I implored him to give me a chance. Again the reply was negative. Stubbornly, I made the suggestion that he let me prove myself and my linguistic talents by working for three days without pay. Again my German perseverance paid off! He could not resist my suggestion. The quality of my voluntary work must have impressed him, because he offered me the job without further hesitation.

Once on the job, I had to convince the printers that, although a foreigner, I knew how to spell, even though my ways of expressing myself and my German accent may have sounded somewhat clumsy and awkward. I quietly did my job with a great deal of dedication and pride, every evening from seven through midnight. Once in a while, a printer would come up to me to question some of my corrections. Good-naturedly, I looked up the spelling in question in the dictionary, although I was convinced of the correct spelling, and invariably I was correct. I really succeeded in establishing my reputation as a competent proofreader.

Besides working evenings for the Eugene *Register Guard*, I continued my part-time job at the U of O library, where I stacked returned books. These two sources of income provided me with the money to defray my living expenses and to maintain a comfortable life style, until I had to return to Germany in the middle of September.

The work at the library started at 8 a. m. and I did not get much sleep, but the afternoons were free for me to work, slowly but steadily, on my dissertation. I was extremely busy and did not waste any time. It was very seldom that I saw anyone around the house at breakfast time. However, one morning, I was lucky enough to have breakfast with my landlady, whose name was Mildred Gilson. I rarely had a chance to talk with her because of my work schedule. She seemed to be concerned that I got so little sleep and asked me, "Don't you ever have the urge to sleep in?" The American language played a trick on me. I misunderstood the meaning of the verb "to sleep in" and interpreted it to mean "to sleep inside the home," or better, "at home." I had a hard time restraining my indignation and forced myself to answer firmly but politely, "What do you think of me - I sleep in my room every night."

She smiled and proceeded to explain to me the meaning of "to sleep in." As a school teacher, she did a good job of easing my indignation. We shared a good laugh and became friends. I learned that she had a son named Dale, who studied at the university and lived at home. His girl friend, Roselee, occupied a room at his parents' home as I did. Dale's father, Byron, was a mill worker in a Eugene lumber plant. Dear readers, please do not forget these names, because these wonderful people later on played a decisive role in my life.

In order to start working at the Eugene *Register Guard*, I had to apply for a Social Security card. The clerk in the SS office asked for my name and my birthdate without requiring proof of the veracity of my data. I could have received a Social Security card under a fake name, if for some reason I needed to do that for false identification. Again I was in awe of America and uplifted by the trust put in me, a foreigner. The Americanization of Hildegard gained momentum! How could I ever be the same? On second thought, I really didn't need or even want to remain the same.

After spending one year in the United States, I wanted to stay here for good. When I inquired about the prospects, I received a negative answer. There was no way that a student visa could be changed to an immigrant visa. Reluctantly and sadly, I made preparations for my return to Germany toward the end of August. I had received a train ticket from Eugene to New York City and was given an option of flying or traveling by boat across the Atlantic. The mayor of Roseburg had instilled an enthusiasm for flying in me, when he took me on a ride in his private plane. Apart from that I had never flown before. It was a great temptation to opt for the flight rather than the boat ride. My father, fearing for my safety, had advised me against flying, but I thought it would be a nice change and fun to get home faster and surprise him.

So I ordered a flight ticket, which the Foreign Student Advisor presented to me on my last visit. He wished me "good luck" for the future and it was sad to part with him. I was in a melancholy mood and thanked him profusely for his invaluable services during the year. Taking stock of all those wonderful experiences between my arrival and imminent departure, I felt so overwhelmed - in a way quite undeserving - and I asked him what I could do in return for the numerous favors and good deeds extended to me. He replied, "Just help students who need help in the future and pass the favors on to them." I never forgot these words and made it a point to put them into practice during my long teaching career.

One problem I had not worked out before leaving was finding a sponsor to help me return to the United States. I hesitated to put people on the spot by asking them directly if they would be willing to sponsor me. Becoming a sponsor sounded quite easy, but the responsibilities were rather involved. It was a matter of vouching for the immigrant's moral character and promising complete financial support, up to five years, in case of unemployment, illness, or disability - a risky task to say the least. Americans had proved helpful to me in many situations of less significance, but this was an entirely different matter. Providing complete financial support in case of emergency could have run into many thousands of dollars. Nobody seemed particularly anxious to venture into this undertaking. I knew that Germans who wanted to emigrate to the United States were often sponsored by relatives already here. Expecting the same of people not related to me was asking an awful lot.

I bade all my friends and the university a tearful farewell, not knowing if I would ever see them again. My train ticket could be used for various routes and for an unspecified time without extra • charge, so I travelled to New York City via several interesting cities, including San Francisco, Los Angeles, Salt Lake City, Denver and Chicago. On the way, I made several stops to take in a lot of sightseeing. One evening as we approached Denver, the train ran considerably late, and I missed my connection to Chicago. The gentleman seated next to me was a resident of Denver and, to my surprise, offered me an overnight accommodation in his home with his family. I had such great confidence in the goodness of American people that I trusted him implicitly and gladly accepted his offer.

This shows how conditions have changed for the worse in this country. Nowadays, I would under no circumstances trust a complete stranger to the point of going to his home. He turned out to be a Jew who was gracious enough to offer a German national his assistance. Now I was convinced that there was hope for the world and mankind! His wife had waited up for him and was not too surprised, certainly not upset, that her husband brought a young lady home with him. The next day, I met their children.

After breakfast, we went for a ride to enjoy the beauty of the Denver area. As so many times before, I felt greatly enriched by this American hospitality and almost reluctant to leave. The whole family took me to the train station, and I left for Chicago and New York City around noon. The rest of the journey went off without a hitch.

While in New York City, I did some last-minute sightseeing and spent my last quarter on a milkshake, for which I had developed an addiction. Later, as I was waiting for a bus, a young lady shouted "Hildegard, Hildegard!" Not knowing one soul in the big city, I first thought it must be a mistake. When the lady ran towards me and hugged me, I recognized her as a fellow student from my dormitory at the University of Oregon. It was a happy reunion. We found it extremely unusual that we saw each other again so soon and so far away from Eugene.

The flight was fantastic, almost like a fairy tale. Somehow it helped me over my sadness at having to leave America. The thought of crossing the Atlantic at such an unbelievable height boggled my mind. The service was perfect and I enjoyed being pampered by the stewardesses. How would I ever manage to come down to earth?

Left: Three foreign students in native costumes at University of Oregon, 1951. (Guatemala, Germany, and Panama).
Right: My first place of employment, the Eugene Register Guard, 1951.

17

Back to Dreary Reality

We landed in Frankfurt, and I was only about 140 miles away from home. I arrived about four days earlier than if I had taken the ship. How was I going to break the news to my father that I had travelled by plane? Perhaps he was pleased to have me home several days before we planned? So I decided to give him a phone call and surprise him. I expected a cordial welcome, but instead he said only three words which more than anything expressed his consternation and rage over my disregard of his advice not to fly. In an angry voice, he said *"Du bist geflogen!"* (You flew!)

From Frankfurt I took the train to Nuremberg where my father met me at the railroad station. I was a little afraid to face him, but luckily his disappointment in me had almost subsided. He was grateful to have me home safe and sound.

I arrived in Germany on September 15, 1951, and my passport expired the following day. The expiration was symbolic of my parting with the country that I had learned to love so much. Two days later, on September 17, I wrote a letter to the U.S. Consulate in Munich to request application forms for an immigrant visa, much to the grief of my father. Although I promptly took the necessary steps to ensure a return to the United States, there was a painful waiting period. The German immigration quota for admission to the United States was 26,000 per year. At that time, many Germans took advantage of emigration, because political and economic conditions remained unstable after the war and living standards were low. When my father learned about the long waiting period, he was relieved and expressed hope that I would adjust to life in Germany and give up my emigration plans. Besides, I was still without a sponsor.

In the following weeks, it became apparent that I was extremely unhappy and that I could not make an easy adjustment to conditions at home. I was so homesick for the United States! Quite often I asked myself, "How can you be homesick for a country which is not your own?" The contrast between the United States and Germany was so great that I could not ignore it, not just in material goods but in everything else. I suffered from a thoroughgoing case of depression, to the dismay of the people around me. On Sundays especially, I missed the excitement of American weekends, when there was always a friend eager to take me for a ride through the beautiful countryside surrounding Eugene, or even to the wild and rugged Oregon coast.

I pursued the task of finding a sponsor and returning to the United States with great deliberation. Actually, I was supposed to get my first teaching job upon return from the United States. However, I missed the beginning of the German school year by about two weeks, unwittingly or subconsciously? So I decided to apply for a job in an office of the U.S. occupation forces, which hired young Germans, especially those with a good command of English. My friend, Anneliese, whom I had known since early childhood, worked in such an office and recommended it very highly. I reasoned that working in an American office might present an opportunity to meet - maybe, just maybe - a sympathetic and kindhearted American, who might be willing to help me return to the States by serving as my sponsor.

A job proved easy to get, especially with my proficiency in the English language and my recent experiences in the United States. I worked as a typist, an uninteresting job, to be sure, but I savored the American flavor of the office and cherished the opportunity to speak English again. The new job did not turn out the way I had hoped. Relationships between American bosses and German subalterns were not as relaxed as I expected them to be. Maybe it was only my imagination, but somehow I had the impression that the Americans acted as victors and treated Germans as underlings. Certainly I was treated quite differently in the United States. Once in a while, the Americans gave us American money for an ice cream cone, which was greatly appreciated. Friendships between Americans and Germans, which were so easy to establish in the States, did not develop. I realized that this was no way to find a sponsor. Obviously, I was in that job for the wrong reason and motivation. Besides, the work was boring, and I was overeducated for it. By Christmas 1951, I felt so discouraged that I quit.

Before the holidays, I wrote Christmas cards and letters to my cherished friends in America. I realized that my fellow students with whom I was still in touch wanted to help me return. They were guided by youthful enthusiasm, but in no way were they financially qualified to act as my sponsor. Their parents, on the other hand, exercised more caution and were less willing to help for practical reasons. Besides, they did not know me well enough to make a commitment.

I was so terribly disappointed that I almost gave up on my goal to emigrate. In my despair, I wrote a letter to the Gilsons, my former host family in Eugene. I wrote of my ardent wish to return to the United States and the difficulty of obtaining a sponsor. Again I did not come right out with a direct appeal to their generosity and a request to sponsor me. Frankly, I had almost given up hope of ever seeing my wish fulfilled.

To my surprise, I received a very quick reply to my letter. I opened it with trepidation. Certainly, such a quick response had to carry a very special message - and it did! I cannot express my happiness in words, when I read Mildred's kind offer to sponsor me. I felt as if I had conquered the whole world, not militarily by any means, but with my outreach for friends and love for all human beings. My experiences could be likened to a spiritual experience, in which my life became whole again and took on a new meaning.

It was evident that there was a long wait ahead of me because of the quota restrictions. So I contemplated accepting a teaching job in the meantime. A boyfriend of mine, Otmar, a staunch Catholic, recommended that I apply for a vacancy in a Catholic high school in Nuremberg. The school, the *Institut der Englischen Fräulein*, normally employed Catholic nuns exclusively. I was a Protestant but I applied just the same. After going over my résumé, the Mother Superior called me in for an interview and complimented me on my qualifications, but told me that she would prefer to hire a Catholic.

Otmar realized that it would be difficult for me to land a teaching job in the middle of the school year, so he generously put in a good word for me to the Mother Superior, who was a friend of his. She changed her mind and hired me. I was the only lay teacher in a school of 800 students and the only one not dressed in nun's attire. It was a girls school, and I taught English and French there. I appreciated the daily extra hour that the retreats provided me, because as a Lutheran I did not participate in Catholic worship.

Teaching English to German students proved to be a greater challenge than I anticipated. The students were to be taught British English and I had acquired some Americanisms, but the students were not sufficiently versed in the language to sort out the differences. Whenever I used an American pronunciation or a typically American vocabulary word, the pupils apparently thought of it as a mispronunciation or the wrong choice of a word. As well-disciplined German students, they did not see fit to call my attention to something that might have been an embarrassment to me, the highly respected teacher. Instead, some of them squirmed in their seats to show with their body language that something was amiss. I would seize the opportunity to explain the differences between the two languages and, in the process, show off my newly acquired knowledge of idiomatic English.

In most respects, however, teaching in Germany was extremely easy, because students never questioned the authority of the teacher, but it was also less challenging and more monotonous for both students and teacher.

It was January 1952. I had a teaching job and the prospect of living in the United States again. I dared not think of spending my whole life there, and no one could predict just when my immigrant visa would be issued. Therefore, finishing my dissertation became my new priority. I worked on it feverishly, but did not make much progress because my teaching responsibilities did not leave me much extra time. It was obvious that, at my slow rate of writing, my visa would come long before I would get my Ph.D., which could have delayed my departure considerably. In order to prevent this from happening, I quit my teaching job at the end of the school year to devote full time to my thesis.

Two very sad events marred my happiness and dampened my enthusiasm for research and writing. My father came down with cancer of the stomach and died within three months, in September 1952. Since I had been especially close to him all my life, I took his death very hard. I suffered guilt feelings and felt somehow responsible for his death. In Germany, a psychological theory as to the cause of cancer was popular and endorsed by members of the medical profession, namely that the probable cause of cancer was extreme prolonged stress. I suddenly realized that I had caused my father an undue amount of stress because, due to the influence of my

American experience, I had changed from the "typical" German to a citizen with a broader outlook on life and ideas, which my father, in his "Germanness," could not accept. In his eyes, I was a terrible disappointment to have digressed from my traditional upbringing. The worst effect on my father, however, must have been my obsessive desire to live in the United States.

Although I was thirty-two years old at the time of my father's death, I lived at home. There was still a severe shortage of housing due to the destruction in the war. Unless a refugee or homeless, there was no chance of renting an apartment. Living with my stepmother did not exactly make for a pleasant life. For example, she did not allow me to listen to music on the radio after my father's death, because I was supposed to grieve for him, and music was taboo. Likewise, she resented my conviction that it was not necessary to wear black for one whole year after the death of a loved one. Wearing black was considered a symbol of love for the deceased. I did not own any black clothes, nor did I have the money to buy a new wardrobe, which I could not wear in the States, anyway. Also, I had brought back from America several very good-looking pieces of clothing, which I was proud to wear. To me, the custom of wearing black after a death simply did not make sense, and it did not mean at all that I loved my father less. My stepmother made my life difficult with her narrow-minded and, in my eyes, old-fashioned ideas.

A second event, one month later, proved almost as upsetting to me as my father's death. My *Doktorvater* (thesis advisor) unexpectedly died of a heart attack. There was no other member on the faculty who was as much of an expert in French medieval literature as he. The other faculty members were unwilling or unqualified to take over his role as a thesis advisor. Finally, I succeeded in persuading another professor of Romance Languages to supervise my thesis. However, his specialty was not literature, but linguistics. It did not seem to matter because my dissertation was actually a combination of both. After reading my rough draft, he suggested a couple of changes, which forced me to do some more time-consuming work. I lost about four months in the process.

Eventually, events began to turn in my favor. The timing could not have been more perfect. I received my Ph.D. on May 6, 1953, and my immigrant visa came in the mail a few weeks later. I gleefully made reservations aboard the "Queen Mary" for July 1. The ticket for the passage cost $180.00. Shortly before paying, I received a tax refund from the Internal Revenue Service of the United States.

I was proud of having contributed part of my earnings to the U.S. tax system. It was a special boon to apply the $50.00 tax refund towards my passage. I felt the tax return was symbolic of the willingness of the American government to welcome me back to the land of my dreams.

Freedom beckons. The Statue of Liberty in New York harbor, 1950.

18

Auf Wiedersehen, Deutschland!

Needless to say, I was ready and anxious to start a new chapter of my life, one that promised to hold predominantly positive experiences, unlike those of the first thirty-three years of living in Germany. However, uncertainties lay ahead, and I could only rely on hope and my newly acquired American optimism to keep my spirits up. I was anxious to lay the negative experiences of my earlier life to rest and was convinced that the second part of my life would be more pleasant. Surely I would be able to make it in the New World by relying on initiative, talent and personal resources, whereas in Germany I was forced into a mold set up largely by a government which had no tolerance for individuality and personal initiative.

My stepmother was not able or willing to share my enthusiasm for a new beginning. She repeatedly asked me what I was going to do, if I were not able to find a teaching job in the United States. I stubbornly, yet confidently, came up with the same answer over and over again, assuring her that I would try as hard as I could to find a job in my field. However, if I should not succeed at first, I would work as a cleaning lady, at least for the time being. If I did not succeed at all, I could always return to Germany and teach. I was determined to make it, regardless of effort, and nothing could have deterred me. I may have been the only cleaning lady in the U.S. with a Ph.D., if it did not work out.

All my relatives, without a single exception, strongly opposed my decision to emigrate. They thought that I was foolish to think that a young German would have a chance to succeed professionally in America. There was still a considerable anti-American sentiment prevalent among the generation who grew up in Nazi Germany, which was even more surprising in view of the fact that most of my relatives were not members of the Nazi party. It took a long, long time before Germans dared to develop an interest in Americans and to consider them likeable and trustworthy human beings. No matter how exciting a new venture promises to be, bidding farewell is seldom an easy thing to do. I dreaded saying good-bye to my relatives for obvious reasons. Instead of being happy for me in the fulfillment of my strong desire to live in the United States, they met me with long faces, convinced that I was about to take a terribly wrong step and was just wasting a lot of precious time, before I would certainly come back to live in Germany for the rest of my life. My favorite aunt shouted after me, *"Wir werden uns nie wiedersehen!"* (We'll never see each other again!) and another aunt called me a *"Volksverräter"* (traitor to the German cause).

I can't imagine what my dear father would have said in parting if he had been still alive. As the fine human being he was, I think he would have refrained from making a harmful remark, but would have just suffered in silence. In a way, I was glad that I could not hurt him anymore. Somehow I was grateful to be at a point in my life that I had no longer close family ties that might have made the separation more difficult. This sounds terribly selfish, and in some respect it was, but no amount of love and grief would have brought my loved ones back.

As far as my uncles, aunts and cousins were concerned, I have always held that you do not have to live close to them to love them. Over all the thirty-seven years that I had the good fortune to live in this country, I have never stopped loving my relatives, as far away as they may be. I wish I could say the same about their love towards me. No doubt, they still love me, but they have resented my crucial decision to leave Germany and have never forgiven me for making it.

I was not the only German participant in the special reorientation program for German teachers who came back to live in the United States. Out of the four Germans and two Austrians with whom I studied at the University of Oregon four returned. This no doubt defeated the purpose of the program to re-educate German teachers in the democratic ways, so that they could pass on these new ideas and ideals to the German youth. After I came back to the States, the U.S. Immigration Service revised its policies. Scholarship recipients, who studied under the Reorientation Program, were obligated to teach at least five years in Germany, before becoming eligible to apply for an immigrant visa to the United States. How lucky I was!

I realized that I needed not only to part with my relatives, but also to tear myself away from my native country. The latter proved to be almost more painful than saying *"Auf Wiedersehen"* to my relatives. In my thoughts, I heaped lavish praise on my future adoptive country and dwelled too much on my negative experiences in Germany. My assessment was not exactly balanced.

It was not until the time of my departure that I realized how attached I was to the country of my birth. How grossly unfair it would have been to condemn my fatherland and all Germans because of a dismal record of twelve years of misrule. Granted, Germany can rightfully be accused of and condemned for engaging in more than its share of wars, killings and atrocities. On the other hand, she has immeasurably contributed to the enrichment of the culture and civilization of the Western World. German composers, authors, historians, philosophers, religious leaders, scientists, physicians, inventors have made significant contributions to the rest of the world. Our life would be unthinkable without Beethoven, Mozart, Schubert, Bach, Brahms, Wagner, Haydn, Goethe, Schiller, Mann, Hesse, Böll, Brecht, Grass, Leibniz, Kant, Schopenhauer, Nietzsche, Hertz, Roentgen, Einstein, Luther, to name just a few at random. I feel extremely proud of German culture and civilization, but I have tried to distance myself from all deplorable activities of Nazi Germany, which remain an unpardonable assault on human dignity and an unconscionable violation of the rights of other races and nations, but to a certain degree I still bear the sting of it all deep in my heart.

Pius Wolter, the best friend I left behind.

19

Life in the Land of my Dreams

It was hard to believe that I had reached my goal and my wish had been fulfilled. After an enjoyable train ride through France, this time traveling north, I boarded the ship in the harbor of Calais on July 1, 1953. The *Queen Mary* had previously earned the blue ribbon for crossing the Atlantic in record time. It took us only four days, including the Fourth of July, to arrive in New York. That was a far cry from my previous transatlantic crossing, which took twelve days! Traveling on a British ship on an American holiday, especially Independence Day, was quite an experience. The U.S. citizens aboard celebrated to the hilt, whereas the English people kept quiet and subdued. For obvious reasons, they saw no reason to celebrate. Guess on whose side I found myself!

My journey did not go off without a hitch. In 1953, eight years after the end of the war, life in Germany had not returned to normal yet. Authorities had yet to devise a legal way of exchanging German marks into dollars or taking German currency to other countries. Fortunately, I had been able to pay for both railroad ticket to Cherbourg and ocean passage in German money. My sponsors had sent me a train ticket for my trip from New York City to Eugene. They had informed me that they would deposit a check for additional expenses to general delivery at the main post office in New York City. Unfortunately, I arrived on a Saturday and, to my disbelief, the post office was closed. In big German cities, at least one post office is kept open night and day, as well as on Saturdays and Sundays. How could my beloved adopted country be so insensitive to my needs!

My empty purse forestalled the possibility of staying in the city, so I boarded the next train and hoped for the best. I might have been forced to go without meals for three days - a prospect which I did not dread at all, because I was hoping that I would lose some extra pounds that I carried around ever since I was born as an overweight baby. However, after a couple of skipped meals, I quickly changed my mind. Some fellow travelers asked me why I did not eat, and so I confided in them. Without hesitation, those good souls treated me to all meals for the remaining journey. Luckily, they traveled with me all the way to Portland, Oregon. Again American hospitality and generosity had come to my rescue in a precarious situation.

My sponsors met me at the train station in Eugene, Oregon, and surrounded me with a lot of care and affection. They had moved to Junction City in the meantime, to a beautiful home in a rural setting about twenty miles from Eugene. Mildred was not among those who welcomed me back to the United States. She was in a Eugene hospital recovering from minor surgery. Byron and Dale took me to their new home on Oak Knoll near Junction City, grateful for my companionship and skill in cooking tempting German meals for them until Mildred's return home. At our request, the New York post office later returned the registered letter with the check that I was unable to pick up.

The three Gilsons were just as pleased to have me around as I felt privileged to be in their company. They quickly adopted me into their family circle. Having been raised as an only child and, with the exception of my parents, I had always missed the closeness and warmth of other people around me. Now I especially appreciated the companionship of the family and their numerous relatives, who dropped in quite frequently. Very seldom had I experienced that degree of happiness within my own family. I am tempted to compare the affection I felt towards the Gilson family with the feeling one experiences when first falling in love with a member of the opposite sex. All of a sudden, I felt wanted and appreciated, regardless of weaknesses and faults that had been so frequently brought up in Germany, both at home and in school. Everything seemed to be so right between me and the world. American optimism had reached me sooner than I thought!

Most people tend to prove their appreciation by going out and buying an expensive gift. This was not possible in my case, because I had not a dollar in my wallet or in my name at a bank. Instead, I had to express my appreciation by using my imagination. I thought of many different kindnesses towards each member of the family, or the family as a whole. I got up early and prepared breakfast, not an easy-to-fix continental breakfast that I was accustomed to in Germany, but a hearty American breakfast consisting of bacon and eggs, toast, butter, biscuits, orange juice and various fruits. Then the family rushed off to work in three different cars. This impressed me considerably because, in those days, very few German families owned a car, let alone three!

Left alone at home, I spent the remainder of the working day by doing various chores around the house and yard. I washed the breakfast dishes, made the beds and cleaned the three bedrooms and the kitchen. Remembering my beloved mother's household routine, I never ran out of things to do to keep me busy. Once in a while I scrubbed the kitchen and the bathroom floors and in doing so I was reminded of my vow to my stepmother, before leaving Germany, that I would not hesitate to work as a cleaning woman in case I should not be able to find a job in my field right away. It now seemed ironic as it came true, although under different circumstances from those my stepmother had imagined. I did not mind at all scrubbing floors in the Gilson household. I would have done anything within my power to prove how thankful I was to them for helping me create a new, more rewarding and fulfilling life. Mildred was a very down-to-earth lady, who was not prone to express any degree of excessive feelings. She sometimes even attempted to tone mine down, especially my gratitude, which somehow seemed embarrassing to her. Every once in a while, she said, "You must not go overboard with your gratitude towards us."

Life in an American household proved to be a source of great excitement to me. I especially appreciated all kinds of modern conveniences, such as the use of a refrigerator, a freezer, all kinds of electrical appliances, for example an electric mixer, a bottle opener, a toaster, an oven with adjustable temperatures, running hot water, and - last but not least - the comfort of electric heat with a thermostat in each room.

All my life, I had been a worshiper of nature without knowing anything about it. I took strength from observing nature, because I considered it tangible manifestation of God and direct access to my Creator. In Germany I had very little chance to enjoy nature close-by, because we never owned a yard and my experiences were limited to observation. However, the Gilson house was surrounded by a vast area of trees and grass. Around the house there were flower and vegetable beds in which I took great pride. I watered regularly, pulled the weeds, fertilized the plants and derived a great deal of spiritual pleasure from watching plants grow from seed to maturation. It was quite gratifying to fill several vases with flowers to decorate the various rooms of the home.

One task I was not able to do was to shop for groceries because I did not know how to drive. Once a week, Mildred took me to the nearest grocery store, about five miles away. Shopping proved quite a revelation to me, who, for about ten years, had to get along with an absolute minimum of food supplies. American grocery stores simply overwhelmed me with their easy availability and variety of goods. Indeed, it took an experienced shopper to purchase food efficiently.

The simple activity of shopping was a culture shock and a somewhat intimidating and humiliating experience - intimidating because of the vast variety of items available, the need to compare prices and make the wisest choice; humiliating, because I was an intelligent thirty-three-year-old woman who was not able to carry out the simple task of shopping to satisfy everyday needs. Mildred was blessed with a wonderful empathy and, in her admirable thoughtfulness, introduced me to the intricacies of American grocery shopping by pointing out the important things to look for in making proper choices.

I could not help but admire the multitude of prepackaged items and the freshness of fruits and vegetables. In Germany, grocers scooped the desired food items into paper bags and weighed them before handing them over to the customers. Every housewife came with her own shopping bag, into which she placed the various purchases. There were no checkstands, so one customer was waited on at a time. Here in America, every time we went grocery shopping, the checker provided us with a new paper bag. It seemed such a waste to use a strong paper bag only once.

Another convenience I began to appreciate was the fact that you had to go grocery shopping only once a week, provided you carefully planned your weekly meals in advance and made a reliable shopping list. Coming from a country, which by necessity restricted a large number of food items, it was hard to resist impulse shopping, especially ice cream, which was my absolute favorite. Fortunately, Mildred was in charge and managed the money. I would have certainly gone overboard in my desire to buy more than needed, out of sheer curiosity and to satisfy my unusually great appetite, in an effort - as if that were possible - to make up for being deprived of all those food items for so many years. The mere sight of an egg carton put me into a frenzy. In Germany, a dozen eggs had to last us a whole month; one pound of meat was the monthly allotment per person during the war.

Another surprise for me was the vast array of fruits and vegetables, in orderly display and wonderfully fresh, and customers could reject items that displeased them. To my surprise, shoppers picked up produce and inspected and squeezed it to test it for its freshness. In Germany, this is impossible, and anyone who tried it would be set straight by the owner of the store. When we went shopping there, we told the merchant what we wanted to buy and he, often very quickly, placed the item in a paper bag, in order to hide blemishes from the customer. It was not until we arrived home that we sometimes found that a vegetable or fruit was far from fresh.

Although the Gilsons took care of all my immediate needs, it was difficult to get used to the idea that I had no money of my own. This became very evident when Dale married Roselee, his college sweetheart. I already knew her because she had a room in the home of Dale's parents when I lived there. They both lived under the same roof, but in separate rooms, as was the custom in those days, no matter how much people were in love with each other. Naturally, I was invited to the wedding, but to my dismay I had not the "right" dress for the occasion. Neither did I have any money to buy a wedding present for those lovely people. Later, when I was on my own and taught high school in Portland, I presented them rather belatedly with a wedding gift bought with pride from my own earnings.

I still lived with Mildred and Byron, Dale's parents. They were very busy people, both working full-time. Nevertheless, on weekends they made it a point to introduce me to the beautiful scenery of Oregon, as the three of us shared a love for the countryside. I loved the scenery in Oregon, from ocean, to mountains, to meadows, to rivers, to arid lands. I grew up in northern Bavaria, a region almost devoid of scenic beauty, at least when compared with the diversity of the Oregon landscape. I did not get my first glimpse of the Alps until 1940, of the ocean until 1950 and of the Rhine river until I was fifty-four years old! Any American traveling to Germany today gets to see those three scenic areas within three days.

Perhaps it is characteristic of me that I always desired to venture out into the world and get acquainted with other countries rather than giving my own country first priority. The closing of the borders of Germany during World War II had a claustrophobic effect on me. I felt like a prisoner in my own country. As a prisoner discharged from jail no longer finds prison very interesting, I considered Germany less a home than an institution, so I traveled all over Europe, before I decided to give more attention to my native country.

Back in Oregon, I was fortunate enough to see more of the state traveling with the Gilsons than I had ever before seen of Germany in my thirty-three years of living there. Distances did not seem very important to Americans. After all, what is a *Strassenkreuzer* (street cruiser) for? This was the name given by the Germans to the huge six-seater American cars which they looked at with considerable envy as they viewed them from their small VW's. Actually, most Germans did not even own any car at all. Those who did would not have thought of traveling 500 to 600 miles a day, as we do here. If they did that it would be easy enough to travel all the way through Germany from North to South or East to West in one day. I was used to traveling exceedingly long distances from my student days, so the Gilsons did not surprise me by following the same procedure. They crisscrossed the state with me several times and I fell in love with the Oregon scenery all over again. To this day, I never tire of seeing the same sights, be it Seaside, Lincoln City, Newport, Mt. Hood, or the Columbia Gorge. Nature in all its manifestations has been a source of comfort and serenity to me, and the Gilsons saw to it that I got more than my fair share.

In spite of all this excitement, the fact remained that I was still without a job and income. It was not that I did not try. Although I was a trained high school teacher and had taught in Germany, I was of the opinion that I had a lot to learn before I could venture into a classroom in a foreign country. Most of all, as a German brought up to strive for perfection in all endeavors, I saw a need to improve my oral skills before applying for a teaching job. Therefore I intended to delay entering the teaching profession until a later date. In an effort to learn how to speak like a native American I often felt frustrated. I discovered that Americans in many respects were more polite than Germans. Invariably, my friends in this country would not have been caught dead trying to correct me in spite of my plea to do so. How could you learn anything if you are allowed to make the same mistake over and over again? On the other hand, I myself have the tendency to correct people, when they make mistakes. Germans, as a rule, are more blunt in that respect because they consider criticism as something positive and constructive used to help people improve themselves rather than putting them down. I am convinced that, in my zeal to be helpful in such a situation, I scared away many students who took German, French, or Latin courses from me. I do not even hesitate to correct colleagues of mine when I catch them making a mistake.

A means of learning the language faster and better was to watch TV. It may not always have been exemplary language but it helped me with my fluency, colloquialisms and even slang. Since I was aware that my American friends would not correct my mistakes, I was anxious to listen to their language intently and, in the beginning at least, I never ventured into speaking in a creative and original way but used vocabulary, expressions and sentence structures only after I had heard them used previously. Imitation and repetition was the name of the game!

A few weeks after my arrival, I applied for various jobs other than teaching. Mildred never tired of driving me from one place to another in the Eugene area. I filled out countless application forms which never led to a job. In retrospect, I think I have found an explanation for the phenomenon. One question invariably asked was, "How many years of high school did you attend?" The truthful answer was "nine years." Another one that might have tripped me up was, "What academic degree do you have?" My answer, "Ph.D."

No wonder potential employers were puzzled: What kind of person would attend nine years of high school? And what kind of person with a Ph.D. would apply for a menial or secretarial job? Obviously, I was overeducated for such a job.

One time I surprised an interviewer who had administered a spelling test to twenty prospective employees. It turned out that I, as a foreign speaker, received the highest score of 100 percent. That really boosted my ego, to say the least. I gave my excellent teachers and professors in Germany credit for teaching me so well.

In the meantime, I had kept in touch with my stepmother in Germany, who never believed that American authorities would hire a German for a teaching job. In each letter I received from her she urged me to reconsider and come back "home" to Germany, but I was too determined to become successful in the country of my choice, which I loved so much!

After a few unsuccessful attempts to land a job, Mildred Gilson very tactfully steered me in the right direction. She encouraged me to apply for a teaching job. Although scared to death, I heeded her advice and applied to the Eugene School District. Again

I was unsuccessful in my search, not because there were no openings in my field, but because I had no Oregon teaching certificate.

I learned that the only chance of teaching without such a certificate was in Portland, the only city entitled to issue "emergency certificates," which would enable school districts to make temporary hires of teachers who had not yet earned a certificate. This seemed to be the reasonable track to follow, but it entailed parting with my sponsors, moving to Portland and establishing myself there.

Fortunately, I had a friend by the name of Hildegard whom I had met at the University of Oregon and who lived in Portland with her parents. In the true American spirit of hospitality and cooperation, this family, Charles and Frieda Wagner, offered me a place in their home. It seemed like an historic event, when I reported to the office of the superintendent of Portland Public Schools to find out about an opening at Jefferson High School. After an interview with the superintendent, I was advised to report to the principal of Jefferson the next day, which I did with much trepidation.

Having been trained in Germany, I had an excessive respect for anyone in a position higher than mine, which made it difficult to relax in the presence of superiors. However, Mr. Charles Jones immediately made me feel at home. A vice principal, Mr. Malo, also was in attendance. The interview went very well. I was informed that there was a temporary opening for one year for a teacher of French and Latin. French was one of my majors and I had no reservation teaching it, but Latin was another matter. In Germany, a teacher was authorized to teach only the subject(s) in which she was officially trained. I was perfectly honest when I declared that I could not consider teaching Latin.

The principal did not give up as easily as I did. He pursued the matter by asking me, "How many years of Latin have you had?" Thereupon I answered truthfully, "six years in high school and four more years at the university." He told me he was convinced that I could teach Latin also, besides French, provided I would be willing to give it a try. When I replied that I would, he turned to the vice principal and asked, "What do you think?" Mr. Malo nodded in agreement. Mr. Jones congratulated me on getting the job. I was ecstatic, although still afraid. Another ardent wish concerning my career had materialized.

20

The High School Teacher from Germany

I find it strange that I must start my discussion of teaching in America with the relatively insignificant and even trivial matter of transportation. Living in a city the size of Portland proved an overwhelming experience to me. When I studied at the University of Oregon in Eugene, it was simple to get around on foot within the confines of the campus. Even going downtown on an occasional shopping spree could be accomplished by walking or taking a bus without the need to transfer. When I lived with the Gilsons, getting around the Eugene area proved no special problem either, because there was always one of the three family members able and willing to take me around.

Living in Portland and on my own, I found transportation difficult, to say the least. It took me quite some time, three years to be exact, before I could afford to buy a used car and to muster enough courage to learn how to drive. Certainly, the Wagners, my new "family," could not be expected to provide transportation to and from school on a regular basis. Although my new home was located within the school district, it was still too far away from the school to walk, approximately 30 minutes. Yet, it was a comforting thought that, in an emergency, I could get to work on foot.

I was greatly relieved when, towards the end of my summer vacation, a lady called to offer me regular rides to and from school. She turned out to be a fellow teacher of mine, who had learned about my joining the faculty in the upcoming school year. She proved to be most kind and helpful. I should have been used to the graciousness and generosity of American people by then, but one of my distinct character traits has always been an overdeveloped urge for independence. I found it difficult to accept the kind offer of my future colleague without insisting on paying her the amount of the bus fare. It seems trivial now, but maybe I felt the desire to be in charge of every little happening in my life after having been dependent on so many people for such a long period of time.

Faye Chavez came by my house every morning to take me to school and in the afternoon she dropped me off at home. This arrangement not only fulfilled a practical purpose, but provided me with a chance of talking with an experienced American teacher and exchanging various ideas and opinions about school. Obviously, teaching in a new country in a different language under an unaccustomed educational system brought about more problems and questions than I had anticipated.

Actually, thinking about too many potential difficulties ahead of time would have been unwise. So I decided to throw myself *in medias res* and learn to roll with the punches. If I had not developed that kind of attitude I would have found myself frozen stiff, while standing in front of those hordes of American teenagers.

It was not half as bad as I make it sound. The "kids," as I learned to refer to them lovingly, approached me with a certain good-natured and natural curiosity. Certainly, they were not deliberately mean to me as we were towards our teachers in Germany when I went to school. We sometimes teamed up against teachers in the classroom and made life miserable for them. Fortunately, no such thing happened to me on my new job. So apparently I treated the students in the customary and expected way. That gave me a great sense of confidence and gratitude towards my charges.

I was at first somewhat surprised by the apparent lack of respect shown to me. Students walked in, chattering away, sometimes cutting up and always more or less indifferent to me. When they did speak to me it was almost as an equal, and I cherished the occasional "good morning" that was casually flung my way. On the other hand, when students would confide in me, or when they opened their hearts on the details of their personal life, my spirits soared.

Over the years I learned to feel comfortable with the informal, egalitarian character of American education and eventually I came to realize that at the heart of the American educational system lay a deep respect for the integrity of the individual and an almost pathological hatred of tyranny, whether exercised in the name of national greatness or in the petty forms of manipulation and control practiced by arrogant teachers. To me the American schools were more humane, the students more sincere and their respect for me and my own integrity more deeply felt than anything I ever experienced in Germany.

With all those new experiences, the first academic year passed quickly. I was sorry to learn after a few months that the lady for whom I served as a full-time substitute died of cancer. I must have done a satisfactory job in my first year because I was hired as a regular teacher for the second year. However, three additional years on a probationary status lay ahead of me before I was eligible for tenure.

According to my contract, my assigned subjects were French and Latin for the first four years. German was taught by an American colleague until that time. Thanks to my excellent academic background provided by superior teachers and professors in Germany, I never had any difficulty imparting the subject matter. I had the definite impression that, in general, students respected me for my proficiency. There were five classes to teach every day plus one study hall. The school enrollment amounted to 2,000 students and my classes were large, up to 144 pupils every day.

Teaching languages became a pleasant routine without any problems. Study Hall was another matter. During my school years in Germany, first as a student and then as a teacher, study halls did not exist, so I did not quite know what to expect. Judging by my experience as a student and my customary daily study load of up to six hours of preparations for the next day, I was confident that American students would welcome an hour to get started on their assignments. Far from the truth! A small minority in my study hall tried to socialize and chat with their friends, instead of applying themselves and doing their home work. I sized up the situation in terms of how these occasional disturbances might affect the hardworking students. I did not want to aggravate the situation by calling for silence. So I just lifted my head from my reading to give the troublemakers a serious look and make them aware of my assessing the situation.

When German teachers encountered discipline problems, the administration always backed up the teacher. In American schools this was not always the case. At least in the beginning, I did not know how to handle discipline problems. The greatest difficulty was that I did not know the students in study hall by name, which made it impossible to refer the matter to their counselors. In some cases, the students simply refused to give me their name and some gave me a wrong name. Study hall became an absolute nightmare, because I was not accustomed to having my authority as a teacher challenged. Students in Germany seldom created an open scene for me. Fortunately, the enrollment in study halls varied from year to year, and after establishing myself as a respected teacher, I had fewer behavior problems.

Challenges to the methods of my teaching and criticism of length of assignments were something else that I needed to get used to. Furthermore, it was astonishing that a student was authorized to complain about a teacher to a counselor or an administrator. While I opposed unwarranted criticism, I welcomed any discussion, positive or negative, of the subject matter. In Germany, such practice was not customary. Discussions gave me a chance to express my appreciation of the students' intellect and judgment and to reinforce good learning habits. My students taught me a lot over the years, more than they realized, I am sure.

Criticism was not always easy to take, especially when it involved an attack on the subject matter. I remember one student who referred to Latin as "a lot of flimflam." Latin has been so valuable to me, not only in my study of Romance languages, but also in learning English, a Germanic language whose vocabulary is about 60 percent of Latin origin.

It made me happy when students displayed enough confidence in me to feel free and uninhibited talking to me and discussing all kinds of matters, including personal problems. In the process, I learned to take myself less seriously and to laugh at myself. Those occasions when I made mistakes in my use of the English language must have been amusing and sometimes distracting. That was my greatest concern when I first started out teaching, but it never provided a problem, with only one exception. One day we studied German music and were concentrating on Beethoven in particular. I asked my students which ones of his works they were familiar with, at least by name. One of my favorites is the "Moonlight Sonata" (German *Mondscheinsonate*). You guessed it, I asked my students if they knew the Moonshine Sonata. Instead of giving a logical answer, the whole class of about twenty-five students burst out laughing. I stood there, red-faced and dumbfounded! Obviously I had committed an embarrassing error. To ease my embarrassment, a brave student gave me a lesson on the meaning of "moonshine." I was grateful for the information and I never made the same mistake again. Each time the *Mondscheinsonate* came up in my subsequent teaching, I shared the episode with my students, to their delight.

Every teacher learns that the job is not done at the end of the day. In the opinion of German educators and parents, classroom teaching is a first priority in the educational process. The remaining tasks, such as character building, developing social graces and instilling a workable value system, were the responsibility of parents and clergy. American schools shoulder a much greater burden in the development of young people. In this respect, too, I had a lot to learn. For the first time in my life, I was introduced to extracurricular activities. As a beginning teacher, I was exempt from participating in non-teaching tasks, which gave me a chance to watch my colleagues from the sidelines and learn by observation. In the following years, I did my share by forming and advising a German Club to which my students gave the name *Edelweiss*.

The first election of officers for *Edelweiss* stands out in my memory because the students carried out the task with a dedication and dignity that I never observed among my classmates and students in Germany. For a person having grown up under a dictatorship, watching the democratic process in action under such humble circumstances was a touching experience. The members of the newly founded club were a constant source of inspiration to me, as they discussed their business and came to decisions in their democratic ways, which seemed to be innate! I was so proud of them!

We met four times a month for two business meetings and two social gatherings. The business meetings took place in the classroom after regular hours. For the social functions, we gathered in the home of a member or my apartment. All of us brought refreshments. Sometimes the students invited a guest speaker, or I made a presentation on a topic suggested by students. This gave us a chance to practice our German, but I made it a point to please my students rather than making it a learning experience.

The club activities forced me to reassess my primary role as a teacher. In Germany, the teacher was always the center of attention in any group, but here I learned to place myself in the background as a spectator, give students a chance to act on their own and provide guidance only when needed.

The students cooperated very nicely when it came to sharing rides to the evening meetings, but after three years I enjoyed showing off my newly acquired car and my driving skills by gathering some of our members at their various homes and taking them back safe and sound after the meeting. They knew their way around better than I and gave me excellent directions. Socializing with students was not without risk, especially when the weather was cold and wet, and road conditions were hazardous. Sometimes there was snow on the ground, the streets were icy, and I could have been easily involved in an accident in which students might have got hurt. However, I would not have dreamed of canceling a meeting because we all enjoyed our gatherings so much.

The highlight of the year came before Christmas. Several weeks before the holiday, I taught the club members German Christmas carols. A few days before Christmas, the young people made arrangements for us to appear in a retirement home or a nursing home and cheer up old people by caroling for them. The students had prepared themselves well by memorizing several carols. Quite a few of our listeners turned out to be of German descent and still spoke the language to a certain degree. In some cases, our singing must have reminded them of Christmases decades ago. Very seldom had I seen so many tears being shed - tears of joy and remembrance, of course. The very bravest in the audience, who knew the German text, joined us in singing. Then we wished them *Frohe Weihnachten* and went on our way, as delighted and moved by this cultural and humane experience as the old people, who were listening to us.

In addition to serving as faculty advisor to the German Club, I prepared students of Latin for the Roman Banquet which they put on once a semester. They tried so hard to disprove the popular notion that Latin was a "dead language." The banquet was planned and staged by students of Latin, but everybody was welcome. We hoped that some students might become motivated to pursue the study of Latin after sharing in the festivities. My students enjoyed doing research into Roman customs, meals and costumes in preparation for the feast. The day before we had a dress rehearsal, which lent the event a professional character and gave us confidence that everything would go off as planned. All participants, including faculty members, were required to dress in authentic Roman costumes. This entailed wearing a toga and a tunic. The toga consisted of a large piece of wool or linen and was draped around the body. The tunic was a short straight sleeveless shirt worn under the toga and reaching a little below the knees. The Romans scarcely distinguished between men's and women's garments. Some inventive students made it easy on themselves by artistically draping a bed sheet around the body. Holding the toga and tunic in place became a major concern of shy students, but those young men unconcerned about letting the opposite sex have a glimpse of their chests did not always try to hold the unaccustomed garments in place.

I, too, wore the Roman costume. In this country a teacher must never be a wetblanket. I learned that early on. Let me assure you, however, that I belonged among the shy ones when it came to holding up my garments. If my students in Germany had seen me in that outfit and my carefree "undignified" mood - unbecoming of teachers - they would have been convinced that I had flipped my lid. "Why shouldn't teachers be entitled to some fun, too?" was the question with which I tried to justify my venture into my "unladylike" conduct.

First-year students had to dress as slaves, while some of the more imaginative second-year students dressed as Roman senators, soldiers, officers, political leaders, or even as emperors. The banquet room was decorated with Roman banners and an array of pictures of well-known classical monuments and Roman buildings. Latin mottoes and proverbs covered the walls. The food "from soup to nuts" was cooked by the students and beautifully displayed. It did not differ substantially from American meals and it looked inviting and appetizing. We did not pretend it to be authentic, but the main thing was that it tasted delicious! However, according to Roman custom, it had to be eaten with spoons and fingers. Some adventuresome students tried to speak Latin to each other, although we realized that the oral expression of the language is no longer used as such anymore - therefore the expression "dead language" - but lives on in the various Romance languages.

One of the most rewarding experiences of teaching is witnessing students' progress. This was especially true in the case of those students who studied language with me exclusively. They were truly my own product, and I was extremely proud when they performed well in contests. Some of my high school students used to take part in the annual state-wide Foreign Language Field Days held at the University of Oregon. In 1957, four students of mine received Honorable Mention. The following year, one of my students became first-prize winner.

Two of my classes were invited to appear on Portland TV with me for a half-hour program each. A first-year class performed admirably on KOIN-TV in 1956. A third-year class made an outstanding appearance on KGW-TV in 1960. Not a word of English was spoken during these programs. Needless to say, I was thrilled with their performance.

Teachers trained in this country are used to numerous committee assignments, which are always time-consuming, frustrating and sometimes nerve-racking. In German schools of my time, committees did not exist at all. They now do, I am sure, because West Germany has been good about imitating everything American, both good and bad. When I grew up, the principal, assisted by a vice principal, made decisions pertaining to his particular school. More far-reaching decisions affecting all schools were made by the State Department of Education and dutifully and unquestionably carried out by teachers and students alike. After all, that's what "experts" were for!

At Jefferson High School in Portland, I served on most of the faculty committees during my ten years of tenure. Committee assignments were not my favorite activity. In most instances I considered them frustrating and a waste of my precious time. The same was true of most faculty meetings. I sometimes had the impression that important changes and decisions were made by the administration ahead of time and that the faculty, bored and waiting for the end of the meeting, finally gave its sanction just to bring the meeting to an end. On the other hand, I always enjoyed the meetings of the foreign language department because the teachers were most personable and made meetings very pleasant. We had so much in common!

The work performed by city-wide committees also appeared to be meaningful and worth the time and effort. I served on several of those committees when I became head of the foreign language department of my school. The committee I found most interesting was the Textbook Selection Committee, whose members evaluated several textbooks new on the market and then decided which one was to be used by language departments of all public schools of the city. When time came to change textbooks, the task of evaluating and selecting new textbooks required innumerable hours which I gladly spent as a service to what I considered a most worthwhile project.

Attendance at PTA (Parent-Teacher Association) meetings was more or less expected of us teachers. This was also new to me, because in Germany school affairs are left to teachers and administrators. There again the "experts" were allowed to make all the decisions. It was unheard-of that German parents ever protested against or - Heaven forbid - interfered with educational matters.

Because of my regular attendance at PTA meetings in this country, I became quite well acquainted with the leadership and also with many parents. They occasionally invited me to speak to the organization about all kinds of educational issues. I had several standard speeches that I had ready to fit different occasions. One involved a comparison between the U.S. and German school systems and another an introduction to various methods of teaching foreign languages. These were real favorites which I was willing to present upon request, not only to the Jefferson PTA but also to various AAUW (American Association of University Women) groups in Portland, as well as to the Portland branch of the American Overseas Education Association.

Another duty unknown in Germany was what could be called "continuing education" for teachers who had to acquire a certain number of "in-service" credits within a specific period of time. This was an ongoing requirement and failure to fulfill it resulted in the repeal of a person's teaching certificate.

I was also instrumental in training a number of student teachers. They were generally well-prepared in their field, and I enjoyed their company and watching their progress under my guidance. A few of them turned into long-time friends. Unfortunately, two of them passed away in their prime of life.

One extra duty I was asked to perform and which gave me untold headaches had nothing to do with my expertise in languages. It entailed figuring four-year grade point averages of approximately 300 senior students who, if qualified, were to receive special honors during graduation exercises. It was an excruciating task that was assigned in addition to teaching all my regular classes. The calculator had not been invented yet, and so I did the work without one. In order to avoid any errors, I had to double-check the results, which again required an enormous amount of additional work. I performed this duty for several years in a row.

A last activity to be mentioned here is several stints of teaching summer school at Lincoln High School in Portland. I was assigned to teach French, Latin and German. Summer school was set up for students from all Portland high schools who wanted to earn extra credit as well as for those who needed to make up a failing grade in a subject. This dichotomy and lack of homogeneity of students made it difficult to coordinate the preparations, but I found the work challenging nevertheless.

Becoming a successful high school teacher in a foreign country was a monumental task. I venture to say that, at least in my first years, I probably had to work twice as hard as a teacher trained in this country but it was all worth it. Fortunately, I had a lot of assistance from my fellow teachers, who were aware of my special difficulties. I would not have been able to make it without their invaluable help. Two of them, assigned to me by the administration when I first started to teach at Jefferson, were members of the foreign language department, one a teacher of Spanish and the other one of French. Their names were Grace Deierlein and Marian Kilborn. Without hesitation they welcomed me within their ranks and were always willing to assist me and answer any questions. They even went out of their way to help me become a successful teacher in a minimum amount of time. We became the fastest friends and still see each other on a regular basis.

The Jefferson faculty displayed a wonderful school spirit and an unusual pride in their school. I felt as if I belonged to a big loving family. Socializing among teachers was not practiced in Germany. Here I was welcomed with open arms not only by teachers in my field but by educators of all disciplines. Many invited me to their homes, introduced me to their family and served me delicious meals. I became a genuine "social butterfly," a term untranslatable into German for obvious reasons. In addition, there were regular faculty dinners and summer picnics in which all members of the faculty took part. I still pride myself in continued friendships with those lovely people. Once a year, the Jefferson faculty meets for a picnic at Laurelhurst Park in Portland. Although I no longer know most of the faculty who were hired after I left in 1963, I am still invited, along with a number of "old-timers" who taught with me. The memory of my first experiences at Jefferson High is still vivid in my mind, and it seems incongruous that I am now termed an "old-timer."

So far the description of my various teaching activities sounds like a real success story, but there was one significant ingredient missing: a valid teaching certificate. I was one of several teachers with an excellent educational background who were denied teaching certificates because of outdated rules of certification. Eventually, a thorough study and overhaul of the whole teacher certification rule book was undertaken, but it was too late for me to profit from any subsequent changes in the rules. The Portland *Oregonian* covered the various proposals concerning rule changes in a detailed article entitled "Archaic Rules Bar Certification of Oregon

School Administrators With Wide Experience" on December 4, 1955. My case was written up in the following way:

"A Portland German teacher who was educated in Germany and took her doctorate in French there, including supervised teaching, can't get a state certificate as a high school teacher because she was not graduated from an 'accredited teacher training institution,' as defined by the state department.

"She like a good many others, would not be teaching in Oregon if it were not for the fact that under the law Portland, because of its size, is the one system in the state that can certificate its own teachers. She could go to work here, then make up deficiencies in her credentials for state certification. The 30 hours she has done in extension and at the University of Oregon still hasn't won a certificate."

After my credentials were evaluated by the Oregon State Department of Education, I was required to repeat all education courses that I had taken in Germany. In addition, twelve semester hours in German literature were required, as well as Oregon History and Oregon School Law. It is a fact that I was a native German, attended grade and high school in Germany, hold academic degrees, including a Ph.D. in Romance languages and had spent the first thirty-one years of my life in Germany. I was proud of my background in German literature and, of course, I had a perfect command of the language. What I lacked, however, was university credits in German.

The State Department gave me five years to acquire the prescribed credits. A person with less determination than I might have thrown in the towel, but I was made of better stuff and I was going to prove it! I cannot recall how much time I allowed myself to reach my goal, but it was less than five years. During the summers I was able to accumulate additional credits. As a crowning achievement, I finally attended two successive summer sessions of German literature at the Summer School of the Pacific held at Reed College. Two of my professors, also native Germans, knew me personally and were familiar with my case. They occasionally poked fun at me and seemed to enjoy chauvinistically their superior position, but nothing could deter me from my goal. When I signed up for their course in "Methods of Teaching Foreign Languages" I happened to be the only one enrolled. At our first session, they gleefully exclaimed, "Isn't it wonderful! Now we are finally going to learn how languages are taught in high school." I had signed up, because the State Department of Education had required it, and here they expected me to teach something to them. As a good sport (or a fool?), I went through the motions, just to get the credit needed. After I had met all the requirements, I promptly received my first Oregon Teaching Certificate and eventually tenure.

Some of the best and brightest of my students, 1956.

*The teacher from Germany,
Jefferson High School,
Portland, Oregon, 1956.*

21

On the Road to Self-Sufficiency

The elder Wagners and I had quite a bit in common. All three of us had been born in Germany, came to this country as immigrants and spoke with a German accent. Maybe that was the reason that they treated me like one of their own children, who were about my age. One unmarried daughter still lived at home with her parents. Imagine, two women by the same name of Hildegard - very rare in this country - living under the same roof! That was unusual, indeed.

Frieda Wagner was a typical German housewife, who took excellent care of the household and the family, in which she included me, too. She also was an outstanding cook. I was privileged to eat breakfast and dinner with the family, including Sundays. During the week, I was in school from 8 a.m. through 4:30 p.m. In the evenings, I corrected student papers and tests and prepared my assignments for the following day. There was not much time for conversation. On Saturdays, I often went shopping downtown or went out with my friends. Sundays were quite unusual. All family members were devout Baptists. As a matter of fact, the father, Charles Wagner, had been an ordained Baptist minister until changing to the more lucrative occupation of a house painter. After breakfast on Sunday mornings, the four of us went first to Sunday School and then to the main service. Although I was a Lutheran and would have preferred to attend a church of my own faith, I felt honor bound to worship with the Wagners.

On our return home, the whole house smelled heavenly. In our absence, a succulent pot roast, including vegetables in a casserole, slowly cooked to perfection in the oven. The timing was just right: before leaving for church, Mrs. Wagner put the meat in the oven, set the temperature on low, and presto, the finished product awaited us around one o'clock. She finished a full-course dinner in no time by adding dumplings to the gravy. Dessert, usually pie, prepared ahead on Saturday, gave the finishing touch to a delicious Sunday dinner. In the evening, it was off to church again for the late service.

Never in my life had I spent so much time in church and I am not at all sure that the experience was good for my soul. Frankly, I often felt the need for a little more freedom, especially on Sunday evenings when the time came to prepare my school work for the next day. It seemed unnatural that, at the age of 34, I still lived within a family circle and that I was so closely tied to their routine. I soon suffered a little from an overdose of religion. Moreover, since I had only one room in the house, I was not able to invite friends to reciprocate for their many kindnesses to me.

One day, I met a German woman, a little younger than I, who lived in her own apartment within walking distance from me. She was also an immigrant from Germany. Her name was Friedel and she was anxious for me to see her apartment of which she was justifiably proud. Since both of us worked during the week, Sunday seemed the best day to get together, Sunday morning, to be more specific. I realized that the Wagners would regret my breaking away from their routine, most of all if I did not attend their church anymore. When I told them that I would like to attend a Lutheran church for a change, they understood. Friedel and I were eager to get better acquainted and to talk about our experiences in Germany and our adopted country. So we decided to skip church and spend a few pleasant hours in her apartment. It turned out that she suffered from too much religion too, because she was a minister's daughter. Her father lived in California. This first Sunday morning with Friedel became a comfortable routine for many weeks to come.

Some well-meaning friends assessed my rather confining life with the Wagners and convinced me that the time was ripe to make a change. They introduced me to a lovely couple who had an apartment for rent in the second floor of their very cozy home. It did not take me long to make the decision to move from my one room at the Wagners' to this new place. I shared the kitchen and the bathroom with another woman, but we each had our own room. It constituted an improvement for me insofar as I could now do my own cooking and was free to invite a few friends in on occasion. Mrs. Stella Nelson and her husband were quite hospitable and allowed me to use their dining room whenever I wanted to have guests. They were of

Norwegian descent and Lutherans like myself. We became very close and I enjoyed the freedom that I had, coming and going as I pleased.

Stella invited me to attend Central Lutheran Church nearby, and I gladly accepted. The minister gave outstanding sermons, and I felt so much at home that I decided to join the church choir. We had choir practice every Thursday evening, and I always walked to church, a ten-minute walk. Even then, in 1954, I was warned not to walk at night, although it was still relatively safe. There was no direct bus service between home and church, and I did not own a car yet. Stella was like a mother to me. She grew very fond of me and spoiled me in every way possible by giving me homemade cookies or other goodies, inviting me to meals and even sewing for me on occasion.

One exciting event happened in my life during that time: I became the proud owner of a car! I saw the need for convenient and timesaving transportation but was scared to death learning how to drive. The heavy American traffic really frightened me, but finally one day I decided to shop for a used car. Nobody in the whole United States knew less about cars and what to look for than I did. I went more by appearance than by the quality when I finally chose a nice-looking Studebaker with seating capacity for six. Did I ever feel Americanized!

The car was delivered to the Nelson home and there it stood parked in front of the house because I did not know how to drive it. Neither was I anxious to learn. So it stood there for a few days while I longingly looked at it from my upstairs window. I continued to take the bus to school. This lack of action on my part became ridiculous. After a little while, a very helpful gentleman friend of the family offered to teach me how to drive. I was overjoyed but still fearful. Andy took me out to less-travelled roads and very competently introduced me to the skills of driving. The car had an automatic transmission, so I did not have to learn how to shift gears. Nevertheless, even after a few lessons and a little practical experience, I still felt ignorant and afraid to venture out into the streets. Every time I came to a stop sign I sized up the traffic coming from both directions. Whenever just one car approached the intersection from a distance of 200 yards, I did not have the courage to cross. So it went on and on, until Andy thought I was ready to take the driver's test. But I was still hesitant. One day, he did not say a word, but very adroitly steered me in the direction of the Motor Vehicles Division and asked me to park. He left the car, and I stayed in the driver's seat. To my surprise, he came back with an examiner in tow. I finally realized what was going on. The two gentlemen got into the car. I started driving following the directions of the examiner. It all went very well, until he asked me to park in a small space between two cars. This was difficult for me and I did not do a good job but the examiner remarked that my driving was satisfactory and he would have a license issued, provided I promised to learn how to park. I faithfully gave my promise but today, thirty-four years later, I still cannot park unless I have a lot of room.

Andy was proud of his teaching and my achievement. His parting statement was, "Lady, you are on your own, but never forget that driving is a full-time job." That was good advice, which I was grateful to heed over my long years of driving. The Nelsons welcomed me on my return home and later threw a party to celebrate the occasion. Papa Nelson thought it would be a good idea for me to venture out into heavy traffic the same afternoon, in order to gain even more confidence. This was an excellent idea and, with trepidation, I took the Nelsons over to Union Avenue, a very busy thoroughfare, to practice my driving skills a little more.

My vehicle seemed in good shape when I bought it from a used-car dealer. It had only 32,000 miles on it. However, after a while, I was concerned that someone had taken advantage of me and possibly turned back the odometer. I cannot remember all the details of the many troubles the car gave me, but it seemed to be in the repair shop longer than I was able to use it. Nevertheless, I kept it for three years.

In 1958, the Nelsons felt that their home was too much of a responsibility to keep up and decided to sell it. The "For Sale" sign on the front lawn and the prospect of having to leave the hospitable home almost broke my heart. Just the same, I faced reality and started to look for another apartment, this time much closer to school. I moved into my own apartment before school started in the fall.

For five years, I had enjoyed the companionship of three different but nurturing families. While living with other people, as kind and gracious as they were, I subordinated my own wishes to their family routine. However, at the same time I was appreciative of their moral support. Now I was wondering how I would fare when living on my own. Any doubts I might have harbored were soon dispelled. I was ready to enjoy my independence and unlimited freedom.

My "declaration of independence" and naturalization happened within a matter of two weeks. For five years, I had been waiting for 1958 to roll around. Five long years was the waiting period for foreigners, before they could apply for U.S. citizenship. In preparation for this significant event, applicants could attend a formal course which, free of charge, was offered by the Immigration and Naturalization Service to applicants who wanted to prepare themselves for the examination required of prospective U.S. citizens. The course covered American history and taught the structure and functions of the government. I attended a couple of times, but soon found out that the course was geared mostly to the needs of those who still had language difficulties. I concluded that I would be able to study on my own by utilizing the reading material distributed by the instructor, as well as by additional recommended reading. As it turned out, I was indeed well prepared for the test and had no difficulty responding to the questions posed by the examiner.

One of the most impressive events in my life happened to me at 10 a.m. on September 4, 1958, when I was sworn in as a U.S. citizen. It was the time when the new school year was just about to start, and the faculty was assembled for its first meeting. I informed the principal ahead of time that I would not be able to attend. Instead, I drove my own car, in true American fashion, to the naturalization ceremony in downtown Portland. There I joined 139 other happy and lucky aliens from thirty-six different countries to be sworn in. Little did I realize at the time that the man whom I had the good fortune to meet later and marry in 1965 also became a U.S. citizen in the very same ceremony but I did not know him until 1960.

Did I feel different when it was over? Happy and elated, certainly, but not different, at least with respect to my native country, which I continued to love. Just as we may have a place for many people in our hearts, we can also love two countries. I find it easy to live with loyalties to both countries, but difficult to measure one against the other.

After the ceremony, I walked back to my car, a proud and happy citizen of the United States of America. I checked the time, hoping that the faculty meeting would not be over yet because I was so anxious to share my happiness with my faculty friends. Sure enough, my wish came true. I threw the door wide open and greeted the faculty and administration with a victorious smile on my face. They responded by giving me a standing ovation.

On February 22, 1959, the Portland Americanization Council welcomed new citizens with a public reception in the Portland Public Auditorium. The date, the 227th anniversary of George Washington's birthday, was appropriate. The mayor of Portland, Terry D. Schrunk, gave a speech in our honor and Mark O. Hatfield, then Governor of Oregon, shook hands with each and every one of us. It was another memorable day and my spirits soared, as I chatted with my fellow citizens.

After coming down to earth again, I faced the challenge of an empty apartment. The kitchen was in good shape because I already owned dishes, pots, pans and all kinds of kitchen utensils, but the living room and bedroom stared at me accusingly. My previous accommodations had been completely furnished. Now I did not even own a bed! A friend of mine loaned me a cot on which to rest my weary bones at night.

The thought of putting to good use the money I had saved over a period of five years was exciting. I even invested in a piano to replace the cherished one I had to leave behind in Germany. Certainly I knew nothing about buying furniture, but I felt much more confident and more sophisticated as a shopper than I did when I first went grocery shopping about five years previously.

In Germany, cash was used for all purchases and credit cards were almost unknown. A German proverb that everybody believed in was *"Borgen macht Sorgen"* (Borrowing brings sorrows). Germans never made it a practice to go into debts and they scrupulously lived within their means.

After my arrival in this country, I always paid cash for all my purchases. Now that I needed to buy quite a few items, I thought it would be convenient to establish a credit rating. Endowed with tremendous self-discipline and will power, I trusted myself not to overspend, even if I had credit cards. I made an effort to become more Americanized step by step. When I planned to buy a record player for $94.95 at Meier and Frank's department store I did not take my check book or enough cash along, in order to make myself acquire a credit card. But how do you go about taking the first step? Obviously, somebody had to trust me. I told my story to the salesman at Meier and Frank's, who very efficiently had me fill out an application form. The purchase of the record player had to wait a few days till the application was approved. But I was used to waiting!

Since then, I have acquired a few more credit cards. They have come in handy at times, but I never allow myself to buy anything that is beyond my means. I have bought several cars - cash only, to the amazement of the car dealers. The biggest purchase which my husband and I made was a home in McMinnville for which we took out a loan from Linfield College at five percent interest. Even at this low rate we paid back the full amount as soon as we had saved up the money, instead of making monthly payments. Actually, it might have been wiser not to pay up so quickly, but we both felt more comfortable without a mortgage hanging over our heads.

Spending money was so much fun - would this Americanization process ever stop? - that I decided to buy my first new car, a Rambler American, bright red "like a fire engine", as my prospective husband used to say. But I am getting way ahead of myself! I was already forty years old and still unmarried. There were a couple of reasons for this. During World War II, all young German men were drafted and millions of them killed, so that the number of returning men had considerably dwindled, and millions of young women had to go without a husband. Furthermore, it was not customary for a woman to have a family and pursue a career. Growing up under extreme parental pressure to succeed academically, I did what was expected of me, and so career took precedence over marriage and a family.

But despite all those plans, I would not have hesitated to shock my parents and relatives by getting married and giving up my career, if the right man had come along. In my younger years, I fell madly in love with two young men but marriage did not materialize. This sounds unbelievable nowadays, but the main reason for not getting married to either one of them was that they were Catholics and I was Lutheran. Most Germans were either Lutherans or Catholics. The Lutherans led the Catholics in numbers, a fact that is understandable, considering that Luther, who founded the religion named after him by breaking away from the tenets of the Catholic Church, exercised a considerable influence on his countrymen.

Should religion be allowed to come between two young people who seriously and sincerely love each other? Certainly not! Nevertheless, marrying within one's faith was considered a prerequisite for marriage and an almost automatic guarantee for happiness. Catholics especially were adamant about marrying a partner of the same faith, and I must say that parents exercised a big role in approving or disapproving a future marriage partner. When a Catholic displayed enough courage to disregard parents' disapproval, the Catholic Church stepped in and insisted that children resulting from the marriage be raised in the Catholic faith. This was deeply resented by Lutheran church officials, who feared that they would eventually lose their following to their Catholic rivals.

But love would find a way to bring a wonderful man and exquisite happiness to my life, and although our time together would be short, if measured in terms of fulfillment and bliss, we reached eternity.

I am the proud owner of my first car, a 1958 Studebaker!

22

Max - Love and Marriage

Despite all odds, I never gave up hope that I would eventually meet a Lutheran partner. Little did I realize that he would enter my life in the United States rather than in Germany. One day in 1960, I received an invitation for dinner from a German family in Portland. Their name was Heinz and Margaret Nowak. That particular day, March 6, was meant to be another milestone in my life. One of the other guests was an extremely good-looking, tall German gentleman, whom I took a fancy to right away. However, I was puzzled by his strange ways of moving about with his camera and taking pictures of me from all directions. Who was he, a Hollywood movie producer who wanted to hire me for the next film because of my good looks? Then, when it was time to go home, he decided to leave with me. He asked where my car was parked and after escorting me there, gently took my car key out of my hand, opened the door for me, and bade me good-bye as we parted. I was impressed by his gentlemanly ways, but did not give it much further thought.

The next day, he called to ask me to go to a symphony concert with him. I did not know what possessed me, but I told him that I had tests to correct for the next day, which was absolutely true. Never was there a more dedicated (or foolish?) teacher than I, or so it seemed. In the course of our conversation, I informed him that I had planned a trip to the San Francisco area the following Friday, to visit some friends during my spring vacation. After two days, a small package arrived by mail with a few rolls of film to take along on my vacation. I was impressed by this token of thoughtfulness.

Grace and Marian took me to the Union Station in Portland to catch the train. I had told them about my new acquaintance, and they seemed very interested. As we stood there on the platform, Max Reinhold Kurz appeared out of nowhere. I said to my friends, "There he is!" After introducing everybody it was time for me to board the train. To my astonishment, he followed me into the compartment. First I thought he had decided to accompany me on my trip, but any such thought was just wishful thinking and completely ridiculous. I sat down in my reserved seat, not knowing what to make of the situation, when suddenly he placed a box of chocolates and a magazine into my lap and kissed me for the first time!!! I had hardly time to thank him for the gifts because the train was just about to depart. As the train began to roll, he jumped off, leaving me completely flabbergasted and overwhelmed with joy, happiness and a feeling of sadness for having to leave him now, even though only temporarily.

When Germans do something they do it thoroughly and I was thoroughly in love with the man. Why, oh why, did I have to leave him now? One week of vacation lay ahead of me, but oh, so far away from him! My friends in the Bay area showed me a wonderful time, but nothing seemed to matter to me. I did not hear from Max for more than a week, an eternity for me, because he did not know the name or the telephone number of my friends. His phone number was in my wallet, but I could not possibly have called him. As an old-fashioned gentleman he would have frowned on this, because a well-bred lady should not take the initiative and call a gentleman first. The initiative lay strictly in the hands of the man. How customs have changed in just three decades!

At night, I would lie awake thinking of this wonderful man. I simply could not sleep and so I spent the night listening to a radio station which broadcast nothing but love songs! The week seemed to go by so slowly!

Finally, the time came for me to take the train back to Portland. I left Oakland on Saturday at 4:30 p.m., sat up all night and arrived in Portland at 8:30 a.m. Sunday, dead-tired, got off the train, and - to my complete amazement - Max waited for me with a bouquet of twelve roses to take me home, or so I thought, at least. Not so - he insisted on taking me to breakfast at Rose's restaurant, a venerable delicatessen in northwest Portland.

It was all so romantic! After breakfast, he took me home so I could get some rest, but reminded me that he would be back by 3 p.m. to take me for a ride to the Columbia Gorge. After losing a whole night's sleep, I needed to sleep for hours on end, but the prospect of seeing Max again gave me the inspiration to get up in time. The love of a man of the caliber of Max against the backdrop of the beautiful Columbia River Gorge was almost impossible to bear.

This was the beginning of a loving and most beautiful relationship. He was certainly worth waiting for and he was Lutheran! I was on cloud nine! We kept seeing each other as often as we could and, like all lovers since Alexander Graham Bell, we called one another every evening to talk for hours on end.

I had never been so totally in love, but nothing is perfect in this world. At times, Max was still grieving over the death of his wife, who had died sixteen months earlier. I tried to help him overcome his grief as best I knew how. I understood what was going on in his mind. According to German custom, it was inappropriate to date again soon after the death of a spouse. Another one of those German societal quirks: it just was not done! But how long a waiting period was enough to satisfy the expectations of your fellow men, who had no business judging your private life by their unreasonable standards?

Max was a conservative German, holding more to the traditional German values than I, who was more willing to make a changeover to American customs and habits. After all, we now lived in American society, and it seemed only fair and justified to embrace different values. Strangely enough, I recognized his desire to conform to tradition as a holdover from the Nazi times. These were not the only differences between the two of us. Others involved discrepancies in education and age, which Max felt deeply about, but which were meaningless to me. In my opinion, our love was so strong that it would overcome all obstacles. The ancient Romans used to say, *"Amor vincit omnia"* (Love conquers everything), and I think that is true. Although we loved and enjoyed each other thoroughly, marriage was not in the picture for a long time. We spent all weekends together. Max was great at planning various activities. I liked to be surprised but I never knew what occasion to dress for. It happened that we went hiking, with me being dressed as if I were going to a concert and, vice versa, sometimes I was dressed casually when we attended a theatrical performance.

One very hot summer evening, Max took me out for a ride. Again he did not say where we were going. I was dressed in a casual sleeveless dress, was not wearing nylons and, to put it mildly, I glowed all over. Max kept on driving, destination unknown to me. We finally ended up on Council Crest Drive in Portland, where he stopped in front of an attractive home. What was I getting into? He rang the doorbell, and we were greeted by his brother and sister-in-law, Karl and Pauline Kurz. This was the fist time I met any of his relatives. The idea of moving one step closer to them appealed to me for obvious reasons. But I was so ashamed of my sloppy appearance. Fretting over matters of little significance was another typically German habit that I had to learn to drop. Karl and Pauline made me feel relaxed. We sat on the balcony in the back of their lovely home, refreshed ourselves with ice-cold soft drinks, and enjoyed the breathtaking view overlooking much of Portland, as well as Mt. Hood, Mt. Adams, Mt. St. Helens and Mt. Rainier.

On weekends, we usually drove to the beach, Mt. Hood, or Central Oregon. Max never ran out of surprises. He really spoiled me! I missed him badly during the week and could hardly wait to see him again. Sometimes we met on weekdays, too, mostly on Wednesdays, when we went out to eat or to shop downtown. It was a very fulfilling life for me and lots of fun. The more we saw each other the more I wished we would get married but that was a long time in coming. Unfortunately, Max acquired various health problems, which worried me no end.

Another important date that sticks to my mind because of its psychological impact was December 3, 1962. It was three days after my 43rd birthday. Max had visited me in my apartment to celebrate the occasion. We had dinner together, and he left for home around 9 p.m. It was a blustery evening, and I aired the apartment by opening front and back doors, with screen doors locked. I was in the kitchen washing the dishes when suddenly I heard a rattling noise, which made me think that I had better close the doors. The light was on in the kitchen but not in the living room. As I walked to the front door, a man came from the bedroom towards me. Since it was dark, I was not able to make out details of his appearance. All I could see was a tall man with a coat on and wearing a hat. I was so frightened that I ran out of the front door to alert my neighbors, but was unable to scream. It was probably wrong to leave the apartment but all I could think of was my safety. My flight gave the thief a chance to search all my belongings thoroughly. I ran over to my next-door neighbor but she was already in bed and did not answer the door. Then I dashed across the street to ask some other neighbors to let me call the police. As I stood there at their front door waiting to be let into the house, I saw the burglar leave my apartment with his loot. I did not enter my place until the police arrived. The two policemen questioned me about details of the burglary, but I knew so little and could be of no help. The burglar had stolen my genuine German jewelry of gold and silver - Germans did not believe in wearing costume jewelry - my parents' wedding rings, my wallet containing about $100, credit cards, driver's license and, strangely enough, a large fancy bottle of Eau de Cologne.

While I was over at the neighbors' to call the police, Max tried to phone, as he always did to tell me that he had arrived at home safe and sound. When he did not receive an answer, he was afraid that something might have happened to me. So he decided to drive back to my place, all the way across town. When he saw the police car in front of my apartment, he did not know what to make of the situation. Exercising his German reserve - do not interfere with other people's affairs if it is none of your business - he did not think it was up to him to get involved. He drove home again, and it was not until much later that I collected my wits to tell him all about the burglary. Frightened, I spent that night with a neighbor in her apartment.

The police were never able to find the thief and retrieve my lost items. However, I could not dismiss the idea that I had been singled out by a student of mine as a potentially "rich" woman. He was later arrested for a burglary in my neighborhood, where he had stolen the same type of things that were missing from my apartment. A few days later, I received in the mail my wallet minus the money and credit cards. It had been found at the school grounds of Ockley Green grade school, only two blocks from my apartment.

The remainder of my stay in that apartment was miserable. I was afraid to go to sleep and every time I walked through the living room I conjured the thief, over and over again. In order to restore my peace of mind, I decided to move into a large highrise apartment building, where a desk clerk monitored every person who entered the lobby after a certain hour in the evening. The new apartment was much more expensive than the previous one and it was far away from school. The only mitigating factor was its closer location to Max's home. When I first moved into the building, I did not realize that I would live there only from January through the middle of August 1963.

The year 1963 brought about another important event in my life. I had taught at Jefferson High for ten years. Every few years, high school classes were evaluated by college and university professors. Early in 1963, a professor of German, Dr. Helen Emerson from Linfield College, visited my classes and evaluated my teaching. The reports must have been good because, after some time, I received a letter from W. W. Dolan, Dean of Faculty at Linfield College. He asked me if I would be interested in a teaching job at Linfield. Previously, some of my friends and fellow teachers at Jefferson had asked me why, with a Ph.D., I did not teach at a college or university.

I had never before contemplated teaching college, due in large part to my German background. It was true that I held a Ph.D., as about 60 percent of German high school teachers do. In order to teach at a German university, a candidate had to pursue three more years of academic work beyond the Ph.D. For that reason, I did not consider myself qualified to teach at the college level. I simply lacked self-confidence to think that I would be able to carry it out.

Now there seemed to be an opportunity to accept a great challenge. The very thought of holding an academic job in this country beyond my reach in Germany without additional study intrigued me. This is indeed the "land of unlimited opportunities" as we referred to it in my own country!

At Linfield's invitation, I was allowed to observe a few courses to get a feel for college teaching in this country. I was grateful for the opportunity. The experience almost felt like a reprise of my student days at the University of Oregon, which I had enjoyed so much, with the only difference that I was no longer a student. Helen Emerson took me on a tour of the campus and its facilities and introduced me to a few people on the way. Somehow I felt very much at home on the campus. When Helen invited me for coffee and a doughnut, that did it to me! Little things mean a lot, especially for somone who had come from the rigidities of German society.

Linfield College is a Baptist institution with ties to the American Baptist Church. Somehow I liked the idea that religion constituted an integral part of campus life. Helen explained the role of religion at the college as we sat down for a few minutes in the chapel and observed a short period of silence away from the hustle and bustle of the rest of the campus. I sensed a comforting and soothing feeling coming over me. At Jefferson, a public high school, the very mention of religion was taboo. On one occasion, I was reprimanded by the vice principal for allowing the father of two of my students to speak to one of my German classes. He had indicated that he would be speaking about growing up in Austria. Instead, he exclusively talked about the Jehovah Witnesses Church, of which he was a member.

I thought this rather strange, but did not take it too seriously because I was not accustomed to the practical implications of separating church and state and, as an educator, I regarded information on comparative religions as interesting and informative. But even my best friends told me in no uncertain terms that I had committed a *faux pas* which was not to be repeated under any circumstances.

At Linfield I felt a spiritual atmosphere surrounding me and I must admit I liked it. Maybe it was not so surprising because I grew up with thirteen years of religious instruction in school and I attended church every Sunday at the request of my parents. When I met Max, I became more profoundly and sincerely immersed in spiritual matters, especially when the two of us attended church every Sunday. He was a deeply religious man, whereas I was still more or less groping, in an attempt to establish my faith as a stabilizing factor in my life. I speculated that, perhaps, teaching at Linfield would help me overcome my last doubts.

I was interviewed by Dr. Paul Gebauer, professor of German, Dr. Carle Malone, the head of the Modern Language Department (unmarried and a Lutheran - I could not resist the temptation to mention these two facts), Dr. W. W. Dolan, Dean of Faculty, and Dr. Harry Dillin, the President. Interviewing with these men was a heady experience. In Germany, we were trained to show deep respect for authority, a habit which to this day I have not been able to shed completely, although I am working on it. Yet here I was, a lowly immigrant, (self-effacement is another German characteristic, for the individual, if not for the nation!) introduced to and talking casually with people so far above me! I almost felt like a VIP myself! After the interview, Win Dolan (note that I dropped the Dr. in front of his name!) asked me to consider accepting the teaching position at Linfield. To my knowledge, no committee decision had to be made and hiring seemed to be in the hands of the administration and the language department chairman.

I drove back to Portland, pondering the implications of changing positions. The idea of giving up my roots in Portland and living so far away from a wonderful group of friends was disconcerting to me. The thought of thirty-eight miles separating me from my beloved Max was devastating. Furthermore, what if I did not enjoy college teaching as much as I did teaching at Jefferson High? The latter doubt was quickly dispersed when the office of the Superintendent of Portland Public Schools graciously granted me a one-year leave of absence from my job with the option of returning to Jeff, in case matters did not work out at Linfield, or if I did not like living in McMinnville, which at the time had a population of only 8,000. Indeed, I had some reservations about living in such a small town, which was by far the smallest of all cities I had ever resided in. Besides, I wanted so badly to live where Max was.

Perhaps Max would discourage me from moving away from him. Oh no, no such thing happened! As a matter of fact, he strongly encouraged me to accept the job offer, which was in line with his previous assertion that he did not ever want to stand in my way, if and when time came to further my career.

How could I make a rational decision amidst all this emotional turmoil? Here he came to my help again. In his sweet gentle ways, so reminiscent of my father's treatment of me, he laid out his plans about continuing to date me and visit me in McMinnville, as he had done so far in my apartment in Portland. He succeeded in convincing me that our relationship would not fall apart because of distance. After all, "Absence makes the heart grow fonder."

Since I had the assurance that I could move back into my job at Jefferson after a year, I decided to give Linfield a try. After all these deliberations, I sent my letter of acceptance to the Dean's Office. I received a warm letter of welcome after a few days. To prove again that Latin is not a dead language, at least to me, I want to apply an appropriate proverb, "*Alea iacta est*" (The die has been cast).

The response of the Jefferson faculty to my transfer to Linfield College was overwhelming. I received many notes of sincere admiration, encouragement and best wishes for the future. The number of parties in my honor exceeded those which originally welcomed me into the Jefferson family. In a way, I felt sad to have to leave all those lovely friends, but on the other hand the parting was sweet, and, after all, Portland was only 38 miles away.

One afternoon, upon returning to my apartment, the desk clerk greeted me with obvious excitement, "Have you seen your picture in the paper?" No, I had not. So he opened *The Oregonian* and showed me my picture accompanied by a description of my background under the heading "Post Filled at Linfield." I was puzzled because I knew *The Oregonian* had not taken my picture or interviewed me. Later I learned that the newspaper obtained my picture and pertinent information from the Public Relations Office of Linfield College. Aren't American practices wonderful?

Moving to McMinnville was an easy matter. It was my fifth move in eight years and I had acquired some expertise. The Mayflower moving company took care of the smallest detail. Renting an apartment in town was done in one day with the assistance of Mr. Elliott, the owner of Pioneer Real Estate, whose wife Virginia taught music at Linfield. From the beginning, I was in good hands and well taken care of. At Mr. Elliott's recommendation, I rented a very nice court apartment on South Baker Street and there made my first friends, who also lived in the small court. They were Edith Reynolds and Sybil Seward, better known as Duffy and Tex. Duffy was a professor in the Linfield Home Economics Department and Tex taught grade school in Dayton. The very first Sunday in McMinnville, Carle Malone, head of the Language Department, invited me to attend a Lutheran church with him. We arrived in the nick of time just before the service was about to begin. The church was pretty much filled with only two rows unoccupied, the one in front and the one in the back. Carle had a hearing difficulty and he decided in favor of the front row. All the worshipers had their eyes on us, so it seemed at least, as I walked down the aisle with Carle. I felt a little embarrassed, but was I again overreacting in my German way?

Max and I developed a certain *Schlachtenplan* (battle plan) for our weekend activities. We agreed that he would visit me on Saturdays and I would drive to Portland to spend Sundays with him. Note that we each returned to our own abode in the evening. Staying together overnight without being married was unthinkable at the time, at least to two ultra-conservative Germans, I less so than he! Besides, as an educator, one had to set a good example at all times, When I was first hired at Linfield, I was asked two personal questions which made me think that emphasis was placed on good morals, " What is your church affiliation?" and " Do you drink alcohol? "

I still was not fully convinced that I had made the right decision in accepting the Linfield position and move away from Max. My hope of getting married to him was completely shattered. Which man, I asked myself, would let a woman move away, if he intended to marry her? He owned a beautiful home in the southwest area of Portland. Why should I have to live in a rented apartment if I could have been his wife and the mistress of his home?

At least in my imagination, we might drift apart. Max had always loved me from the bottom of his heart, but he could not come to grips with the difference in our education. Like so many bright

Germans, he worked his way from the bottom up and was trained on the job at the Robert Bosch Company in Stuttgart. Later he worked as a tool and die maker for Mercedes-Benz. When he came to this country he took a similar job at Sawyer's, Inc., in Progress, Oregon. In addition, he worked as a research engineer in the photography department of the company. When he explained to me the challenges of his work I could have listened for hours. I admired him for his unusual intellect and his wide range of technical experiences. In my way of thinking he had the makings of a potential Nobel Prize winner.

In addition to his technical training, Max was well-read and extremely interested in a great number of subjects. To me he was the most intelligent man I had ever met. What he lacked, however, was a college education. He may never have been more aware of this until he met me. I did not see things that way at all. Max was a self-made man and the discrepancy in our education did not matter to me in the least. I did not even think of it. But have you ever tried to change a German's mind after it was made up? It is next to impossible! The teaching job at Linfield was a step up in my career. Deep down in his heart he admired me, but he lacked confidence that we would be compatible once we got married.

When I moved to McMinnville, we faithfully followed our *Schlachtenplan*, and we called each other almost every evening. Our telephone bills were outrageously high, but it was all worth it. Would it go on like that indefinitely? I was afraid so. As happy as I was in the relationship, I found it quite stressful. I almost gave up hope.

Our relationship went on like this for another year and a half, until one day in January, 1965, when I visited Max in Portland. He always enjoyed surprising me. This time he really swept me off my feet. To my complete surprise, he proposed to me. Words cannot describe my happiness. It happened to be January 30, 1965, a day which, during the Hitler regime, was celebrated as the anniversary of Hitler's ascent to power, *Machtübernahme*, as we called it. Max and I jokingly asked each other, "Which one of us is going to exercise power over the other?" We both could not believe that we would finally tie the knot. In the evening, Max took me out to Rose's, by now our favorite restaurant. Afterwards we went to see Pauline and Karl and celebrated our engagement with a bottle of red champagne.

At that time, Linfield was between semesters, and I had two days off plus the weekend. I needed the time to get adjusted to my new situation. Setting the date for the wedding was an easy matter. I suggested March 6, the anniversary of our first meeting. This day proved to be inconvenient because it was in the middle of the semester, so we decided on April 10, a Saturday followed by a week of Linfield's pre-Easter vacation.

We arranged to be married in the First Baptist Church in Portland in the presence of six of Max's relatives and some of my closest friends. Neither Max nor I wanted an ostentatious wedding. The reception took place at Karl and Pauline's home. The next day, Max and I left on our honeymoon to the Oregon coast, which we both loved so much. The Linfield spring semester started the following week. I moved to Max's home in Portland, which meant commuting between Portland and McMinnville.

Commuting was not a big problem to me because I like to drive. What I did not like was the fact that I had to get up at 5:15 to prepare breakfast and to be in McMinnville for my 7:40 class. Max never liked the idea of my doing so much driving, because he reasoned that, the more I drove, the more likely I would be involved in an accident. Good practical thinking, to be sure, but I kept on driving till the beginning of December, when it started to snow and traveling became hazardous. Max decided that we had better move to McMinnville to spare me the driving. He acted quickly and put his home up for sale. We bought a home in McMinnville and moved in before Christmas, 1965. Now it was Max who commuted, and I worried about him. Fortunately, he and a gentleman who also worked at Sawyer's took turns driving.

We soon settled down like an "old couple." Max was happy to meet my colleagues and their families. I made it a point to give frequent dinner parties, because he did not have any friends in McMinnville yet and I wanted him to get to meet as many people as possible within a minimum amount of time. He was a very gregarious person and had no difficulty getting acquainted and making new friends. I was so very proud of him! We had such good times together. I enjoyed cooking for him, especially those German meals which he had not eaten since the death of his first wife. For the first time in my life, I had a house of my own and a yard in which we grew plants, plenty of flowers and some vegetables. Life could not have been more rewarding.

Unfortunately, our happiness was marred by Max's illness. The physician, who treated him, did not seem overly concerned at first. The problem was not diagnosed for a long time. Max was able to go to work in spite of his feeling not too well at times. As the illness progressed, it was diagnosed as a rare blood disease, which had to be treated with occasional isotopes. But the treatment was only temporarily successful. Once in a while, the physician removed a pint of blood. Both of these measures did not produce lasting effects. When we celebrated Christmas in 1966, I had a terrible premonition that it would be our last Christmas together. Max was now no longer able to work. He had to see a blood specialist frequently and spent a few days in the hospital, off and on. His condition was diagnosed as polycythemia vera, which led to a stroke at the end of March. Max died on April 4, 1967 in the McMinnville hospital. To me, it was just like the sun going down, never to rise again.

My grief was overwhelming, but my work at the college helped to distract my mind. Time heals all wounds, but in my case it took a long, long time. I now feel that Max's love will always be with me and I have derived much comfort and strength from the most wonderful man I ever knew. At his funeral, a friend of mine told me that I had received more love in the short years of our courtship and marriage than many women ever get in a lifetime - and I fully believe that.

Max Reinhold Kurz, my idol and beloved husband, 1958.

23

College Teaching - Upward and Onward

    I taught German and French at Linfield. To my dismay, Latin, my third expertise, was not offered. Three years later, I took on an overload in French after Dr. Carle Malone unexpectedly died of a heart attack in the middle of September, 1966. Dr. Paul Gebauer and I worked diligently to increase the German enrollment. When we had reached our goal, my full teaching load was in German, which I enjoyed tremendously. I was able to give my students infinitely more of my native language and I could draw more fully on my rich experience in German culture, civilization and modern history.

    I very much enjoyed teaching on the college level for various reasons. First of all, the students were more advanced and goal-oriented than my high school students. I was able to communicate with them on a much more mature level than at Jefferson High. I also appreciated the fact that they frequently came to me during office hours, not only to discuss their progress, or lack of it, but also to confide in me about their personal problems. In high school, teachers did not have office hours because most of their time was devoted to classroom teaching. The only time we were able to communicate with high school students on a personal basis was after school hours. That was the reason why students went to the counselor when they were in need of discussing personal matters.

    While teaching high school, so much of the teaching material I had accumulated while studying at the university lay dormant and submerged in my mind. Now I could use it! A lower teaching load enabled me to prepare my lessons with greater diligence and sophistication. There was also a better chance to continue furthering my education by reading more extensively in German literature, attend courses in other disciplines and evening lectures, as well as cultural events at the college. It was so gratifying to branch out and expand my horizon and interests. Not only were there fewer courses to be taught, but the average number of students in each class was lower than in high school. The less-structured time schedule gave me more time to get better acquainted with my colleagues and engage in discussions of mutual interest. In high school, on the other hand, I was confined to the classroom from 8:15 in the morning till 3:15 p.m. with the exception of thirty-four minutes for lunch.

I also appreciated the academic freedom I enjoyed as a college professor. The choice of subject matter and special emphases was entirely in my hands. The same was true of textbooks. In high school I had no choice of textbooks at all, but had to accept the decision made by a city-wide Textbook Selection Committee, which chose and recommended different textbooks to be adopted by all city schools every four or five years.

During my tenure at Linfield, the Language Department initiated a special requirement of a one-year study abroad for all language majors. The purpose of this was to give students an even better chance to learn the language because they could hear it and were forced to speak it on a twenty-four hour basis. Furthermore, our students abroad were exposed to customs, culture and civilization of the foreign nation whose language they studied. This study abroad was required during the junior year.

Not all language majors chose teaching as a career, but I especially enjoyed those preparing for the teaching profession. I was in charge of teaching them the German language, civilization, literature and some history. In addition, I taught the course in Methods of Teaching Foreign Languages, not only to my German students, but also to prospective teachers of French and Spanish. After these students had fulfilled the requirements in the subject matter and the education courses, I cooperated with the Education Department in finding competent high school teachers, who were willing to serve as supervising teachers for our students. This involved a visitation once a week to the school to which our students were assigned. The purpose of the visitation was to observe student teachers in action, follow their progress and discuss problem areas with them and their supervising teachers. This task, which usually involved only a very small number of students, was especially time-consuming but also most challenging and gratifying.

In addition to my teaching duties and related responsibilities, I was engaged in many additional activities at Linfield. I served on numerous committees over the years and as head of the Language Department from 1967 to 1970 and again from 1973 to 1976. Along with my colleagues, I travelled all over the state of Oregon to attend annual state-wide foreign language teaching conferences as well as additional meetings of the Pacific Northwest Conference on Foreign Languages.

I periodically spoke to various groups of students about my many experiences under the Hitler regime and during World War II. This involved especially students who were enrolled in courses on German history. Sometimes I was interviewed by a staff member of the Linfield student paper, the *Linews*, about my life in Germany and my travel experiences in Europe.

Under my leadership, the Language Department initiated the Language Tables in French, German and Spanish. Once a week, interested students gathered for lunch with the intention of speaking a foreign language exclusively for one hour. These meetings are still going strong after at least twenty years of existence, and now also include Japanese and Chinese.

I was especially proud of my participation in the inter-semester conference "Man and the Land: Humanities Perspectives," which met on the campus January 13 to 15, 1972. It was attended by approximately 500 participants. Various speakers from Linfield and other colleges and universities throughout Oregon presented topics for discussion at the conference. My topic was *"Blut und Boden"* (Blood and Soil): Slogan and Reality in German Culture." My esteemed colleague, Dr. Vincil Jacobs, spoke about "Land, Peasants, and Proprietors on the Eve of the French Revolution." The two of us were subsequently invited to appear on KOAP-TV for a discussion of our topics and to present a slide show to illustrate our presentation.

Another honor came my way in 1975, when I was awarded a scholarship stipend to attend a summer seminar on "German Literary Existentialism" at the University of Minnesota. Sponsored by the National Endowment for the Humanities, a major emphasis of the seminar was on the relationship between literature and philosophy and the approaches of each discipline to fundamental life problems. I was especially proud of the fact that I was one of only twelve recipients from across the United States who were chosen on the basis of "their quality and commitment as college teachers; their qualifications to do the work of the seminar and make a contribution to it, and the conceptions, definition, and organization of their proposed programs of personal study."

The seminar lasted from June 17 through August 7, 1975. The scholarship took care of all my expenses, including transportation, room and board, numerous required books, plus a generous amount of spending money. I lived on campus in Centennial Hall. This was one of the few dormitories without air conditioning, and did I ever suffer in the hot and humid Minnesota summer! The professor in charge of the seminar was Dr. Leo Duroche, whose books on German literature I had read and used in my literature courses. We met as a group on a regular basis with sufficient time for preparation for the next discussion and for independent study. Each of us was assigned a specific topic on which we did our own research, and we then met individually with Professor Duroche to discuss our findings with him.

The concentrated nature of our studies helped me tremendously to enrich my courses in German literature. At times, I found some of the participants a little intimidating because they held a Ph.D. in German Literature, whereas mine was in French. I made up for it by studying diligently for long hours into the night.

The NEH seminar enabled us to attend cultural events offered by the university and the city of Minneapolis, especially concerts and theatrical performances. Minneapolis is a big city, and it was hard to get around without a car. Fortunately, the bus system proved to be quite efficient. In spite of the murderous heat, I did a lot of walking. This was especially necessary to get around on the huge campus. It took me twenty-five minutes to walk from my dormitory to the air-conditioned comfort of the library. I spent a lot of time there because of the air conditioning and did not go back to my room until late at night because the heat there was intolerable.

But all good things (even those not so good) have to come to an end. On the way home, I took the southern route back to Portland to visit my in-laws in the Los Angeles area. I marveled at the policy of airlines and railroad companies which allowed customers to choose their own travel route without extra charge.

All foreign language teachers periodically feel the need to travel abroad to study language in its native setting, where they can ferret out neologisms and changes in grammar, vocabulary and customs. I went back to Germany for that reason but also to keep in touch with my relatives.

Visiting with my relatives again after such a long absence aroused mixed feelings within me, and I am convinced they felt the same way about me. We were happy to see each other again, but there still seemed to be resentment in their hearts and guilt feelings in me. Most of my relatives had opposed my earlier decision to emigrate to the United States. Once an aunt of mine took a Bible passage out of context and applied it to my situation, *"Was hülfe es dem Menschen, wenn er die ganze Welt gewönne and nähme doch Schaden an seiner Seele?"* [For what shall it profit a man if he shall gain the whole world and lose his own soul? (St. Matthew, chapter 16, verse 26)].

In every letter that I received in the United States from Germany, my relatives asked me the same question, *"Wann kommst Du wieder heim?"* (When are you coming home again?). I was the youngest child among my cousins, and somehow my aunts and uncles took it upon themselves to look after me, even after I had become an adult, and they never learned to let go. Now that I am approaching the final stage of my life, the question has changed to *"Willst Du nicht lieber bei uns wohnen?"* (Wouldn't you rather live with us?) - the implication being, "Wouldn't you rather be buried on German soil?" Being buried on foreign grounds used to be considered a disgrace and becoming only to German soldiers who had died in battle.

Although I could not understand my relatives' attitude towards me, I somehow feel that I have let them down. In this country, individuals have the right to shape and live their own lives as they see fit, provided they live within the law. Separating from the family and striking out on your own is never easy, but it is a natural occurrence. No matter how much the family hurts when the separation happens, such a decision should not be followed by accusations. My relatives could never get used to my referring to this country as "home." Home in their eyes continued to be Germany, not the United States.

In spite of all these disagreements and squabbles, my relatives always treated me with a certain admiration - or was it envy? German families with relatives in the United States refer to them by *die Tante* or *der Onkel in Amerika* (the aunt or uncle in America), who were looked upon as somewhat odd, but who were willing to help out those left behind when they got into a pinch. This view helped put German expatriates in a superior position. My relatives eagerly introduced me to their children, some of whom had been born after I left Germany, as *die Tante aus Amerika*. German children in general are much more shy and reserved than their American counterparts and easily intimidated. Although I relate well to American children and they like me - or at least talk to me - I had difficulty getting a few words out of those German children, even though I spoke to them in a friendly way and in their own language. Some of them did not even have the courage to bring a brief *dankeschön* over their lips when I brought them a gift. All I got out of them was a stare filled with curiosity. Some of them did not even speak to me without the encouragement on the part of their parents. I sometimes wondered what kind of bizarre stories their parents had told them about me. Maybe it is a good thing not to know!

During my last trip to Europe in 1973, I travelled all over West Germany, to East and West Berlin, to Austria and Switzerland on a Eurail Pass. Two rather strange episodes stand out in my memory. Both had to do with my confusion as to whether I was a German or an American. Whenever I ate in a restaurant at noon, I ordered a main meal, as German custom dictates. In the evening I very conveniently became aware that I was actually an American and ate another main meal, as I do in the States. The consequences were horrendous: within six weeks I put on eleven pounds! But it was fun just the same.

The other episode had to do with the use of language. Whenever I travelled by train I had fun listening in on conversations among Americans, while I pretended not to know any English. On the other hand, when travelling with Germans I listened in on their conversation as an American, who acted as if she did not know any German.

Although I enjoyed college teaching tremendously, there were a few practices that, from my German perspective, I did not understand. I loved my students but I probably made some mistakes, the greatest one being applying German standards of learning to them. All too often, I heard the remark, "But that's no fun!" as referred to assignments, academic projects, research, term papers, etc. To me education was the most uplifting and gratifying experience in my life; therefore I could never understand why American students wanted everything to be "fun."

Then of course, many of us went through the rebellious 1960's, during which time students wanted to be in charge of everything pertaining to their life. Respect for elders and authority, never strong in this country, was just about to go out the window. The young people came down on the older generation with a vengeance that was hard to bear. In one of my courses, an undercurrent of dissatisfaction developed which I was not even aware of. Later, I wished students would have had the courage to approach me and talk things out. Instead, they appointed a spokesman who referred their grievances to the head of the department, again without my knowledge. My colleague could have saved me further embarrassment by calling me in and sharing the complaint with me but, shirking the responsibility, he sent the student to the Dean of Faculty. I was completely surprised when I was summoned to the Dean's office. The Dean, in a most gentlemanly way, explained the nature of the complaint which had to do with my standards - much too high in the eyes of the students - and my method of teaching.

Granted, language teaching requires different methods from those of other disciplines. A small group of students complained that learning in my classes was nothing but "regurgitation." My reply was that, in the case of language learning, regurgitation is indeed practiced and students should not have resented it. Language, whether native or foreign, is learned by imitation, which is akin to regurgitation. You cannot utter a word or phrase that you have not previously heard, to be assured that it is correct. I was deeply hurt by these childish and unfair accusations, especially in view of the fact that they had been launched just a few days after my husband's death. In addition to my grief over his passing, I had to cope with this unfair attack on my professional integrity. As it turned out the following days, I took this student attack all too seriously.

The Dean suggested that I have *all* my courses evaluated to give him a better perspective of my performance as a teacher. I followed his suggestion without telling my students the reason for the unexpected evaluation. I was generally well-liked and appreciated and did not want students to give me special consideration by answering the questionnaire in my favor. I had already learned - not from experience but by observation - how much Americans favor the cause of the underdog! The Dean thoroughly read the student evaluations, and I could hardly wait for the results. When he called me in, I immediately got the impression that things had worked out for me, judging by his well-meaning and sympathetic smile. He said, exactly in these words, "Hildegard, congratulations, you have come out smelling like a rose."

As it turned out, those students who had created that trouble for me, constituted only a small nucleus of the class. The majority of their classmates had evaluated the course in a very positive way, and so had my other classes. Compared to my overall success, a few negative experiences did not hurt my academic standing.

One more item I want to mention concerning language learning in this country. Generally speaking, Americans, with typical optimism, tend to underestimate the amount of work and patience needed to become fairly proficient in a foreign language. Over the years, I heard numerous remarks from people who considered themselves unsuccessful, because they were not able to learn a language in two years or less. They blamed themselves for being untalented or the teacher for not knowing how to teach more effectively. It does not cease to amaze me that in a country, in which so many different nationalities are represented, the importance of language learning is so greatly underestimated. I realize that, as a speaker of English, you can travel around the whole world without running into communication difficulties. However, it is interesting that people in their later years begin to appreciate languages more than the younger generation. Quite often, I hear people say, "My parents came from Germany (Norway, Italy, France, etc.). We spoke German (Norwegian, Italian, French) at home, and now I am sorry that I did not learn it better and keep it up."

During my tenure at Linfield, four presidents were in office, each one with his own ideas about education and emphases on various subjects. Languages were not ranked among the subjects with any great priority, but never was the situation as grave as it became in the early 1970's. At the time, declining enrollments and rapidly rising costs caused serious financial problems to the college. Instead of raising more funds and attracting more students, the president's action towards solving the problems moved in the direction of personnel cuts in the philosophy, religion and language departments. The foreign language majors and upper-division language courses were to be eliminated and subsidies of the Junior Year Abroad programs to be stopped. Those were grim times, not only for faculty members in jeopardy of losing their jobs, but also for the academic reputation of the college as a whole.

Fortunately, the college weathered the storm and so did the language department, which to this day teaches the three traditional languages and has even added Japanese and Chinese to its curriculum. Nevertheless, the financial crunch continued for some time to come, something that affected me personally. Two professors each carried out the duties of French and Spanish. German, nation-wide the language with the lowest enrollment - a fact traditionally explained as an aftereffect of two world wars and the enmity between the United States and Germany - did not do as well at Linfield as French or Spanish. Left as the sole professor of German, I shouldered the immense amount of work previously carried out by two professors. I worked not only the customary five days a week but took care of school work every Saturday and Sunday, too. I realized that such a demanding work schedule might eventually result in health problems. When the opportunity arose to take early retirement, with one-third of my salary paid for the next three years, I took advantage of it, grateful that I was able to supplement my greatly reduced salary with other sources of income.

24

The Golden Years - No Return to Homeland

Whoever came up with that nonsensical, though supposedly comforting and reassuring euphemism, "the golden years?" Does it refer to the fact that some of us oldsters - what an ugly expression that is! - have been able to accumulate some gold currency and thus enjoy a relatively comfortable life style? Or is it because that particular chapter of our life should be expected to be the best ever - regardless of those little aches and pains creeping up, not to mention more serious painful reminders of advancing age - diseases, such as arthritis or osteoporosis, or - Heaven forbid! - the susceptibility to incurable illnesses, often called terminal, or the inevitable final occurrence - death? Let us not be fooled by euphemisms!

"Senior citizen" is another one of those terms which, although a well-intended term, does not do the trick for me. I know better! "Senior" no doubt sounds impressive to graduating students who have reached a goal in life, which they strove for and looked forward to for years; but does an aging man or woman have an equivalent goal to strive for? Probably not!

Apart from reaping the benefit of a ten percent senior citizens discount in restaurants, I do not like to be classified as a senior citizen. When I still had fewer wrinkles and less gray hair I was often asked, "Are you a senior citizen?" I was proud of the fact that apparently I did not look my age - yet. Now I get the discount in restaurants automatically, which proves something. At least I am spared the agonizing question which I never liked anyway.

We elderly are human beings. Old age is the only criterion that we "seniors" have in common, nothing else. But all this is relative. Ask me anytime and I will tell you that I feel like a sixteen-year-old in my heart, whereas other people my age may feel as if they were ninety! No classification for me, please! I am allergic to it! Reason? I think it has something to do with the first classification I underwent as a member of the Hitler Youth in Nazi Germany, for which I had to pay dearly, not so much in terms of penalty or punishment, but for sharing guilt feelings with hundreds of thousands of my generation. I suffer from overdeveloped guilt feelings to this day. Never having been able to come to grips with the horrendous effects of the government actions under which I grew up, I still carry a sense of responsibility for not only the Nazi misdeeds, but for practically everything that goes wrong in this wide world. In spite of these obviously misguided, but nevertheless still authentic feelings, I have been able to keep them under control and to enjoy life to the fullest.

Despite warnings on the part of my friends about the risks and boredom of retirement, I jumped at the opportunity of early retirement when it was offered by the college. Mind you - the emphasis is on "early." I make that clear when people ask me, "What year did you retire?" and quickly do some arithmetic adding the number of years in retirement to sixty-five and thus come up with seventy-four years. Far from it! At my age there is a considerable difference between seventy and seventy-four, and I enjoy my relative youth as a senior citizen. The classification has crept in again - at my own hands!

Early retirement offered a chance to enjoy life and do things that I never seemed to have time for. My retirement years have not been spent in the rocking chair, as many people who are still in the work force look at it - far from it! The Puritan work ethic is very prevalent in this country. I have no qualms about retiring early and "wasting" my time. Often I jokingly refer to WORK as another one of those four-letter words to be avoided if at all possible.

The opportunity of organizing time and the freedom of making wise decisions add a special bonus to retirement. In the early months of retirement, whenever I showed up on campus in a non-teaching capacity, well-meaning colleagues greeted me as if they felt sorry for me, asking, "What do you do with yourself all day?" The question implies, "You poor soul, all by yourself," as if there were no contacts with other people. The very opposite is the case - after all, there are more than four billion people in this world! Never in my working years was I socially as active as I am now.

After retirement I looked into the possibility of moving to the Oregon coast to be closer to my beloved Pacific Ocean. However, upon close scrutiny and weighing the pros and cons of a move away from the campus and the community in which I am well established and respected, not to mention numerous friends, it was not difficult to decide against such a move. A great honor was bestowed on me when

I was appointed Professor Emeritus of the College, which made me feel proud, humble and grateful at the same time.

Linfield College is like a second home to me, and continued friendships with faculty and students have been a special blessing. Invitations to most activities of the College, including social affairs as well as cultural events, keep me busy, and I have the time to attend and enjoy campus events without having to think about correcting papers and preparing for the next day. I have enjoyed fairly regular participation in weekly Language Tables, which give me a chance to speak my native language with students and some faculty members. I spend many leisurely hours in the library and I enjoy the privilege of checking out books for the duration of the academic year.

Another opportunity the college provides to faculty members, both active and retired, is free admission to courses. I have taken advantage of this bonus by attending classes in Chinese Civilization, History of Germany, Latin American Literature, The Art of Ancient Egypt and Introduction to Film. What a wealth of insights and knowledge I have gained that way! While I faithfully did all the required reading assignments, as a special student I was exempt from writing time-consuming term papers and taking nerve-racking midterm and final exams.

The most exciting event in all those years was the visit of Helmut Schmidt, former Chancellor of the Federal Republic of Germany, to the Linfield campus in the fall of 1988. Herr Schmidt has been my all-time favorite statesman. My admiration for him goes back to the late 'fifties and 'sixties when he first became active in German politics as a defense minister, then joint minister of economics and finance, and from 1974 to 1982, as Chancellor of the Federal Republic of Germany. He was one of the founders of the economic summits started in 1975 to coordinate the policies of major western nations. In 1972, he received the U.S. Medal of Distinguished Service.

He honored us with his visit to the Linfield campus to deliver a most enlightened speech, sharing with the administration, the faculty, the students and approximately 1,300 guests, his great understanding of international issues and his wide range of political experiences.

Needless to say, I was ecstatic and looked forward to seeing him personally and to listening to his speech. However, my anticipation grew immensely when, some ten days before Mr. Schmidt's visit, I was informed by Dr. Charles Walker, president of Linfield College, that two persons had been selected to meet Mr. Schmidt at the Portland airport. One was Dr. Peter Richardson,

Professor of German, Head of the Modern Language Department and my successor when I retired. I was the other lucky person. Time could not pass fast enough for me. The day before Mr. Schmidt's arrival, President Walker phoned me to ask me if I would be willing to express Linfield's thanks to our distinguished guest after his speech. I was overwhelmed, quite nervous, but at the same time very excited. After that was settled, President Walker and I exchanged some opinions about our guest. He told me that, in the summer of 1988, he and his wife had traveled to Norway. During a boat trip up the fjords, he became acquainted with a German gentleman, whom he asked for an opinion of former Chancellor Schmidt. The gentleman responded that he admired Mr. Schmidt greatly for his honesty, his insight into political issues and problems, his way of dealing with them and his ability to make friends with common people as well as foreign leaders.

On October 13, Peter and I left for the Portland airport at 2:45 p. m. and a Linfield student took his own car along to transport three of Mr. Schmidt's four body guards to McMinnville. The Continental Airlines plane arrived from Houston, Texas, at 4:35 p.m. It was exciting to spot Mr. Schmidt as he deplaned. We introduced ourselves and shook hands with him and his escorts, all from Hamburg, Germany. Three body guards and the student claimed the baggage, while Peter, Mr. Schmidt and I drove to McMinnville. The Chancellor and I sat in the back seat and talked all the way. We spoke in German exclusively, and the only English word that was uttered was when I asked him the German meaning of the word "rush hour." The laconic answer was "rush hour." Apparently there was no German equivalent to this obviously typically American phenomenon. However, in the meantime, I was informed by a reliable German source that, indeed, there is such a word. It means *Stossverkehr*, literally "push traffic."

At first it seemed a little difficult to find proper topics for discussion; no small talk and yet nothing too heavy, because Mr. Schmidt still suffered from jet lag after his visits to China and Japan, and was very tired. Getting to know a stranger, feeling one's way and becoming comfortable with him is one thing, but talking with one of the highly regarded world leaders added an extra dimension to my experience and seemed to put greater demands on me, mostly because of my desire of doing well in his estimation. Conversing with him became easier when he asked questions about Oregon and Linfield in particular.

Upon our arrival on campus, there was a brief press conference, a dinner at the president's home, Mr. Schmidt's speech and a question-and-answer period. Then I was summoned to the podium to express our gratitude, in German, as I had been directed, for his visit and insightful speech. I told him, among other things, that I had seldom learned so much within an hour and a half, which brought a genuine smile to his face. At this point, I must insert that Germans, as a rule, do not smile as readily as we Americans do. I like to believe - and I think it is a fact - that this particular smile was the first and only one I noticed on his face all evening. We then shook hands and I began to come down to earth again.

The following day, another question-and-answer period was scheduled, which was limited to students and faculty. It provided one more opportunity to gain more and deeper insights into international issues and problems, as well as possible ideas for solutions. Helmut Schmidt left the campus at 11:45 a.m. and departed for Germany at 1:15 p.m.

The ancient Romans had a proverb saying *"Neapolim videre et mori"* which means "To see Naples and then die." I could not help but think of that proverb, which to a certain degree is applicable to my experiences with my hero. It certainly does not mean that I am willing to die after such a highlight of my life, but it pertains to the depth of my emotions in meeting this man whom I had held in such high esteem for almost three decades.

My words of thanks to Chancellor Helmut Schmidt:

"Sehr geehrter Herr Bundeskanzler,

Als einer Ihrer vielen Bewunderer ist es mir eine grosse Ehre Ihnen im Namen des Instituts, der Verwaltung, der Fakultät, der Studenten und unserer verehrten Gäste unseren tiefgefühlten Dank auszusprechen, dass Sie um die halbe Erde von Waterkant zu Waterkant in unsere kleine Stadt gekommen sind, um uns mit Ihrem Besuch zu beehren. Ihre Ausführungen waren informativ und aufschlussreich und haben uns einen guten Einblick nicht nur in politische und wirtschaftliche Verhältnisse in der Welt, sondern auch Probleme und deren mögliche Lösungen gegeben. Wir sind Ihnen zu grossem Dank verpflichtet. Hoffentlich können Sie uns wieder einmal besuchen. Wir würden Sie herzlichst willkommen heissen. Inzwischen rufe ich Ihnen ein fröhliches 'Auf Wiedersehen' zu".

Translation:

"Most esteemed Federal Chancellor,

"As one of your many admirers it is a special honor for me, in the name of our institution, the administration, the faculty, the students and our distinguished guests, to express our deep-felt thanks to you for traveling half-way around the globe, shore to shore, to come to our little town and honor us with your visit. Your deliberations were informative and instructive and have given us a good insight, not only into political and economic conditions in the world, but also into problems and possible solutions. We are deeply indebted to you. It is our hope that you will be able to visit us again some day. We would most cordially welcome you. In the meantime, I salute you with a heartfelt *Auf Wiedersehen.*"

Obviously I do not fit the stereotype of a retiree. I do not know boredom or depression. The college alone could keep me busy and occupy most of my time but there are a lot more benefits that my retirement years have offered. It has been gratifying to see how easy it is to form new friendships. This is necessary because most of my college friends were still employed when I retired. Several people approached me with suggestions for sharing their time with me, once they learned that I was available for socializing. I especially appreciated new friendships with couples and young people with children.

When I first retired I assumed that my circle of friends would be mostly around my age. Fortunately, this has not been the case entirely. I have several young friends who could be my children or even grandchildren. It feels so good to be appreciated by all age groups and both sexes. My engagement calendar is filled with activities three to five days ahead. However, this does not rule out on-the-spur-of-the-moment activities because I keep my schedule flexible. Whenever the phone rings I guess what kind of excitement awaits me. I sometimes jokingly refer to these calls as "attacks on my time." This is not meant to be interpreted that I dread receiving phone calls - I love them - but another indication of my "weird sense of humor," as my students used to call it.

Germans walk a lot, and I have maintained the custom. I find it unbelievable, when my able-bodied American friends drive around and around, in an effort to find a parking space instead of parking a little farther from their destination and walk a little. When I have to run an errand I prefer to walk, even as far as downtown. Occasionally I spend some hours on the coast without benefit of a walk along the ocean because my friends do not enjoy or are not in the habit of walking. On my return home, I feel cheated when I did not get my walk in.

Some of my friends have developed an interest in genealogy and in the process have discovered that they have ancestors and/or relatives in Germany, Austria or Switzerland. I have helped many people with their correspondence to those countries. Occasionally I do translations on other topics - free of charge, of course. It is good to continue being useful and needed.

I like to indulge in meaningful dialogues with all kinds of people, even lifetime friends whom I have not seen for decades. This, of course, has to be done either by telephone or exchange of letters. For that purpose, I keep up an immense correspondence, including friends, relatives and in-laws in Europe, as well as former students.

I belong to a discussion group consisting of nine members who call themselves "Mavericks," because of the fact that we do not always willingly conform to the run-of-the-mill opinions of the majority of society, and because we do a lot of independent thinking, regardless of what the media want us to believe. We meet twice a month for lunch in a restaurant and discuss whatever happens to be of interest at the time. The group is outrageously honest and outspoken. We often do not agree among ourselves and are not afraid to admit our disagreements to the point of savagely attacking each other - verbally, not physically, of course. The more sparks are flying, the more interesting and rewarding the meetings get to be.

Fortunately, I do not feel lonesome when I am at home alone. On the contrary, I welcome quiet hours which I use for contemplation, taking stock of my life and keeping a proper perspective. I am grateful for the time I have to play the piano, read interesting books, magazines, the daily newspapers, go shopping, listen to talk shows, or knit.

Increased leisure time has also given me chances to travel. After I retired I took two superb trips to Alaska and China with Dottie, my good friend, who is a marvelous travel companion. We have also travelled extensively all over Oregon, Washington and up and down the Pacific coast as far south as San Francisco. I also travelled several times to British Columbia with other friends.

I am often asked if I have any plans to travel to Europe or, "How long has it been since you last visited Germany?" A little sheepishly, I answer "no" to the first question and "seventeen years" to the second one. The responses are usually followed by a short period of silence. Then the dialogue resumes with another question, such as, "Don't you WANT to see your native country and your friends and relatives more often?" This question cannot be answered with a simple "yes" or "no," because the circumstances surrounding the problem are based on my psychological make-up.

I approach Germany with the same dichotomy of thinking as it has presented itself to the world. Most people love and admire Germany for its culture and contributions to the Western world and, on the other hand, criticize it for its ideology, warfare and serious mistakes it has made in politics. However, I do not have to live or spend time there to appreciate the positive features of Germany. I

can honestly say that, for many years, I have enjoyed sharing my
roots and background with hundreds of students, who were enrolled
in my courses on German Civilization and German Literature, more
so than a visit to Germany would have afforded me. Another reason
for not being overly keen to travel to my country lies in the fact that
most of my relatives do not live anymore. Those who still do indulge
in a form of worship of the dead, which I find a little morbid. This
involves visits to various cemeteries, decorating the graves and
engaging in prayers. I can and do love my deceased relatives without
this outward show of affection and do not think I need to prove my
love in such a disconcerting fashion.

A third reason for not choosing Europe as a travel destination
is a more practical one. I spent thirty-three years there and after
World War II travelled extensively through most European countries.
When I was about fifty years old I decided it was time for me to
branch out and see other countries instead of paying repeat visits to
places that no longer offered me new experiences. I thoroughly
enjoyed visiting the Soviet Union, Turkey, Greece, Bulgaria,
Romania, Italy and - most of all - China. My travels to numerous
countries afforded me the opportunity to indulge in one of my favorite
hobbies, which is photography. I took thousands of slides and
snapshots on those trips. During my years of teaching I tried to
instill in my students the same love of traveling and admiration for
foreign cultures which I harbor in my heart.

Fortunately, my continued good health has contributed to the
enjoyment of life during these "golden years." I have appreciated the
efforts of several excellent physicians to keep me well and let me live
a relatively long and good life. However, the maverick in me tells me
to follow the practices of German doctors who treated me whenever I
was ill as a child and teenager. This included a minimum of
medication. To this day I refuse to put any chemicals into my body,
including the over-the-counter pain killers. My very competent
physician honors this quirk of mine but periodically examines my
vital organs for signs of deterioration. Someday I may have to resort
to medications or undergo surgery, but so far I have found the side
effects of medicines harder to tolerate than the medical problems I
have suffered from. In my opinion, pills often cover up the symptoms
instead of helping a patient fight the actual disease.

After my immigration to the United States, I planned not to
visit Germany until I received my citizenship, in order to be able to
view my native country and people through the eyes of an American
citizen. After living in a foreign country for six years, the need to
make necessary adjustments and to conform to a certain degree

becomes apparent. In the process, outlook, customs and habits undergo changes. The Germans have a proverb for every situation in life and the appropriate one in this case is *"Andere Länder, andere Sitten"* (Other countries, other customs). I became personally aware of the validity of this adage when I visited Germany again in 1959.

Many of my relatives welcomed me at the Nuremberg airport. After the first greetings I was immediately told that no German in his right mind would fly from Frankfurt to Nuremberg because taking the train is so much easier due to the distance of the airport from the city. Certainly my relatives, most of whom did not have a car, found getting to the airport by taxi expensive and inconvenient. It would have been much easier for them to take a streetcar to the main railroad station, where the trains from Frankfurt arrive. So here I was, the troublesome American, being told in no uncertain terms that I should have arrived by train. Germans, as a rule, are quite blunt, needless to say. In my opinion, my arrival should have been met with joy and cheers rather than with stern criticism, but I understood.

Germans used to have an aversion to wearing glasses. I began to develop a case of myopia when I was still in high school. Without glasses I was not able to read the teacher's notes on the blackboard, but I wore glasses only for that purpose and took them off immediately after they had served their purpose. Never did I wear them at home, let alone for social functions. It was considered a misfortune for a girl to have to wear glasses. Society was of the opinion that no man would fall in love and marry such a girl.

When I came to the United States I had my eyes tested. After the examination, the ophthalmologist said, "Frankly I can't see how you can see." Despite my countrymen's prejudice against glasses, I felt very comfortable wearing mine in this country and was well accepted by everybody. My self-esteem grew and I even dared to think that I might even find a gentleman who was willing to marry me. It took a little while, but it happened!

I wore my glasses for six years from morning till night every day, but the thought of arriving in Germany with them was bothersome. So I decided to have prescription sunglasses made which I would wear on my arrival. Fortunately, the sun was shining brightly. I do not know what I would have done if it had rained. Of course, rainy days caused problems, but I went without glasses, in order to be presentable to my relatives.

My preference for bright colors and more stylish clothes than German women used to wear also caused problems. I was still young enough in 1959 to get by with American idiosyncrasies. However, when I went out in public, I often noticed curious looks on the faces of German women. Somehow they sized me up by looking at every piece of my clothing from top to toe and classified me as an American, sometimes with a friendly look and other times with disapproval, depending on their attitude towards America.

When I visited Germany again in 1969, I was fifty years old. I was told by my stepmother that, at my age, I should wear more subdued colors. I could not believe my ears. Politely, I responded by saying, *Andere Länder, andere Sitten.*

My use of the German language also came under scrutiny. Germans have one language in common, which is High German. It is the formal language taught in schools, used in writing and by the media. On the other hand, the spoken German is a dialect of the region in which one lived. Some dialects differ from one another almost as much as if they were foreign languages. I remember overhearing a Berliner and a person from Munich trying to converse with each other, to no avail. Neither of them was educated enough to be able to speak High German, which could have served as the common bond.

The division of the German language into at least fifteen dialects has been explained by the political division of the country into 350 principalities after the Thirty Years War, which resulted in a lack of communication among the various German regions. It was not until more than two centuries later that Germany was united and dialects became less pronounced. Another noticeable reduction in dialectal distinctions resulted when millions of refugees from the Eastern part of Germany fled into West Germany after World War II and mingled with people who spoke differently.

Foreigners learn only High German, which enables them to be understood by all Germans, no matter what dialect they speak. When I taught German in this country I spoke High German exclusively, which became so deeply ingrained in my mind that I found it difficult to shed when talking to my relatives. They found it amusing that I spoke High German. It took me up to three days, until I confidently lapsed into my Bavarian dialect. Oddly enough, I was accused of speaking German with an American accent, whereas in the United States people often comment on my foreign accent when I speak English. What a "mixed-up kid" I am!

My stepmother, with whom I stayed whenever I was in Nuremberg, was interested in learning more about my American life style. She found it outrageous when I told her that I did not clean one room of my apartment a day as she did. One day I shocked her by describing my practice of cleaning windows. I find it relaxing to use the garden hose to remove quickly the dirt clinging to the outside windows. She lived on the third floor and could not possibly have done that. My description provided grist for her gossip mill, and she went around to neighbors to show off her knowledge of American customs and habits.

When I visited relatives they often invited their closest friends to meet me. Most German families take pride in having a *Tante aus Amerika* (Aunt from America) who, in most cases, shows off her wealth when visiting her homeland by showering everybody with gifts. In visiting my relatives after more than ten years, I found them searching for signs of the Americanization process that I had undergone. Most of them acknowledged changes in a positive and friendly manner, although I sometimes heard some chuckling behind my back. It did not bother me in the least. As a matter of fact, I was amused and proud to be the center of so much attention.

Most of my relatives never quite understood the reasons for my emigration to the United States. Some consider me somewhat ungrateful and disloyal, but they respect and love me as I do them. They have forgiven me for "deserting" them, but in conversations with others I could detect a little thinly-veiled resentment. Nevertheless, they all treated me royally and wined and dined me beyond all expectations.

After so much conforming in my youth, both to government, family and teachers, I took pride in making my own decisions as soon as possible, especially those of great magnitude, such as emigration. Very seldom in my adult life have I made a wrong or unwise decision. It did not take me long to refer to this country as "my home," even in correspondence with my German relatives. Because of this I was severely taken to task, "You must never forget where your home is. Certainly it is not America."

A few encounters with some strangers in Germany struck me as odd and are worth relating. One day, I took pictures of the beautiful countryside near Wiesbaden. Next to me stood a German with a camera in his hand. In my American exuberance and enthusiasm over the lovely scenery, I started talking to him in German. His reaction was hostile. Without uttering a word he turned away from me, not even taking time to shoot his picture. I had completely forgotten that a lady does not speak to a man first.

German bus drivers and streetcar conductors are known to be rude, because they feel they are in charge, which is true to a certain degree, but it does not justify their rudeness. I had one unpleasant experience with each one of them. One day I travelled to my Alma Mater in Erlangen and in the evening I visited some relatives in the same city. We had a good time reminiscing and chatting, and it got quite late. I had to catch a bus back to Nuremberg that same evening, so I raced to the bus stop and was lucky enough to catch the last bus of the evening. Since I had planned to take the same trip a few more times during my visit in Germany, I asked the bus driver for a schedule. He did not have one, so I asked him a few questions about how often the buses were running, etc. He became impatient with me and asked me the reason behind all those questions. I responded that I wanted to learn about the schedule. He shouted at me, "What is there to learn about a schedule? It's the same every day!"

American bus drivers are more service-oriented and anxious to please. In Germany they lord it over the passenger. I was lucky that I was the only passenger on the bus. Not so on the occasion of a streetcar ride to downtown Nuremberg. I wanted to get off at the same stop that I had used every day for three years when I worked for the telephone company. When the stop approached I stepped out to the platform, ready to get off. I raised the protective railing but the streetcar did not stop where it used to. The stop had been changed to a different location about twenty yards away. I was in no danger of falling out and did not attempt to get off. You should have heard the conductor scream at me in front of about thirty passengers, "What's your hurry? If you had fallen off, you would have had to go to the hospital, which would have taken a lot longer than waiting for the stop." I was embarrassed and completely devastated. Incidents like these make me feel grateful for the pleasant treatment I get in the good old USA.

Early in 1984 I received an invitation from the *Gustav-Adolf-Kirche*, the church in Nuremberg in which I was confirmed at Easter 1934. The 50th anniversary of the event was to be observed in 1984. I had not been in touch with the particular church since I left Nuremberg in 1943. I felt honored by the invitation but was not able to attend. How the church kept track of me to the extent of knowing my married name and my U.S. residence was beyond me.

Another exciting day I had to miss because of distance and expense was our 50th high school reunion in March 1989 and, according to the letter I received from my classmates, I was *"sehr vermisst"* (sorely missed).

25

Culture Shock

My experiences both as a student and an immigrant to this country were overwhelmingly positive and have continued to be so. Even before arriving at my destination in Oregon, I was deeply impressed by the warmth, openness and gentleness of the people, even complete strangers I met on the train. But I did experience culture shock and as I bring this story of my life to an end I feel compelled to reflect on the changes that have occurred in my life and in American society. In some measure these changes are a result of my German upbringing impinging on my American identity and in some ways they are a function of advancing age and a recognition that those values that I absorbed may no longer fit the circumstances of modern life.

Little did I realize that the culture shock I experienced was not just temporary but, in certain aspects, a lifetime matter. Contrary to the dictionary definition of culture shock, I maintain that it is not always negative but a positive reaction to the negative feelings you harbor against your own society. In some cases, I was not even aware of those negative feelings about my country until I was given a chance to compare the two countries and societies. I found life in the United States so much more attractive and I continue to marvel at the diversity of life styles and values to be found in America. Democracy here offers a means to bring happiness and fulfillment to everyone. It is so humane, and I remain deeply grateful for the hospitality that has been extended to me. How I wish my relatives and friends in my native land could see it the same way!

While traveling from the Atlantic to the Pacific through several different states, some of which exceeded the size of my country, I was deeply impressed by the vastness of the United States. Being familiar with the number of square miles (13, 618,770 versus 95,908 of the Federal Republic of Germany), is one thing, but actually traveling from coast to coast through a vast area and varied landscapes illustrates the reality of sheer numbers. In comparison, the area of all European countries combined is only 3,800,000 square miles. Even today, when traveling in this country I marvel at its size.

One advantage of a large country with its wide-open spaces is the opportunity to own land and to enjoy greater privacy than Europeans. My present home has more floor space than any apartment I lived in with my parents, and it has a back yard, a front yard and a garage. When I lived in Germany I never in my wildest dreams envisioned such generous living space. The great majority of Germans live in apartments, not so much because they cannot afford their own homes, but because there is no space for individual homes. The density of the population is approximately 247 persons per square mile and still growing, as compared to 17 in the United States.

The number and dimensions of highways and freeways, as well as the size of cars and trucks, also made an immediate, terrifying impression on me. However, in comparison to European traffic and driving habits, the United States is much better organized. Traffic is well regulated and American drivers in general are well-disciplined and have more driving experience than the majority of European drivers, many of whom acquired their first vehicle as late as the 1950's and 1960's. The mortality rate due to traffic accidents in West Germany is a staggering fifty-eight per day, and this on an area slightly larger than Oregon. German drivers as a whole are maniacs behind the wheels. I simply refuse to drive in Germany. On many occasions, I have ridden with friends and spoken many silent prayers to God to help me survive the highly competitive race. There are no speed limits on *Autobahnen*, the minuscule version of American freeways, so everyone wants to show his superiority over the other fellow by passing him at all costs. The poor guy who is not brave enough or too sensible to keep up with the speeders is given a signal, that he is just a wimp to be despised or at least looked down on. It consists of the fast driver tapping his right temple with the middle finger of the right hand. This silent signal is universally understood in all of Germany and not only limited to situations pertaining to traffic. Translated from sign language it means "you fool!" There is also an unwritten law according to which only the bigger and more expensive cars, such as the Mercedes or Porsches, have the right to pass the Volkswagen owner under any circumstances. This means that Volkswagens are limited to the use of the right lane almost exclusively.

As I became acquainted with more and more Americans, I studied their outstanding character traits and compared them with those of the Germans, who are characterized, mostly by other countries, as warlike, power-hungry, stubborn, chauvinistic, self-centered, rowdy, noisy, uncouth, uncaring. Note that these characteristics traditionally attributed to Germans are all negative. How can a nation be all that bad? While I agreed with some of these attributes, I found myself looking at my own people in the light of this rather unbalanced view. In all fairness, Germans tend to be hardworking people who, against all odds, are accustomed to pull themselves up by the bootstraps without relying on outside help. Welfare is acceptable only under rare and difficult circumstances.

This attitude is accompanied by a sense of personal responsibility, iron discipline and pride in achievement. Germans generally live well within their means and they save first before buying or accumulating debts. In relationships, they work hard to straighten out their personal problems. They do not turn to divorce so readily and they continue to regard an education for their children as the key to a successful life.

Part of that education involves becoming acquainted with German culture, which the government subsidizes generously. Opera, operettas, theater presentations and classical music are to be found in rich profusion in Germany, and they are made accessible to the children of rich and poor families alike.

Loyalty is another deep-seated German trait and it has a positive side in relations with friends, family, employers and community leaders. The negative side is present as well, because many Germans, in their unquestioned loyalty, will follow their leaders blindly and without moral discrimination, as the Nazi era so tragically attests.

This list of positive German qualities is not complete by any means. Americans have these traits as well, although often in a less intense and binding way. Americans as individuals have proved to me friendly, outgoing, generous and tolerant. I never experienced any open or hidden prejudice, as my father had predicted I would. American hospitality knows no limits, and I have been fortunate to be invited to countless families and homes.

Privacy, whenever needed or desired, is respected. Germans, on the other hand, have a tendency to interfere with other people's business to the point of becoming obnoxiously inquisitive. People with time on their hands sit by the window and watch everything that is going on in the streets - who goes out with whom, what people are wearing, what time they leave or come home, etc. Such superficial knowledge about neighbors leads to delicious gossip to which Germans are perhaps unusually prone. Americans tend to respect other people's privacy and gossip much less - or have I not met the "right" people yet?

Americans feel free to talk to strangers and smile at each other. I enjoy talking to people now, even to strangers, but it took a little getting used to, and smiling even more so. On my occasional visits to Germany I must watch myself, lest I be considered too forward (for a woman!) or even aggressive.

The high regard for human life is impressive in this country. As a matter of routine, every effort is made to save the life of a premature baby or a child who needs an organ transplant. This concern for the individual also manifests itself in the treatment of the mentally and physically handicapped, who receive a lot of attention at the taxpayers' expense. They can enroll in special programs and are encouraged to compete with each other in sports, such as the Special Olympics. In Germany the handicapped are kept separate as a special class of people, instructed and trained in their own schools, and do not compete with other children.

We know from observation and news reports that individuals in primitive societies do not enjoy this high regard for human life. The individual there is not all that important. Maybe it has something to do with the fact that those societies produce more children than they can support, which cheapens the life of the individual. Germany stands somewhere in the middle of these extremes. The regard for individual life is not as high as it could and should be. This became most obvious in the wars that Germany engaged in and in the willingness of society to make untold human sacrifices of young lives.

The American life style is overwhelming. Food is more than plentiful and despite rising prices still relatively affordable. The choice of various brands of the same product can make your head swim. Everybody who works needs a car and has one. In Germany a person can easily do without a car, which is considered a convenience, if not a luxury. My parents and I never owned more than one radio. In my American home I have four radio sets, one portable radio and a short-wave radio - six radios for one person! But it is nice to participate in this consumer-oriented American life style. I also own two TV sets and two telephones. How spoiled can you get!

Society makes every effort to make life pleasant and comfortable. I am thinking of the many free community services and senior citizens activities. The service of libraries is also free of charge. In our relatively small college library one can read numerous magazines and newspapers from all over the world in the browsing room - no charge. In Germany, public libraries charge the reader a small fee for every book he checks out.

One of the most significant treasures of the American people is the constitution of the United States. I lived under a totalitarian regime for twelve of my formative years (1933 to 1945). Under Hitler, no individual rights and freedoms were guaranteed to us. Finally, four years after World War II, the Federal Republic of Germany adopted a constitution, the "Basic Law" which put a person's freedom above state authority. It guarantees the freedoms and human rights of every citizen and corresponds to the Bill of Rights of the U.S. constitution. In the Weimar Republic, the period preceding Hitler, several attempts at forming a viable government had been made. The Germans were used to a sequence of political changes and experiments, all of which turned out to be more or less unsatisfactory. That may have been the reason why the new constitution did not inspire much opposition. People suspected that it might not last. Even when it proved to be viable and successful, Germans did not see it as the embodiment of the governing ethos of the country.

When I first came to this country, I studied the United States constitution and was impressed by what it had to offer. It was written in a more specific and forceful manner than the German "Basic Law," which deals more in generalities and it has proven to be a very resilient guide to political conduct. To this day I marvel at the facility with which the United States surmounts serious crises, often so severe as to threaten the very foundation upon which the government of this country is based.

Since I continued to be a German citizen for five years after my arrival, the U.S. constitution did not speak specifically to me. The first few words "We the People of the United States" sounded impressive but they did not include me. My heart swelled with pride five years later when I became a U.S. citizen and the constitution applied to me, too. I finally belonged! It was an uplifting feeling to realize that my personal freedoms and rights were equally guaranteed to me, as they were to citizens born in this country. However, I regret that I am prohibited by law to become President of the United States!

While Germany still adheres to a class system, the United States is much more democratic, which has led to a leveling of classes within society. As a high school teacher in Germany I was put in the same category as physicians and lawyers. I felt that, even as a college professor in the United States, I did not enjoy the same status as I did as a high school teacher in Germany. It seems to me that doctors of philosophy hide behind their academic achievements for fear of being called "eggheads." This leveling of class distinctions - if indeed they ever existed - led as far as students calling their professors by their first name. Frankly, this bothered me initially, but in time I looked at my students in a different light and regarded them as potential intellectual peers.

Can this first-name basis be carried to extremes, especially when you do not know the other person? The other day I chuckled when I received a letter from the office of the Governor of Oregon. I was addressed by "Dear Hildegard." My initial reaction (German thinking) was the question, "Who knows me personally in the governor's office?" The signature simply said "Neil," which was the governor's first name. At first I thought "How nice to be on a first-name basis with the governor!" But then I realized that thousands of form letters had been sent out in the same way. The governor requested in a sweet and personal way to vote "Yes" for a ballot measure in the upcoming election, which I would have done anyway. Somehow the letter made me feel good, but I could not help but think that it would be impossible for a German politician to address his constituents by their first name. It would be considered cheeky and undignified.

Watching Americans act in group situations proved just as exciting and sometimes as puzzling as individual behavior and as interesting to observe. Since I am a maverick, I especially appreciate being "adopted" by families, their children and grandchildren, and included in family affairs, such as picnics and reunions. I bask in the informal atmosphere of such events and enjoy sharing their love for one another. Sometimes relatives of American families travel farther than the length or width of Germany to participate in such occasions. Some of them had never even met before. This kind of devotion to family is admirable, indeed.

In Germany, family reunions of such magnitude are practically unknown. Family gatherings are usually observed by the closest members only. Germans seem to feel more comfortable within smaller groups. This practice may have arisen from the fact that German households cannot accommodate large crowds for lack of space or even a backyard. It could also be a matter of expenses. I grew up on such a tight budget that we could not afford to entertain on a grand scale.

The multitude of clubs and social, professional and religious organizations which cater to all-encompassing interests was also something I had to get used to. In my estimation there must be a club or an organization for every American's needs. And Americans are great joiners! When the Germans became acquainted with the American democratic system, they were puzzled and at times even amused. We used to joke by saying "Whenever three Americans meet, they form a committee." And there is some truth to it!

Sometimes I found the rules governing those groups unnecessarily restrictive and even undemocratic. Once I was rejected as a prospective member of a professional organization of teachers to which I applied because I had graduated from a foreign university. Another organization rejected me because I was retired. I felt that I would have had something to offer both groups and rejection hurt my feelings considerably. Generally speaking, I am not a joiner, because I vividly remember the very first organization I joined and its implications for the rest of my life. I am speaking of the Hitler Youth. Of course, this reluctance is foolish, because I am comparing apples with oranges, but the feeling of having made a wrong decision is still deeply felt. Church groups would probably be glad to accept me within their flock. Perhaps not, if they found out that I harbor doubts concerning some teachings of the Christian religion.

Another positive phenomenon that I have had the privilege to follow has been the establishment of equal rights for women in American society. Few, if any, other countries have gone as far as the United States in this respect. Although some dissatisfied women maintain that the Equal Rights movement has not gone far enough and some think they have not been hired or lost their jobs on the basis of sex discrimination, I believe that a woman can get and hold any job, provided she is sufficiently qualified and willing to carry out her obligations according to management's expectations.

When I was hired as an Assistant Professor at Linfield College in 1963, three of my colleagues in the department were men, who willingly and graciously accepted me as their equal. To my knowledge, I was never paid a lower salary than my male colleagues.

About twelve years ago, I was asked by an officer of a female student organization to speak to the group. It had always been my attitude to be of service to students in any way I was able to, so I agreed. However, when I was informed that the topic of my talk was to be "Discrimination against Linfield Women Based on my Own Experiences," I had to decline. The student was completely baffled when I informed her that I had not been discriminated against. Obviously, I would not have been able to satisfy students' expectations if I had accepted their invitation.

When I grew up in Germany students did not participate in the decision-making process. Rules and regulations affecting the school were made by the principal and dutifully carried out by students and teachers alike. Similarly, society as a whole was governed by laws made by the leaders of the Nazi party and accepted by the followers who had no input whatsoever into political or legal processes. There were no committees to gather information on an issue, to weigh the pros and cons in discussions, to formulate a proposal and vote for or against it.

I have been trying to come to grips with four greetings which we hear many times every day. What exactly does "hi" mean? Maybe I should not look for a meaning of a greeting, as long as it is addressed to you in a friendly and well-meaning fashion. All greetings in German - and there are considerably more in existence than in English - have a meaning which is even translatable into other languages. For example, there is *Guten Tag, Guten Morgen, Guten Abend, Gute Nacht,* as well as *Grüss Gott* (May God be with you) and the almost universally known *Auf Wiedersehen* (Till we meet again).

I never know how to respond to "How are you?" Instead of answering, "Fine, thank you", which in many instances is a falsehood, shall I actually say "miserable," "I got a headache," "my arthritis is acting up," if one of these applies? It really perturbs me when I am forced to lie because the well-meaning greeter expects a positive reply. Germans take *Wie geht's* literally and expect a straightforward answer. They actually take the time to stop and listen to possible complaints about a person's health, which may well have a therapeutic effect. So why not tell the truth?

Once a friend criticized me for taking leave of a person by saying "good-bye." She knew that I would see the friend again the following day, but she still said "Are you going away or is she?" implying that "good-bye" refers to a long-range or permanent separation. I thought it was the equivalent of the German *Auf Wiedersehen.* We often use the short form "bye-bye" which does not seem to imply a long-term separation. But it is baby talk and as such not very impressive. I must admit that I use all these greetings without hesitation, but somehow I don't always feel good about it.

I have further questions or doubts pertaining to language. Why do so many people say to me, "Drop in any time?" Should I take this as a serious and open invitation? How about dropping in around midnight on my way home from a movie or the theater? Or maybe I could see these good people at dinner time inviting myself to a free meal? I have a hunch that this friendly invitation may not be meant seriously and that no invitation is intended. But then why say it at all? Why not a direct invitation, if indeed my presence is desirable?

I have also perceived a lack of sincerity in compliments and praise, both of which, in my opinion, are too frequently expressed in this society. Germans extend compliments only when they are meant sincerely and honestly. When you dislike my dress, do not compliment me for some phony reason, maybe to solicit my friendship or some other inappropriate motivation.

On the basis of my teaching experience, I came to the conclusion that praise is often expressed when it is not justified, perhaps as a means of encouragement to do better. In my opinion, praise should be given only for superior achievement, not for average performance. Students should not get confused about expectations and should know exactly where they stand.

I also have trouble with people who are hedging, in order to avoid the truth. But what if I want and need to hear the truth? Germans are much more direct and outspoken when it comes to telling the truth but, here again, at least you know where you stand. Being pleasant to one another at all times is unrealistic, so why not try not to hedge?

"Friend" is another word which does not coincide with the German *Freund*. Just for the sake of conversation, I sometimes asked my students how many friends they had. Invariably, they came up with astronomical numbers, upwards of 100. When they in turn asked me the same question I answered matter-of-factly and in all seriousness, "Maybe three or four," whereupon they felt sorry for me and asked, "How come? Don't people like you?" Then followed a discussion about what constitutes a "friend" in this country and a *Freund* in Germany. In the American fashion, my students called everyone a friend with whom they may have had a one-time short conversation without hardly remembering the person's name. But he or she was a friend! In German a *Freund* is a person who over the years has proved his or her friendship in difficult situations. In addition, a friend cannot be called a *Freund* if he is not a confidant to whom the deepest secrets can be entrusted. This must be a two-way street, and the experience must continue. A *Freund* is a person of long standing, possibly a lifetime. After this discussion I asked my students the very same question again, and the admitted number of friends decreased dramatically. Aren't linguistics wonderful, especially when you look behind the scenes of cultural connotations and differences in the usage of a simple word!

A phenomenon that keeps puzzling me is related to good manners. I realize that most social gatherings in this country are generally less structured and formal than they are in Germany, but I cannot get used to the practice of guests leaving a big party without saying at least a casual "good night". I am often at a loss when I am looking for a person with whom I had an especially good time, to no avail. When I ask the hostess she will tell me "Oh, he (she) has left." This practice should be acceptable to me, but are you ready to accept the German custom, which takes you in the opposite direction? It requires that party-goers shake hands with all those whom they knew or met at the party for the first time. Which is more acceptable? I should learn to be less hung up about seemingly unimportant customs and habits, but *"Keiner kann aus seiner Haut heraus!"* (Nobody can get out of his skin).

I hope my readers will forgive me for disclosing another (and the last) puzzling observation. This deals with jokes that are told at the beginning of serious speeches and sermons. What purpose do jokes serve in an otherwise serious context? It seems so incongruous or at least unnecessary. Is it to woo the attention of the audience whose minds might otherwise wander off?

When it came to my efforts to accept bothersome or irritating American idiosyncrasies I ran into some trouble, no matter how hard I tried. Even Americans often say with a shrug, "This is typically American" in a less than complimentary way, meaning that is the way it is, and we had better accept it. That has been my approach too.

The generosity of the U.S. government towards other nations is commendable when, without ulterior motives, it arises with a genuine desire to help other less fortunate peoples. But would the government really be so generous, if no profit or advantage could be expected? For example, after World War II the economic recovery of European war zones was made possible only with the generous help of the Marshall Plan. Germany was deeply grateful, but there was a diplomatic angle attached to the economic aid. Even though Germany was almost completely destroyed, the U.S. government saw a potential and strong ally in a rebuilt and even re-armed Germany and went for it. The NATO alliance would have been less effective as a bulwark against the Soviet Union without West Germany as a member.

This worked out well for both the United States and the Federal Republic of Germany, although many Germans now believe that armament has gone too far, especially on the part of the U.S. military, which has saturated German territory with war equipment and troops, who frequently engage in large-scale maneuvers and war games. If Germany, in case of World War III, were to be used as a battle ground, it could be completely annihilated, and the destruction suffered in World War II would look pale in comparison.

Democracy is a great form of government, but it does not suit all nations and many are not ready for it. Therefore the United States, in my opinion, should not impose it on other countries by means of financial rewards which are tantamount to bribery. The same goes for religious propaganda. We should be aware of the fact that other religions have the potential to provide as much comfort and spiritual uplift as Christianity. American missionaries in foreign countries, as commendable as their work is, could make important contributions, if they stayed at home and help our homeless, downtrodden people, drug addicts, criminals, prostitutes and juvenile delinquents. Of course, I am fully aware of Christ's admonishment to his disciples after his resurrection when he said, "Go ye into all the world and preach the gospel to every creature" (St. Mark, chapter 16, verse 15).

Many individual character traits have been developed in the education which our schools provide. I miss the thoroughness of information that German students receive and are held accountable for. Relative to this is a lack of attention to detail, which manifests itself mostly in misspellings, misprints in newspapers and misquotes.

I was trained to take full responsibility for everything I do. No teacher ever reminded me of anything, once the information was passed on to me. In this country, even highly intelligent people will say to me, "Please remind me of this again." Some people even need to be reminded of regularly scheduled meetings.

In Germany, rules and regulations are made clear and no exceptions are granted. Here there are hardly any rules or even laws that are consistently enforced. Being aware of this relegates rules to a lesser degree of effectiveness. People realize that there are loopholes and mitigating circumstances and therefore will not always come up with expected behavior. I found this especially disconcerting in teaching and I must have frustrated and even alienated many students by strictly enforcing the rules without exceptions.

Another phenomenon I have found difficult to understand is the lack of long-range patience and the need for instant gratification. Patience is such a wonderful virtue and helps us reach goals in life which are otherwise not easily attained within a short period of time. This is especially true of learning a foreign language, which cannot be accomplished without hard work. If people want to learn a language in a jiffy as preparation for a trip abroad, they had better save their efforts and the small amount of time they are willing to put in.

Sometimes students would come to my office and say, "I have taken two semesters of German and I still don't speak it fluently. Is there anything wrong with me?" Worse yet, some would blame me for being an ineffective teacher. I studied three languages simultaneously in high school, one for nine years, one for six, and one for four years. After spending thirty-seven years in this country I am still learning English and add new vocabulary words to my knowledge on an almost daily basis.

American teachers are anxious to make learning easy and even entertaining to students. My contention is that learning is hard work and cannot be made easier by gimmicks. The other day I heard an announcement over the radio that a greeting card company is publishing children's greeting cards with printed messages. Why deprive children of the thrill and creativity of formulating their own message to be sent to people they love?

We lead such busy lives and there has been an information explosion since my high school days. Today, we cannot afford to devote a lot of time to just one particular issue. This accounts for the surge in instant gratification and quick fixes. Examples are announcements over the radio of the availability of "Ten Commandments for a Successful Marriage" or "Ten Symptoms of Mental Illness."

Germans are well-known for their self-discipline and their will to succeed. Personally, I have been grateful for my iron discipline, which has enabled me to reach several goals in life that otherwise might have been unattainable. Self-discipline is also desirable in small ways, especially when consideration of other people is involved. I find it disconcerting when people come late to concerts or stage plays and when they talk during the performance. Maybe I am too sensitive but this type of behavior is entirely foreign to me. German audiences are well-disciplined. In concerts, American audiences sometimes applaud after each movement, a practice not customary in Europe. Even less educated and unsophisticated Germans are familiar with this custom. Musicians need the few seconds between movements to concentrate and should not be distracted by applause.

Church organizations fulfill a great need to provide companionship to lonely people, and caring for fellow human beings is an integral part of the Christian religion. But in my opinion, there is just a little too much socializing in churches, which takes away from the primary purpose of a church, at least the way I see it. In German churches the main emphasis is on worship, and socializing is kept to a minimum.

It has always been amazing to me how much my German upbringing and my parents' values have stayed with me all my life.

In some cases, even if I later disagreed with my learned behavior, I found myself extremely reluctant to change. The German proverb *"Keiner kann aus seiner Haut heraus"* again is applicable in this situation.

In Germany, as soon as you enter a church, you are silent. There is no speaking, even a whisper. Children under fourteen are not taken to adult worship services. They have their own Bible instruction under the supervision of adult volunteers. I prefer this practice by far and get annoyed by screaming babies or hyperactive children, who are bored, and interfere with my right to pay attention and hear the words of the minister or concentrate on my worship. In a democratic system it is often difficult to determine where one person's rights end and somebody else's begin.

I find it amazing that many individuals rely on groups of other people to help them with problems which they could handle themselves with an extra dose of will power and self-discipline. For example, I believe that people can lose weight by means of exercising their will power instead of resorting to expensive weight loss clinics. The same is true of stopping an addiction to nicotine and alcohol. The medical profession now claims that alcoholism is not an acquired habit but a disease, which has to be treated as such, an attractive source of income for physicians. I do not happen to agree with this assessment. My contention is that self-discipline can help you overcome almost any obstacle.

It has also been fashionable to put the blame for personal problems, such as criminal behavior, on negative childhood experiences. This is just another case of shirking responsibility for behavior by putting the blame on other people. This is tough medicine, but I for one am convinced that it can be done.

In this country, the media have lost their way. They gather both important and insignificant information around the clock, and they mercilessly bombard us with their findings. I dislike the senseless repetition of the same stories. You would think that after two or three days of detailed reporting everybody would be thoroughly informed, but in some cases the harping on the same subject goes on for weeks, even though there are no new developments. This is especially true of mindless talkshows, although I admit that I am a talk show addict and no amount of German will power has helped me overcome this addiction. I seem to contradict myself by claiming that you can overcome any addiction by means of will power. Anyway, I often feel I should spend my time in more edifying pursuits. However, if there were a convincing reason for ridding myself of the talkshow addiction, I would be able to accomplish it on my own, I am sure.

In the case of celebrities or politicians, I wonder where their individual right to privacy begins with regard to the merciless revelations of private matters. It seems to me that the media often overstep their limits in that respect.

Television companies and radio stations are financed by commercials, which bombard the viewers and listeners with never-ending frequency. In Germany, the customers pay monthly fees for the use of their television and radio sets. This money goes to the companies, which in this way are able to function with a minimum of commercials. I would be glad to contribute my money in exchange for commercial-free programs, instead of watching those mindless, excessive, effusive, silly, unrealistic, repetitious commercials. Sometimes, in true American fashion, I eat my dinner from a tray sitting in the living room and watching TV. Invariably, the Preparation H (hemorrhoids, in case you should not know), the tampon or the diaper commercials show up on the screen, a practice which cannot help but spoil my appetite. I dislike unrealistic commercials, as when people float way up in the air and come down with $100 bills raining on them. What would we consumers do without a silence button or remote control?

I remember that in the early days of German TV a full hour of commercials was televised from 2 to 3 p. m. No, the viewers did not turn off their set, but watched with great gusto because the commercials were so well done, entertaining and in such good taste that people actually enjoyed them. Can you imagine a whole hour of American commercials? You would have to send me to the insane asylum!

I have difficulty getting used to reminders to observe specific events or make us aware of special interest groups. Some of those, such as National Osteoporosis Prevention Week, National Real Estate Month, National Ambulatory Foot Care Week, June is Eye-Wear Month, were designed with profit in mind. Others serve special interests, *e.g.* environmentalists with their Safe Drinking Water Week, Clean Air Week, Asian Pacific Inheritance Week.

I sometimes wonder if the dramatic and frightening increase in violence cannot be attributed to the violence shown on TV. Certainly young people could and should be exposed to more programs that serve to build moral character rather than contribute to crime. I gather that many viewers have come to expect sex, violence and crime on TV screens, if what the broadcasters are telling us is true.

Where do we draw the line between personal rights and the public good? I remember a recent news story about a blind passenger who delayed a flight for eighty minutes by insisting on being seated near an emergency exit. He protested the airline policy of not allowing a blind person to sit by an exit because of safety concerns. As much as I sympathize with the plight of this blind person, he should have realized that 147 persons aboard had rights too, namely a prompt departure. The delay ruined vacation plans and made passengers miss flight connections in other airports.

The Supreme Court has ruled that a person who desecrates the flag of the United States cannot be prosecuted. A crucifix was dipped in urine. How disgusting! Is nothing sacred anymore? A woman sued a liquor company because the bottles of vodka which she consumed in great quantities during her pregnancy did not display warning labels. If, indeed, this had been the case, the question remains if she would have heeded the warning. She had given birth to a mentally retarded and physically handicapped child. Whose fault was it, certainly not the liquor company's! Freedom to sue - yes, but not under such ridiculous circumstances. Sometimes I get the impression that criminal law is stacked in favor of rights of the criminal, while rights of the victim are not acknowledged.

A few rather trivial, but nevertheless important personal experiences, may illustrate how my personal rights are sometimes disregarded. A neighbor boy owns a motorcycle but is not old enough to get a license. He cannot resist driving, not on the streets, but on the lawn around his house, around and around for hours on end. The motor is especially noisy.

Other neighbors, while enjoying the outdoors, turn on rock-and-roll music full blast, which I find hard to tolerate. A good friend of mine, an excellent concert pianist, calls rock-and-roll "so-called music." Right on, Richard! On sunny days, I like to sit on the deck behind my home and read. The noise forces me to sit indoors when I could enjoy fresh air and the sunshine. Even staying indoors does not help much because the noise is so penetrating.

Lack of good manners can result in a slight infringement on my personal rights. Sometimes I walk down the street near a school which just dismissed its students. The children are walking towards me in groups of threes or fours and do not make room as I approach. I have to step down the sidewalk on to the street or sometimes on a completely rainsoaked lawn. Bicyclists are dangerous when riding on the sidewalk. Every so often I have to step aside in a hurry to avoid being hit. Another one of my pet peeves is doors slamming in my face, especially when I carry something heavy.

Following his religious convictions, a father refuses medical aid for his ailing six-year old daughter. He hides her and does not disclose her whereabouts to authorities. As a consequence, he is arrested and put in jail. Should parents have unlimited rights over their children, or shall the government be allowed to interfere in such cases? Government intervention in life-threatening situations has been a thorny issue for quite some time.

The preceding observations are not meant to be critical, but viewed as honest revelations of personal experiences. Sometimes I spoke tongue-in-cheek to make a point. My case of culture shock has not been so severe as to create serious problems. On the contrary, I have lived a happy and well-adjusted life in this country. Culture shock has a way of making life more exciting and interesting. Comparing the customs of two different societies adds enrichment because it is almost tantamount to living two different lives. Who can ask for more? I have enjoyed every minute of it!

No doubt, my adopted country is beset with seemingly insurmountable problems. Looking back to the 1950's, when I first spread my wings, and comparing conditions between then and now, I very sadly have to admit that our society has undergone signs of decline. All of us are aware of changes to that effect, very painfully so. I could throw in the towel and return to my homeland and live where the breakdown of the family structure is less pronounced, where the number of crimes is lower, where the sale of drugs and drug addiction is more under control, where greed and corruption have not made such inroads into politics, where overexposure to sex has not produced so much teenage pregnancy, where the costs of medical care are quite affordable by the majority of people, where young people still value education as a privilege and a highly desirable goal, where the budget deficit is manageable, where children are not afraid of strangers.

I think that all responsible citizens are aware of the problems that beset us, but we have not been able to come up with any solutions - yet. In the name of individual freedom, we must allow cranks, misfits and madmen to threaten our peace of mind and to drive us into electronically protected sanctuaries. When will it all end?

BUT I love this country with all my heart and want to make my small contribution to help it extricate itself from the morass it is in. Collectively, we must pull ourselves together, dwell on the strengths that made this country great and help it survive.

26

Germany - A Nation Divided

The preceding chapters of this book were largely finished before the historic events took place in the fall of 1989, which led to the dismantling of the Berlin Wall. Since these happenings greatly changed the political picture in Eastern Europe and rekindled my hope for reunification of my native country, I decided to report about my emotions concerning the loss of the Eastern part of Germany after World War II.

When I first had to face the fact of a divided Germany and the loss of some of its Eastern territory to Poland and the Soviet Union after World War II - both rationally and emotionally - I experienced a strong feeling of grief. In my mind, a nation is a living entitiy, and dividing it resembles physical mutilation of a human body, an action from which it would be extremely difficult to recover, if at all.

Like so many of my countrymen, I often literally shed tears over the division of my country and the ensuing conditions that my compatriots in East Germany had to undergo for an undetermined period of time, adjusting to a Communist system entirely different from the one most of them had lived under since their birth.

Despite these sad, compassionate feelings I found myself lucky and happy to live in the U.S. occupation zone of Germany, probably for the rest of my life. Occupation is never pleasant, but at least ours was tolerable and at times even pleasurable. All my relatives and friends also lived in West Germany, which saved us the pain of separation without a chance of seeing each other for decades to come. Many families, who lived in two different occupation zones, were faced with that dilemma.

Nevertheless, I still suffered emotional pains with regard to the fate of the country I loved. I clearly remember that I harbored a feeling of hope to see Germany reunited in some distant future, preferably before my death. I realized that this was a long-range hope. I was 25 years old when World War II ended, and we were plunged into almost intolerable pains caused by the division of Germany. Frankly, I did not believe that my ardent wish for reunification would be fulfilled in my lifetime. Needless to say, I now feel extremely happy over the recent events that will lead to reunification of the country and the realization of my hope and dream.

As previously mentioned, I had no friends or relatives in East Germany, but I very soon became acquainted with two lady refugees from the East. They were given no chance to stay where they were born and had lived all their life, but forced to leave by the Russians.

There were two types of refugees who inundated West Germany after World War II:

1. *Volksdeutsche* (ethnic Germans), who had lived as minorities in such countries as Poland, Yugoslavia and Czechoslovakia. They left those countries because, on account of their German citizenship, they foresaw problems ahead on the part of the majority.

2. *Heimatvertriebene* (expellees or displaced persons), Germans who were expelled from former German land annexed by Poland and the Soviet Union. All territories East of the Oder-Neisse-Line, including Silesia, were given to Poland, and East Prussia was divided between the Soviet Union and Poland.

All in all, about 13 million German refugees and displaced persons filtered into West Germany, which was ill-equipped to accommodate them. People in West Germany did not greet refugees with open arms because they aggravated the miserable living conditions caused by almost six years of warfare, such as almost total destruction, severe housing shortages, inadequate food supply and deplorable economic conditions.

After 1945, I made the acquaintance of two lady refugees, one from Silesia and one from East Prussia. Since I as a West German was not permitted to travel to East Germany, let alone to former territories annexed by Poland or the Soviets, those two ladies became a precious source of information concerning their treatment on the part of the Poles and Soviets and their early experiences on their arrival in the West.

One of the two ladies, by the name of Annemarie, had come from Silesia and married Georg, my favorite cousin. She became a constant source of irritation to Georg's mother, who could not get used to the fact that Annemarie was not "one of us", with a different background and speaking a Prussian dialect. Georg's parents had spent every penny on his educaton and training as a medical doctor and orthopedist, with the hope that he would some day be able to marry into a rich family. Instead, here came along this refugee girl, who had lost all worldly goods and whose only possessions were the clothes she wore on her body. And she had the gall to sweep Georg off his feet! Speaking of daughter-in-law and mother-in-law friction! It would have provided material for a soap opera, if such a thing had existed in those days. I was caught in the middle between Georg's mother and the lady from Silesia, for whom I felt a great deal of compassion, but could not be openly friendly and decent to her because I did not want to risk losing the love of Georg's mother, the woman who treated me like a daughter, but with whom I disagreed as to the hostile treatment of her new daughter-in-law.

The other lady whose acquaintance I made in West Germany after World War II hailed from East Prussia, a German territory for centuries, but now Russian and Polish. Her name was Elsbeth, who was a superpatriot. She could never get over the fact that she and her family would never see her beloved East Prussia again as long as she lived. Understandably, she hated everything Russian.

Mere words cannot describe the emotional baggage caused by the division of Germany, but it was not until my first visit to Soviet-occupied East Germany and East Berlin in 1973 that the full impact of the development subsequent to the division hit home.

Previously, in 1959 and 1969, I travelled extensively in West Germany and made it a point to go by car to the West-East German border with two German friends of mine. Yearning for contacts with the East, we just stared across the no man's land in the direction of the "other Germany" that we loved as much as the Western part. We stood there at the barriers, which separated West from East, while border guards suspiciously watched us through their binoculars. It was a moving but disconcerting experience.

In 1973, I travelled by train to Berlin through the Russian-occupied Eastern zone. The train, coming from West Germany, was not scheduled to stop at any East German railroad station but went directly to West Berlin. There, it was checked by customs officials. German shepherd dogs sniffed underneath the train, in an effort to locate persons who might have planned to seek refuge in West Berlin, which again was a booming metropolis in stark contrast to lifeless East Berlin.

Since my early childhood, I had the desire to visit Berlin, because it had been the capital of Germany but, for lack of opportunity and money, I was not able to do so until I was already 53 years old. I rented a hotel room in West Berlin, and it was fun to take in all the excitement that a prosperous city could offer, such as movies, stage plays, concerts, as well as much sightseeing. It felt good to identify with the city and be able to say *"Ich bin ein Berliner"*, as John F. Kennedy had done before. Previous to the war, the part which is now East Berlin was considered the truly cultural and historic part of the city, and I was anxious to see what it was like after 28 years of Russian occupation and Communist rule, so one day I decided to pay East Berlin a visit. The Berlin Wall had been built in 1961, so there was no longer free access to East Berlin, even for those people living or staying in West Berlin. I took a bus to the Berlin Wall where all passengers had to get off at Checkpoint Charlie and present their passports to the Russian border guard. He meticulously compared my facial likeness with the passport photo. I wore sunglasses. The border guard removed them and was puzzled because my passport picture showed me with regular glasses. He looked a couple of times back and forth from me to the passport picture and seemed to suspect that I was using somebody else's passport, until I freed him from his suspicion by putting on my regular glasses. Voilà, I was given permission to walk across into East Berlin. Those were some unnerving minutes!

The bus stayed on the American side of Checkpoint Charlie, so that we had to explore East Berlin on foot, which did not get us very far. I could not help but think that this was done deliberately, in order to prevent us from seeing much of East Berlin. Whatever I saw was enough to satisfy my curiosity, however. Crossing the border from West to East Berlin was a difference like day and night. In East Berlin there were few people on the streets and hardly any cars. The people looked somber and unsmiling. The apartment houses and other buildings, even those erected after the war, were already in disrepair, likewise the streets and sidewalks. I saw a class of schoolchildren marching along like an army, carefully watched by the teacher. The stores were not fully stocked, and queues lined up in front of some of them. The overall impression was far from uplifting, and I was glad to go back to the bus after four hours of walking around, looking in vain for the "economic miracle" that West Germans, but certainly not the East, had experienced after the war. I felt sorry for the 17 million East Germans who had to live under those depressing conditions day after day, month after month, year after year. If I had told them that their enslaved circumstances would end in 1989 they would have shaken their heads in disbelief.

And it did happen - quite unexpectedly and sooner than anybody would have surmised. As Communist regimes in Eastern Europe were crumbling in the fall of 1989, East Germany relaxed

travel restrictions to the West and, on November 9, the Berlin Wall
was opened. The whole Western world rejoiced.

The Berlin Wall had been erected in 1961 to prevent East
Germans from migrating to the prosperous Western part of the
nation, where economic opportunities and attractive lifestyles were
waiting. At the time it was feared that East Germany would be at
risk of being depopulated by an excessive exodus of its residents, and
the wall was built to prevent this from happening. The fall of the
Berlin Wall in November 1989 was a victory for democracy and
freedom and signified the end of the Cold War.

It was a touching experience to be able to watch the
happenings on American TV. Jubilating people from both sides, in
most cases complete strangers, embraced each other and shed tears
of exultation and happiness. East Germans, for the first time in
almost 45 years of Communist rule, were able to visit West Berlin
and enjoy a wide array of products easily available and unrestricted
in West Berlin. The West German government even provided a
certain amount of *deutschmarks* for those long-oppressed visitors
from the East, to enable them to go on shopping sprees.

Besides allowing short-term visits to the West, the opening of
the Berlin Wall had the following consequences for the East:
1. migration to the West and gainful employment there;
2. the end of Communism;
3. the origin of new political parties;
4. free election after 44 years of Soviet occupation;
5. eventual reunification with West Germany.

Miraculously, all this has been achieved. When the prospect
of a reunified Germany came up, many optimistic peple, including
myself, were euphoric. However, the many problems and hurdles to
be overcome on the road could not be overlooked in the long run.
Euphoria has given way to cautious optimism in the minds of many
Germans.

When the Berlin Wall first came down, 60 percent of West
Germans were in favor of welcoming East Germans unconditionally.
Shortly thereafter, the number went down to 25 percent. The main
problem was the already overcrowded housing conditions. The new
arrivals had to be accommodated in empty army barracks,
campgrounds, school gymnasiums and rundown hotels. Many
Easterners insisted on special privileges and preferential treatment.
This kind of behavior irritated the otherwise hospitable West
Germans. It provided a feeling of *déjà vu* because they were
reminded of their experiences with *Gastarbeiter* (guest workers) from
foreign countries, such as Italy, Yugoslavia, Greece and Turkey.

Because of a severe shortage of German workers, due to the losses of
human lives in the war, those foreign workers had been invited by
the West German government decades before to help rebuild the
German economy. They found the West German lifestyle and living
conditions so attractive that many refused to return to their
respective native countries after they were no longer needed. The
West German government even paid them to entice them to leave
Germany and go back but they resisted, which led to feelings of
hostility and even hatred.

Owners of apartment buildings in the West openly expressed
their prejudice in rental ads by specifying which prospective renters
were undesirable. Some ads read *Keine Ausländer* (no foreigners).
Others even went so far as to exclude children, pets, middle-aged
women, etc. I am asking myself, "Is this democracy?" Americans
would not stand for this kind of blatant prejudice. The same problem
presented itself again when the number of East German immigrants
increased considerably, so that West Germans referred to them as
"new Turks."

This kind of problem was the first one which West Germans
had to face after the opening of the border, but there were more to
follow, for example skyrocketing rental rates and food prices,
increased unemployment, high costs of social services and
lackadaisical work habits of East Germans, who up to then had not
had a chance to exercise initiative on their jobs.

In the following, I wish to share an excerpt from a letter,
dated December 13, 1989, which I received from Elsbeth, the lady
who had been expelled from her native East Prussia. For that very
reason, her impressions and opinions are quite subjective and even
hostile but certainly there is at least a grain of truth in her
observations.

Before I cause any confusion, I need to explain the terms
used in the letter with reference to East and West Germany. Since
Germans were not able to come to grips with the division of their
country, they never used the terms "West Germany" or "East
Germany", as we do. Instead, they referred to what we call West
Germany by *Bundesrepublik Deutschland* , abbreviated BRD or in
English "Federal Republic of Germany" (FRG). Likewise, Germans do
not call East Germany *Ostdeutschland,* but *Deutsche Demokratische
Republik* (DDR) and in English "German Democratic Republic"
(GDR). I had no qualms accepting the name "Federal Republic of
Germany" for West Germany, but the term "German Democratic
Republic" given to East Germany was an outright misrepresentation

of facts and an insult to anybody's intelligence. What was democratic in that Communist part of Germany?

In my correspondence to Germany, I used to write "West Germany" or "East Germany" on the envelopes, whereupon I was taken to task by my German friends and relatives, who asked me in no uncertain terms to use the "official" terms *Bundesrepublik Deutschland* or *Deutsche Demokratische Republik,* whichever applied. I realized that, if I did not comply with these requests, I would have been suspect of tacitly approving the division of Germany. In order not to confuse the employees of the U.S. postal service, who may not have been bilingual, I used the English terms ("Federal Republic of Germany" and "German Democratic Republic", respectively) with the consequence that my letters were returned to me. Apparently, the postal clerks were not familiar even with the English terminology. I felt caught in the middle and gave up in frustration. Now I am using "West Germany" and "East Germany" again, at the risk of hurting the feelings of my patriotic friends and relatives in Germany. Fortunately, I have never again received a complaint concerning my use of the "wrong" terminology. Elsbeth used the German terms in her letter to me, and therefore I considered it necessary to explain the somewhat confusing geographic names first. Here are her observations (in translation):

"Politics are quite hectic at present. You probably know that the Wall between us and the German Democratic Republic has developed holes and that about 200,000 persons from over there came to us. Of course, this has caused many problems due to scarcity of jobs and housing. Besides, it requires a lot of money. Nobody has any idea if and how all this will work out. The Germans are split regarding unification. Our conquerors still consider us an immature nation. They talk a lot about self-determination and human rights; but all this does not apply to the German people. The victors are afraid that a united Germany will become too strong economically. They want to incorporate us quickly into the European Community, since we are the great paymasters. Personally, I would favor a united neutral Germany, united only with the German Democratic Republic and the Eastern provinces." (My comment: "Eastern provinces" refers to those territories annexed by Poland and the Soviet Union, including Elsbeth's home province of East Prussia. Of course, the Poles and Russians would never give their consent to such an irrational and idealistic wish). "The victors want the exalted Poles to retain the territories which they snatched from Germany after the war. Even many who call themselves Germans, such as members of the Social Democratic Party, the Free Democratic Party and the

Environmentalists, called the Greens, are in favor of this. No country on earth other than Germany would stand for this kind of treatment. The Atlantic Charter with which the Americans were coaxed into entering the war, provided that no territorial changes were to be made as a consequence of war. Naturally, this again does not apply to Germany. There are sensible Poles who admit not being able to take care of the land they now own, as far as the economy is concerned. Consequently, they let it go to waste, at least parts of it. Neither did they do much for the protection of the environment. But the Germans will help and see to it that Poland will recover. We are living under more and more crowded conditions. Every day, additional people, immigrants, foreign emigrés and asylants come to us. In a few decades, the 'real Germans' will be in the minority."

With all due respect to the memory of Elsbeth, who passed away in February 1990, I wish to make the comment that her emotional letter was quite an eye opener. It clearly expressed the hurt feelings and prejudices of a war victim but also her thoughts obviously reminiscent of Nazi propaganda (such as reference to "real Germans"). Her sentiments also reveal the difficulties a united Germany will have to face regarding ill feelings and unjustified prejudices among the population. Reuniting Germany will entail overcoming lots of problems but the situation will become more challenging yet, should a United Europe be established.

The creation of a United States of Europe, more than 200 years after the formation of the United States of America, is my lofty ideal and my sincere hope. Of course, I realize this goal will not be reached until all the problems related to unification of Germany will have been solved, which will be a long time into the future, not within my lifetime, I am afraid.

But one step at a time. Therefore, in the following I will proceed more or less chronologically to describe the future developments necessary to lead to the unification of Germany, which in turn is a prerequisite and a steppingstone towards the European Community and eventually the United States of Europe.

27

German Reunification - Pros and Cons

Some European countries, despite their fear of a powerful united Germany, do favor reunification. Their fears are certainly justified but, in all fairness, they do realize that Germany's division after World War II was unnatural and put the two Germanys into an untenable position in the long run. Therefore they conclude that self-determination granted to all free nations cannot be denied to Germany. However, they fear it would rekindle nationalistic flames and again breed resentment among her former enemies. On the plus side, reunification will free her from domination by two foreign powers, the United States and the Soviet Union, who never managed to achieve a peaceful balance, let alone stability, in Europe after World War II. The imbalance and instability caused by the constant disagreements between the victors has been referred to as the "Cold War."

Unification seems inevitable and even necessary, if the faltering economy of East Germany is to be saved from collapsing. Prosperous West Germany will be the rescuer, because no other country would have the interest or resources to do the job.

There are grave fears among countries, which were attacked and invaded during the two world wars and in previous centuries, that German unification may again result in a strong superpower politically and militarily. Even now, before unification, West Germany is the dominant economic power on the continent. Her trade surplus in 1989 amounted to $81 billion as compared to a U. S. trade deficit of $9.33 billion. A united Germany will have the potential to become the predominant industrial power, not only in Europe but in the world. It is feared that economic superiority may result in an increased political and military might which, in turn, is bound to lead to heightened political tensions in Europe.

Many interpreted the euphoria that accompanied the opening of the Berlin Wall on November 9, 1989, as the Germans "throwing their weight about" and begrudged East Germans their happiness of attaining their freedom after being subjugated by a Communist regime for more than four decades.

Under these circumstances, fears of an overpowering united Germany on the part of former enemies are understandable. The Soviet Union lost 22 million people in World War II. France and Germany were involved in three bloody wars within the last 70 years. Miraculously, these two nations have succeeded in overcoming their hostility and have approached each other with trust, understanding and good will over the past decades. However, it will be increasingly difficult for France to accept a united Germany, whose renewed strength will upset the balance in Europe and push the center of gravity eastward towards friendship with the Soviets, signs of which have already manifested themselves. After World War II, anti-German feelings ran high, especially in France and the Soviet Union, but it is the Jews who harbor the most hostile feelings against German reunification. After all, they lost six million of their people in the Nazi holocaust. They still hold the Germans accountable for what happened under Hitler, although the majority of present-day Germans were not even alive when the Jews were persecuted by the Nazis.

Germans are difficult to fathom and understand, even for me as a native daughter. There is this constant question of the existence of a German national character. Is there such a thing as hereditary wickedness and aggressiveness in the German character? The British just recently have referred to the Germans as suffering from "anxiety, aggression, lack of consideration, smugness, an inferiority complex and sentimentality." With such an assessment the doubt remains whether European nations will ever learn to live in peace with one another.

After World War II, Germany's enemies severely criticized the German national anthem and still misunderstand it because of the misinterpretation of the beginning words *"Deutschland über alles"* (Germany above everything else). It must be realized that the text of the anthem was written in 1848, long before there was one Germany, but only a confederation of 22 loosely connected states. In the 19th century it became the ardent wish of Germans that their states be united and the desire for unity should be paramount to anything else in the world. It had nothing to do with any desire of ranking first among all other nations, as Germany has been accused. Unfortunately, the Nazis themselves added fuel to the fire and contributed to the misunderstanding of the anthem, because their interpretation fit right in with their scheme of things, namely their desire for world supremacy. To eliminate any misunderstandings, a new practice of singing the national anthem has been established: instead of singing the first stanza, around which the controversy centers, Germans now sing the third stanza only, which deals with unity, justice and freedom, which nobody can deny any nation.

In the course of history, many atrocities were committed by countries other than Germany, but hardly any mention of them is made anymore. It seems that victors are not accused of cruelty as much as those defeated, who have no chance to defend themselves. Germany did not invent wars. Yet, the emphasis of the media has been placed on German aggression. The whole world knows what misdeeds and even crimes were perpetuated by the Germans in two world wars, but very few are informed about what was done to the Germans, especially by the Russians to German women and children, who were fair game to be raped and then shot. 13 million Germans were driven from their homes by the invading Russian troops. Three million Sudeten Germans were expelled from Czechoslovakia after World War II. The forced exodus of those people who lived in the territories seceded to the Soviet Union and Poland was sanctioned by the allies, who won the war. The expulsion of Germans has since been called "a crime against humanity for which history will exact a terrible retribution" (Anne O'Hare McCormick of the New York Times). West German Chancellor Helmut Kohl asked Poland to acknowledge, as President Vaclav Havel of Czechoslovakia did, that it inflicted injustice on innocent Germans who came under Polish rule after World War II. James Bacque in his book "Other Losses" claims that five million German prisoners of war were encamped and 30 percent starved to death in allied camps under subhuman conditions. Communist countries, such as the Soviet Union, Yugoslavia, Romania and Albania are reported to have killed tens of thousands and even millions of their own people. By bringing up these statistics I did not mean to justify the dastardly deeds committed by Nazi Germany, but to put matters in perspective.

It is not only foreigners, who are suspicious of German resurrection, but even some Germans view their own shortcomings with reference to other countries with suspicion. Germany has nine neighbors, and the more neighbors there are, the more potential exists for misunderstandings, quarrels and outright atrocities. Of course, this phenomenon should not constitute an excuse for starting wars.

Günter Grass, a well-known German author and severe critic of German politics in the past, said, "We have every reason to be afraid of ourselves." Germans of the older generation, who personally experienced the wars and their suffering, are more cautious in their hope for a unified and more powerful Germany for fear that history might repeat itself. The younger generation is more relaxed in their expectations.

The success of Germans in several peaceful areas has justifiedly resulted in great pride in their achievements. However, excessive pride is a dangerous phenomenon and can lead to an exaggerated image of oneself and subsequent megalomania, and that is something to beware of.

The greatest danger I see in the future is the Germans' hurt pride over lost territories. It is generally agreed that German land lost to other countries as a consequence of the Treaty of Versailles led to the rise of Adolf Hitler, who promised his followers to rectify what was conceived by Germans as injustices of the treaty. Land is a precious commodity, because the country has suffered from severe overpopulation for so long. A feeling of nationalism is a delicate matter and a powerful emotional force, especially in the form of empathy with Germans living outside the borders. It is a little-known fact that a large number of ethnic Germans still live outside the borders of recently united Germany. About two million live in the Soviet Union, one million in former German provinces, now part of Poland, and substantial numbers in Yugoslavia, Romania, Hungary and Czechoslovakia. These people are proud of their German heritage and national identity and have continued to speak their native language. There is a new surge underway to return to their homeland. Last year alone, the number of returnees from the Soviet Union and Eastern European countries to West Germany exceeded the one of East Germans who took up residence in the West in 1989, by 300,000. More will follow in the future. This is in addition to the 13 million expellees driven out by the Soviets towards the end of World War II, and who were graciously and generously accommodated by the West Germans despite their own debacle of defeat and their inability to feed and clothe themselves. The danger I see in the future is the likelihood that Germans want to reconquer lost territories, especially those in the East where they lost 44,000 square miles.

Lost territories has become a political issue in West Germany. One-third of what is now Poland was German before World War II. In an effort to ensure his re-election, which will take place in December 1990, West German Chancellor Helmut Kohl wooed millions of former residents of the area East of the Oder-Neisse Line to refuse, as he did, acceptance of the new border between Germany and Poland. It was only under political pressure on the part of Poland and the Soviet Union that Kohl reversed himself, and the West German Parliament pledged that a united Germany would honor the present border between the two countries. However, in my opinion, this may not keep a German politician in the future from taking up the hatchet and promising to make an effort to reclaim former German territory, just as Hitler did after the Treaty of Versailles. Kohl may have renounced his interest in reclaiming Eastern territories, but the voices of some rightist political elements in West Germany, most of them former citizens of the lost land, have not died down. They firmly believe that territory beyond the Oder-Neisse-Line should be reclaimed, especially in view of the fact that it was developed, populated, governed and inhabited by Germans for 800 years.

Many suspicions remain among European nations as to the future of a united Germany and relationships with her neighbors. However, we cannot overlook the fact that West Germany has been on her best behavior since the end of World War II. She went out of her way to subordinate her national interests to the good of the Western alliance. Chancellor Kohl maintains that his country has learned its lesson from history and he insists that unification take place within a European framework. The main issue is how a united Germany might fit into Europe without dominating her neighbors. West German Foreign Minister Genscher said, "We want to create not a German Europe, but a European Germany." A united Europe would be the best guarantee to contain a united Germany if containment should be necessary.

It is said that learning any lesson from history is difficult, which is probably true with few exceptions. In the case of Germany, I am convinced that she is one of the very few nations which has finally determined not to make the same mistakes over and over again. Now the time has come to convince the rest of the world of her trustworthiness in the future. There are various indications that Germany, indeed, has had a change of heart since the end of World War II.

Unlike many other European states, Germany, over a thousand-year history, was united for only 74 years in one central state, from 1871 to 1945. This relatively brief period was fraught with two devastating wars, World Wars I and II, as a consequence of which Germany suffered a decimated population and severe losses of life and territory. From these painful experiences Germany has learned that the only way to assure her existence among nations was to learn to live peacefully with her neighbors. Only the most humiliating and complete defeat was able to bring about this turnabout in attitudes.

The change from contemptible dictatorship to democracy and democratic values took firm hold in Germany within a surprisingly short time. It was amazing how fast she developed into a sophisticated democracy, considering the high degree with which she was entrenched in Nazi doctrine. Germany now surpasses even the United States in providing medical care for all, a more extensive welfare program, a more effective educational system and higher voter participation. The whole world watched with disbelief and admiration, and possibly concern, the speed, determination and efficiency with which West Germany rebuilt her economy, industrial complex and sorely needed housing facilities. Despite devastating defeat, and maybe because of it, Germans went about this job, brimming with energy and self-assurance. Work ethics and labor skills, outstanding at all times, seemed to manifest themselves in an even heightened degree at that crucial time.

The most important lesson the Germans learned from history was that militarism and nationalism produced nothing but negative results in the long run. The military defeat and subsequent demilitarization were originally felt as great humiliation, especially in view of the fact that the U.S. occupation forces in West Germany did not waste any time showing off their military prowess on German soil. Now heavy spending on armaments no longer meets with popular support in West Germany. It is ironic that both Germany and Japan, the two defeated nations, were able to rise, like the phoenix from the ashes, without their military systems and became economic and industrial leaders, who overpower the nations that won the war.

The age of militarism and nationalism in Germany has given way to responsible cooperation with other nations. After World War II, West Germany became allied with the Western powers without being granted much power herself. She was completely disarmed, had no self-determination in military matters and was deprived of her sovereignty in controlling her destiny. To the dismay of Germans, their country soon became a training ground for American troops. By postwar agreement, the U.S. military forces had a permanent right to be stationed in West Germany. Military activities on German soil escalated to such a degree that the country was soon covered with short-range nuclear weapons, which led to protests against missile installations on the part of Germany, especially among the younger generation. Except for France and Britain, the European states do not have nuclear weapons. West German Chancellor Helmut Kohl proved his moral strength and courage by opposing an American president on a major weapon system.

Besides xenophobic nationalism and blatant militarism, a virulent anti-Semitism constituted the German tradition before World War II. Both West and East Germany have recognized their responsibility for the holocaust, in which an estimated six million Jews lost their lives. So far West Germany has paid $43 billion in reparations to holocaust survivors. Helmut Kohl has been proud to emphasize that the Federal Republic of Germany has for decades maintained close and friendly relations with the state of Israel and been one of its strong supporters.

Thanks to all these positive developments after World War II, there is a considerable sentiment of trust and confidence in the future role of Germany. I have been pleased with pro-German feelings voiced by several U.S. journalists. They have informed the English-speaking world that, since World War II, Germany has done everything expected of her to make amends. In my opinion, she should be given the opportunity to prosper and become a respected and dynamic member within the European community, but be denied any chance to be aggressive again.

My retirement party — a travel bag and flowers, 1980.

Exploring the northern part of Alaska, 1981.

28

Steps Towards Unification

Many important problems had to be solved right from the start. They arose immediately after the initial euphoria caused by the opening of the Berlin Wall had abated to a certain degree. The new problems affected East and West Germany in different ways. In the beginning, mostly young, educated, skilled East Germans left their country to move to the West. Whole sectors of industry were abandoned and hospitals understaffed. After the opening of the Berlin Wall, about 344,000 of a population of 17 million East Germans left immediately. They were greeted with champagne by their West German compatriots, but soon resentment followed when West Germans were faced with the difficult task of providing jobs and accommodations. The East Germans demanded immediate housing for which West Germans were on a waiting list. Further privileges were granted to East Germans which even West German residents did not have. The city of Hamburg, in desperation, eventually decided not to accept another refugee from the East.

West Germans also resented the "integration money," a monthly sum equivalent to $800, which the East Germans secured from the first day of their arrival. All these necessary financial measures put a heavy strain on the West German social and welfare systems. After a few months, the quality of East German refugees declined noticeably. Now people fleeing East Germany belong to lower classes, are less skilled and educated, include criminals, alcoholics, prostitutes and fathers running away from their families to avoid alimony payments. This raises the question whether they are actually seeking freedom or are attracted to the West by the advantages of better living conditions and higher-paying jobs. A speeded-up unification plan was designed to motivate East Germans to stay at home and work to improve conditions in their part of the country. West German Chancellor Helmut Kohl may have been unjustly accused of political expediency when he urged quick reunification. The first step on the road to unification was the economic merger between East and West Germany, which took place on July 2, 1990. This significant event is considered the steppingstone to political unity.

The purpose of the economic merger was fourfold:

1. to save the sagging East German economy from collapsing by integrating it with the strong Western *Deutschmark* and thus operating the two Germanys on one solid currency;

2. to do away with the practically worthless East German currency and eliminate the vast overflow of worthless *Ostmark* in circulation;

3. to rebuild confidence in the East German economy and stem the tide of East Germans emigrating to the West;

4. to bring the divided nation toward unification after being divided for more than four decades.

Citizens of East Germany were granted the following exchange rate from *Ostmark* to *Deutschmark*:

1. Ages 15 to 59 could exchange savings amounting to DM 4,000 (equivalent to $2,400) on a one-to-one basis and the rest of their money at two to one. A West German mark is currently worth about 59 U.S. cents.

2. People over 60 were allowed to exchange 6,000 *Ostmarks* at the one-to-one rate. This higher exchange rate was designed to motivate East German senior citizens to stay at home rather than emigrating to the West.

3. Children up to 14 could exchange only 2,000 *Ostmarks*.

The beneficial effects of this changeover to a common currency can be felt in the following way: East Germans, before the economic merger, earning the equivalent of $190 per month, now make $560 (paid in *Deutschmarks*). West Germans nearly triple that salary, but for East Germans it still constitutes a remarkable improvement in earnings.

The economic unity will bring both positive and negative results to East Germans. Some of the positive sides are:

1. Eventually, a stable economy will replace a government-controlled, centrally-planned economy. Welfare-state thinking and subsidies of all kinds will make way to a free-market economy based on free enterprise, competition and survival of the fittest.

2. A stable currency will be universally accepted and welcomed not only in West Germany but also worldwide. This should

stimulate East Germans to travel abroad, which they were not allowed under the Communist system.

3. East Germans will make more money and pay less taxes under the West German progressive tax system.

4. They will share in economic progress with their West German brothers. It is estimated that living standards will approach West Germany's in about five years.

5. West German and foreign investors will be interested in helping the faltering East German economy by investing there because of cheap labor. However, it is rumored that West Germans are more interested in selling their own goods to the East rather than producing there.

6. A badly needed highway network in East Germany will be built to improve and extend the present dilapidated road system.

Many East Germans, not familiar with the free-market system of the West, view the future with trepidation. Indeed, there are many obstacles to be overcome, for example:

1. Higher prices, especially for groceries, energy, railroads, rents, all of which were highly subsidized by the Communist regime.

2. Unemployment will rise. It is estimated that, out of a population of a little more than 16 million, between two and five million people will lose their jobs, because East Germans will prefer to buy goods manufactured in the West or imported. Antiquated East German companies will go bankrupt and more than one-third of the enterprises are expected to close. Only 15 percent are economically viable and efficient enough to survive on their own. The danger lies in the wholesale rejection of everything East German. "The West is best" is their new slogan. The factory which manufactures the only East German car, called *"Trabant"*, will most likely be among the ones to go bankrupt because East Germans no longer touch it due to inferior craftsmanship. The company used to employ 13,000 workers.

3. East Germany is the most polluted country in Europe. Millions of *Deutschmarks* will have to be spent to remedy this situation. Outdated utilities, poor transportation and shabby housing will require enormous amounts of money.

What rankles West Germans the most is the eroded work ethic in the East, which resulted from the fact that companies guaranteed jobs regardless of performance. People work shorter hours and more slowly for full pay. Punctuality and reliability are no longer universally existent. There is generally a lax attitude towards the job. Workers in the East were not expected to demonstrate initiative and creativity. People were given leading positions in industry because of party connections, not merit, talent and ambition in the workplace. In order to make East German industries compatible with the free-market system, the workers will have to be retrained in many respects. Time will tell if they will be able and willing to adapt to the new Western system.

One interesting aspect in which the two neighbors differ is their abortion policies. In East Germany, first-trimester abortions are performed costfree on demand. The West German constitution has no such provision, and abortions are difficult to obtain. Abortions in the West are restricted to four situations: medical necessity, rape, incest, and dire social or economic hardship. Since the two Germanys plan to unite under the West German constitution, the abortion issue is obviously highly emotional in both Germanys.

Pessimists say that a reunified Germany will be one nation, but two different peoples, after having been separated for more than forty years. The West is prosperous and highly democratic, the East impoverished and undemocratic. The two are like strangers to one another in spite of their claim *"Wir sind ein Volk"* (We are one people). No wonder that many West Germans view East Germans as unwelcome brothers.

An additional change necessary in the West after the collapse of the Communist regime in the East has been in the military field. After World War II, the need of a formal alliance for mutual defense and security in Western Europe became not only desirable but almost mandatory. NATO (North Atlantic Treaty Organization) was formed by twelve European nations in 1952. Its purpose was to defend any of these states against armed aggression. The Federal Republic of Germany was admitted in 1955.

It seemed incongruous that West Germany was not only admitted but, at the same time, given permission to rearm, only ten years after she had been completely demilitarized. The most obvious reason for creating NATO with the inclusion of West Germany was to form a bulwark against the Soviet Union and its East European satellites. Ironically, this led to the Cold War and a deep distrust between the United States and the Soviet Union, the two main countries which, together as allies, brought about the downfall of Hitler Germany. To the consternation of Germans, their soldiers, previously maligned, were trained not in their own interest but to serve the purposes of the Western alliance. NATO member nations were not only honor bound to protect one another in case of war but were also assured of the support of the United States. In addition, West Germany became the recipient of U.S. financial aid, originally to improve her industry and agriculture, but later to build up her military.

Initially, the purpose of NATO was strictly military protection against the potential of Soviet aggression. Now, with the collapse of Communist regimes in Eastern Europe and the planned withdrawal of Soviet troops stationed there, NATO's exclusively military function has become more or less irrelevant. Nevertheless, the United States was not about to give up her military presence in Western Europe. There is too much at stake there. Nothing was easier than switching from a military to a political make-up, and tie in with the political changes in Eastern Europe, to give NATO a new look and, at the same time, to maintain NATO's defensive abilities. The continuation of NATO will assure the United States of political and economic influence in Western Europe, especially in West Germany, which is considered the economic giant. Odd as it may seem, the military occupation, initially considered humiliating, has proved a blessing in disguise for Germany. It has been calculated that the U.S. military pours about 15 billion marks ($9.05 billion) into the West German economy every year. It would be a great financial loss for Germans if U.S. troops were withdrawn. On the other side of the coin, there are many West Germans who would welcome a complete withdrawal.

No other European state fears a united Germany with its potential increase in power more than the Soviet Union, which lost 22 million people in World War II. Therefore, the Soviets were originally strictly opposed to Germany's continuing membership in NATO. However, a neutral Germany, as proposed by the Soviets, would challenge Germany's will to power because she would feel deprived of the protection that NATO guarantees and see the need to arm on her own, thus becoming more of a threat to the Soviet Union than as a member of NATO where her military actions could be carefully monitored. Besides, denying Germany membership in NATO would have a punitive effect by forcing her to rely on her own resources and deny her the friendships contracted while being a member of NATO in good standing for 35 years.

The United States favors Germany as a continued member of NATO, because she can contribute to economic, political and, yes, military stability in Europe. Germany herself is convinced that she would fare immeasurably better within the safe haven of NATO. I suspect that, even after 45 years of peace between Germany and the Soviet Union, mutual trust has not been established, if it ever will after a long history of hostilities. Distrust is precisely the reason why the Soviets would prefer a Germany without access to the support of NATO troops in case of war.

In spite of the Soviet Union's fears of German aggression, she made a most unexpected move and turnabout by suddenly assenting to Germany's membership in NATO. President Bush and other leaders of NATO managed to assure Gorbachev that a NATO strengthened by a united Germany would not pose a military threat to the Soviet Union. According to Bush, NATO is now committed to non-aggression. U.S. troops in Europe will be reduced from 325,000 to 195,000. In addition to this reassurance, Helmut Kohl made some attractive offers to the Soviets which they could not afford to turn down. He agreed to reduce the German military from 667,000 to 370,000. Furthermore, he pledged to the Soviet Union $7.5 billion for the maintenance and withdrawal of the 380,000 Soviet soldiers from East Germany over a four-year period and for financing new housing for the troops when they return home. It is almost incredible that the Soviet Union will be unable to support her troops, if withdrawn, because she has neither adequate barracks, let alone civilian housing or jobs. And what do Germans have to gain by spending such an enormous amount on a former enemy? Foreign Minister Hans-Dietrich Genscher remarked that $7.5 billion is "worth the price of unity."

In addition, West Germany has granted three billion dollars in loans to Moscow for rebuilding the decayed Soviet economy and will try to persuade other Western nations to raise additional money for the same purpose. No wonder Gorbachev caved in and consented to German membership in NATO. He probably decided that Germany's shared wealth is worth the risk of facing the potential of German aggression. Who knows, financial rapprochement may even result in a friendship long overdue that will not end in hostilities again.

On October 3, 1990, unification became a reality. There is no longer any *Westdeutschland* or *Ostdeutschland,* or a Federal Republic of Germany, or a German Democratic Republic, but only **one** Germany. Many adjustments will have to be made in the future, but Germans are hardworking people and used to overcoming crises and meeting challenges, so I am confident that they will manage to solve all upcoming problems pertaining to the reunification of their country.